Danger in the Path of Chic

Fashion: Visual and Material Interconnections

Series editor: Rebecca Arnold, The Courtauld Institute of Art, London, UK

This interdisciplinary series explores the ways that the visual and material interact to create and sustain fashion cultures, both historically and today. Published in association with the world-renowned Courtauld Institute of Art, the series seeks to unpack the ways looking, seeing, wearing and being interconnect with wider visual, material and technological cultures of fashion. Through focused studies of specific themes and case studies in fashion and dress history, the series comprises exciting, new research that foregrounds fashion as a lived, emotional and sensory experience. Including both national and transnational examples, ranging from fashion film to periodicals to fashion photography, it fosters and facilitates new ways of thinking about dress as a local and global phenomenon. Titles in the series draw upon fashion studies and dress history, in addition to art, architecture, design history, philosophy, memory studies and the history of emotions.

Published

The Hidden History of the Smock Frock: Deception and Disguise, Alison Toplis
Danger in the Path of Chic: Violence in Fashion between the Wars, Lucy Moyse
    Ferreira

Forthcoming

Fashion after Capital: Frock Coats and Philosophy from Marx to Duchamp,
    T'ai Smith
*Prêt-à-Porter, Paris and Women: A Cultural Study of French Readymade Fashion,
    1945–68*, Alexis Romano

The Courtauld

Danger in the Path of Chic

Violence in Fashion between the Wars

Lucy Moyse Ferreira

BLOOMSBURY VISUAL ARTS
LONDON • NEW YORK • OXFORD • NEW DELHI • SYDNEY

BLOOMSBURY VISUAL ARTS
Bloomsbury Publishing Plc
50 Bedford Square, London, WC1B 3DP, UK
1385 Broadway, New York, NY 10018, USA
29 Earlsfort Terrace, Dublin 2, Ireland

BLOOMSBURY, BLOOMSBURY VISUAL ARTS and the Diana logo
are trademarks of Bloomsbury Publishing Plc

First published in Great Britain 2022

Series design: Adriana Brioso
Cover image: Models wearing wool suits by Schiaparelli, Vogue, 1936. (© Cecil Beaton/
Condé Nast/Getty Images)

A catalogue record for this book is available from the British Library.

A catalog record for this book is available from the Library of Congress.

ISBN: HB: 978-1-3501-2628-2
        ePDF: 978-1-3501-2629-9
        eBook: 978-1-3501-2630-5

Typeset by Integra Software Services Pvt. Ltd.
Printed and bound in Great Britain

To find out more about our authors and books visit www.bloomsbury.com
and sign up for our newsletters.

Contents

Illustrations

Acknowledgements

I am deeply thankful for all of the support I have received in researching and writing this book. It is based upon my doctoral research conducted at The Courtauld Institute of Art, a very special and formative place, where my studies were funded by the Arts and Humanities Research Council, which I will always truly appreciate. I am also very grateful to the Pasold Research Fund for supporting the images in this publication, and to the institutions who have kindly granted permissions.

I would like to thank Rebecca Arnold for making all of this possible. I am lucky to have been guided by her exceptional insight and enthusiasm over the years, as a wonderful supervisor, colleague, and friend. I am also indebted to everybody else at The Courtauld who has shared their wisdom with me, including Gavin Parkinson and John Milner. A huge thank you to Elizabeth Wilson and Suzannah Biernoff for their kind support and for making my PhD viva a genuine pleasure. Heartfelt thanks to all my colleagues, past and present, who have advised and inspired me, especially Caroline Evans, Marketa Uhlirova, and Jo Morra.

Many staff members at libraries, archives, and museums have helped this project along the way, which I am so thankful for, particularly Kristen Stewart and Julie Lê who made my research trips to San Francisco and New York invaluable. Thank you also to all at Bloomsbury and Integra who have brought this book to life, notably Frances Arnold, Rebecca Hamilton, Yvonne Thouroude, Amy Jordan, Amy Brownbridge, and Viswasirasini Govindarajan, and to my peer reviewers for their generous feedback. This work expands some previously published material, including that in the *Berg Encyclopaedia of World Dress and Fashion* (2014); *BIAS: Journal of Dress Practice* (2016); *Cosmetic, Aesthetic, Prophetic: Beyond the Boundaries of Beauty* (2016); and *The Routledge Companion to Fashion Studies* (2021).

I dedicate this book to all those I am privileged to call family. I would especially like to thank my grandparents, Eric, Doreen, Tom, and Maureen, for all of their love and support; my brother, Toby, for his determined spirit and sense of humour; and my soul sister, Emily, for her boundless heart and mischievousness. A special mention is needed for Darcy, Sandy, Ivy, Tiffany, and Orpheus. To the most amazing parents there could be, Phil and Carole, whom I can't thank enough for their unconditional nurture, encouragement, and strength. And of course, to my incredible husband, Alberto, whose drive and devotion sustain me every day: obrigada por ser meu mais que tudo.

Introduction

Severed heads. Scalpels. Skeletons. These terms are not typically associated with fashion – much less that of the interwar period. Yet, over the course of the 1920s and 1930s, all of these instances of violence, and many more, emerged within the field of high fashion. From fashion magazines and photography, to haute couture designs, violence manifested itself broadly and in multiple forms. This occurred during a period that was consistently marred by violence within wider society on an international level, creating widespread loss and trauma that did not relent. Simultaneously, the march of modernity brought with it dizzying changes and further instability to be contended with. Fashion was far from removed from this and played a critical role in mediating, responding and contributing to this lived experience. As a result, the period also saw the establishment of fundamental fashion trends that persist today, including the colour black becoming officially designated as 'chic',[1] beauty turning to pseudo-science,[2] and the popular coining of the term 'sex appeal' in fashion.[3]

This book examines this proliferation of violence in fashion during the interwar years within British, French and American fashion, focusing on the cities of London, Paris and New York. It explores this disturbing trend, in order to uncover why graphic horror manifested itself in this way, at this time, and in a sphere that is usually perceived as being built on fantasy and escape. Through doing so, it situates fashion within, rather than beyond, the very real traumas of this period.

In particular, this book questions how these developments implicated and were experienced by women, considering the ways in which fashion represented, and contributed to, a sense of anxiety. It assesses the extent to which fashion was a source of violence towards women, and also how it could offer them a means through which to engage with, and actively employ, conceptual violence themselves. It tracks how this phenomenon of violence in fashion changed as the interwar period progressed, and how it differed within the various aspects of the fashion industry. In doing so, it illustrates the construction of a new, subversive form of femininity, which countered the way in which images of women were used within the mainstream. Through this investigation, the themes of modernity, literature, eroticism, art and the discipline of psychoanalysis, which all produced their own manifestations of violence, are also considered. By connecting them to fashion, a deeper understanding of violence in fashion – and culture at large – emerges.

Approach

This book considers violence in several of its different forms, including physical and literal violence, such as the (trompe l'oeil) tears and rips fundamental to the design of Elsa Schiaparelli's 1938 Tear Dress, and metaphorical concepts of violence, including notions of fragmentation, and psychological trauma. In this way, violence towards, upon and within the body is examined.

Similarly, fashion is conceived in a broad sense, following Joanne B. Eicher and Mary-Ellen Roach-Higgins's classification of dress as 'a comprehensive term to identify both direct body changes and items added to the body', therefore including clothing, accessories, cosmetics and skincare products alike.[4] As a result, this research considers manifestations of fashion on three tiers: in dress, upon and within the body, and as represented through word and image.

Accordingly, primary sources are interdisciplinary, including text, image and object. Within this, the material largely focuses upon women's high-end and couture fashion, and therefore engages primarily with elite women. High fashion is crucial for this investigation as it is the platform upon which these themes, from violence to modernity, unravel explicitly, allowing a deep understanding of their relationship to be established. It also directly connects with fine art, particularly Surrealism, which offers useful parallels throughout the book, and is reinterpreted as a result of this association with high fashion. In fact, many Surrealists produced works that crossed over into fashion, and likewise, certain fashion designers, such as Elsa Schiaparelli, are significant for their connections to the movement.

Fashion magazines provided a further outlet for the manifestation of representations of violence. They are vital for their portrayals of fashion, in addition to offering important primary sources within their original context, such as advertisements, illustration and fashion photography. The publications *Vogue* and *Harper's Bazaar* are studied in depth: like this book, each dealt with high-end fashion, and produced editions in the same cities focused on by this project.[5] These titles were contemporaneously regarded as the 'world's two leading fashion magazines', and primarily targeted an elite female audience, who were able to purchase the luxurious items that appeared upon their pages.[6] However, in practice, their readership extended much more widely, and they were also enjoyed by 'millions of women' who consumed them on an aspirational basis, as *Life* magazine remarked in 1937.[7] Furthermore, *Vogue* and *Harper's Bazaar* also held key positions within the fashion industry itself, which formed an important basis of their readership.[8] In addition to recording and reflecting fashion, the magazines were regarded as 'key stakeholders in the industry, able to influence developments in fashion as well as report on them', according to Howard Cox and Simon Mowatt.[9]

This is supplemented with other, more specialized, publications, such as *La Gazette du Bon Ton*, a prestigious French magazine that aimed to emphasize and elevate the cultural positions of fashion and beauty, and connect them to art and literature. Produced on fine paper and accompanied by hand-coloured lithographs, it was, as Mary E. Davis has written, 'required reading for sophisticated Parisiennes who warmed to its tone of elegance and exclusivity.'[10] As with *Vogue* and *Harper's Bazaar*, the *Gazette* appealed to a wider audience due to the escapist glimpse that it provided into a privileged lifestyle, and was also distributed internationally.[11] However, its annual subscription price of 100 francs rendered it more exclusive. Nevertheless, it was a significant fashion publication, and held exclusive contracts with leading couture houses. Additionally, its emphasis on intellectualism, with routine contributions from notable artists and writers, further extended its readership, and its interdisciplinarity offers an important insight for this book.

Whilst fashion magazines represent the primary archive of this book, it also contextualizes primary fashion objects in relation to wider contemporary sources. In addition to art, literature and film, for example, are analysed as another means through which tropes of violence and expressions of trauma reached fashionable, female audiences. As a consequence, primary fashion objects are contextualized with sources as diverse as medical manuals and propaganda posters throughout the book. This places the examples of violence and trauma in fashion within a network of visual, material and documentary representations.

In the *First Manifesto of Surrealism*, André Breton suggested that 'the depths of our minds conceal strange forces … it is in our greatest interest to capture them.'[12] Such strange forces are of particular use to this investigation, and as Breton explained, psychoanalysis can be used as a tool to discover them.[13] Psychoanalysis plays a core methodological role in gauging an understanding of violence and trauma in fashion at this time, and its impact. It was during the interwar period that the discipline first came to prominence and popularity, and within which many of its key areas were first conceived and disseminated. Sigmund Freud's fundamental work was translated into English for the first time just prior to the First World War, and into French only during the early 1920s. Furthermore, medical advances brought about by the First World War increased the discipline's recognition and respect, a powerful factor of change that is discussed in Chapter 1. This was furthered by the later enforced emigration of many European academics to America, bringing psychoanalytic theories to a much wider audience.

Furthermore, psychoanalysis itself relates to this book on a thematic level, as violence was a core feature of many key theories of human development produced at the time (a fact little highlighted by existing literature). Furthermore, gender and sexuality form both a lynchpin of psychoanalysis, and a core way in which to understand violent imagery in fashion and its implication for women. As a result of these parallels, both chronological and thematic, psychoanalysis is used as a tool to both help understand occurrences of violence in fashion, and offer important primary sources and contextualization. It therefore forms the core methodological structure of the book, and psychoanalysts featured include Sigmund Freud, Jacques Lacan, Paul Ferdinand Schilder, Melanie Klein and Carl Jung. This works in conjunction with the material culture and art historical examples discussed above.

Finally, this book considers the various social, political and economic contexts as essential elements in pursuing an understanding of the manifestation of violence in fashion at this time. Geographically, examples are focused upon the cities of London, New York and Paris. These cities are pertinent for several reasons. Firstly, they each served as centres and directors of the international fashion scene. The experiences of modernity and the everyday societal status quo experienced by women in these metropolises are important representations of the wider social and cultural changes. Secondly, the political allegiance of Britain, America and France is an important consideration during the interwar years. Indeed, such episodes as the aftermath of the First World War, the Great Depression, the rise of fascism and the build-up to the Second World War are examined as an integral element of understanding how and why conflating violence and fashion became so relevant in this period.

The First World War and femininity

As the first major conflict to make use of modern, mechanized technologies, such as tanks, in conjunction with nineteenth-century tactics, the First World War caused death and destruction on unprecedented scales. In 1931, Benjamin Crémieux remarked that this led to the 'realisation of the instability of this world',[14] which he specifically linked with the 'power of violence' that the war had inflicted.[15] This affected not just the whole population of each country, but also their culture. For example, in 1919, Henry Seidel Canby explained: 'no war has been so honestly, so faithfully reported as this one. The correspondent has put into words all but his

Figure 0.1 *H. R. Hopps, lithograph, Destroy this Mad Brute – Enlist, 1917*

thinking.'[16] The beginnings of the mass media painted a graphic and gruesome picture of the action, through newspaper articles and photographs, and newsreels, which were accessible in each country involved. Fashion publications were far from immune to the war's devastation, and *Vogue* published a poem lamenting its 'crime and violence', almost one year after it ended.[17]

Canby went on to point out that 'millions of women … flung themselves into the conflict without incurring the passionate reactions of bloodshed, and [were] transformed', acknowledging the war's wide-ranging impact upon women.[18] Certainly, many women's roles brought them into contact with the war, and as Trudi Tate has described, 'the Great War also killed women who worked in munitions factories or volunteered as nurses, workers, and ambulance drivers at the Front. Women civilians were injured and killed in the war zones, in aerial attacks on civilian areas, and at sea.'[19] This did not exclude American women, and Margaret Higgonet has noted that 'a surprising number of American women – perhaps 25,000 – volunteered to help the war effort in Europe.'[20] However, the war also affected notions of femininity on a conceptual and image-based level. Propaganda produced in each country frequently addressed women; and furthermore, as Pearl James has argued, it 'represent[ed] the violence of war through the visual metaphor of a raped, mutilated, or murdered woman.'[21] Figure 0.1, a 1917 US Army poster by H.R. Hopps, is one such example, and portrays a woman in the clutches of an ape-like representation of the enemy, which drew on the wider cultural trope of Bigfoot.[22] The creature wears a helmet labelled 'militarism', and clutches a rough, blood-spattered baton branded 'kultur', as he encroaches onto 'America', having left behind a scene of destruction in the background. The poster attempted to incite enlistment through suggesting that America, despite being further away from the Western front, was not safe from German corruption. It used the representation of a captive, defenceless and beautiful woman as about to be assaulted in order to portray this message. Consequentially, while women could not fight on the frontline, they, like men, were left with considerable wounds. These comprised literal, metaphorical and psychological trauma, which began to appear within violent imagery in fashion and wider culture. As the interwar years progressed, the violence did not diminish, but steadily increased across the period, building its way up to appearing upon the female body itself, through fashion.

Literature

Contemporary historians debate how long the impact of the First World War was felt within society. While the majority agree that fears and anxieties prevailed throughout the interwar years, Richard Overy, for example, has argued that 'their roots lay before the First World War'.[23] While Martin Pugh titled his social history of interwar Britain *We Danced All Night*, its content belied the positivity of its title. Pugh described: 'behind the gaiety, exuberance and irresponsibility of post-war social life lurked a pervasive undercurrent of pessimism, the inevitable consequence of the devastating human impact of four years of mass war'.[24] This book further establishes the way in which the war, its trauma and aftermath persisted many years after the conflict ceased, and introduces violence in fashion, as a vehicle through which this trauma could be expressed and, in various ways, processed.

Whilst the First World War and its impact in general have been the topic of a vast amount of literature, what has not been considered so extensively is the impact upon women. A number of titles have addressed women in relation to the war;[25] however, each largely focuses upon women's roles and experiences during the war itself. Women's implication in the aftermath of the war has received significantly less attention,[26] and a major consideration in this book is to assess the emotional impact of the First World War upon women as manifested in fashion. As early as 1919, this impact was recognized, and the journal *Our Empire* wrote: 'Women … mentally go to the trenches, they see and hear the sights and sounds of battle, they read war books, and they really drift into a morbid mental state which has its reflex on their physical conditions … ',[27] yet there is a distinct lack in the current literature in addressing the significance of this in depth, and particularly in connecting this to fashion.[28]

Ana Carden-Coyne has offered compelling insight into the emotional impact of the war for women, in *Reconstructing the Body: Classicism, Modernism, and the First World War,* using post-war literature to argue that 'through the heroine's feelings and emotions writers examined the deeper social meanings of war, intimate emotions and experiences of loss. Although women could mourn for the nation, reaffirming gender codes, they were also burdened as nurturers, witnesses, and torchbearers for cultural memory'.[29] She goes on to comment that 'women's empathy was distinctly sensory and visual, sponsored by cultural forms. Fathers worried about violent images or depictions of victims in war literature and films. Some preferred uplifting stories of overcoming adversity … still, both women and men were responding to the culture of violent imagery'[30] and 'emotional wounds were slow to heal. Mourning her son, the mother expresses what became a post-war obsession: the presence and absence of the human body'.[31] These observations raise tantalizing areas for potential exploration, which this book aims to further, by investigating the emotional impact of the war in women's realms as defined by fashion. It explores how the emotional impact of the conflict was manifest in representational forms targeted at women. While some studies have explored how women are represented in commercial imagery,[32] this book adds to the conversation by directly addressing the impact of the war, and the role of fashion in particular.[33]

Another significant theme within this book is the role of modernity, which connects to and extends the long impact of the First World War. Indeed, Samuel Hynes has not only argued that the war transformed culture, as mentioned above, but also that its 'process of change determined … what modern came to mean'.[34] Certainly, historians have identified multiple moments of modernity ranging from *c.*1750 to *c.*1950, usually tied to certain locations, an approach that this book affirms.[35] However, the period *c.*1870–*c.*1939, within which the interwar years studied by this work fall, has been noted, for example by Martin Dauton and Bernhard Rieger, as being a particularly significant moment of modernity, due to its great 'social, political, economic and cultural changes, as well as a pervasive sense of crisis', which entailed a 'new phase' of history.[36] This book takes the stance that the years 1919–39 are particularly reflective of, and important in regards to, modernity. They epitomize many changes that are historiographically regarded as 'modern', and in many respects initiated and established systems that are still in place today. For example, during this time, the populations of Britain, France and America (in addition to many other countries) became increasingly urbanized: a process that had begun before the First World War, but gained momentum during the 1920s. Similarly, facilities such as electricity, public transport networks and mass shopping and entertainment venues existed in major cities before the war, but were significantly extended and multiplied afterwards. This was coupled with new forms of transport such as the car and the growing mass media. Altogether, these developments quickened the pace of everyday life, and distinguish the particular form of interwar modernity that this book defines.

One characteristic of modernity that this book explores in particular is the sense of conflict that it triggered, which is connected to the notion of crisis as an identifying element of modernity mentioned above. Pugh, for instance, described the 'combination of greater personal freedom and higher disposable incomes for many ordinary people, and articulated the way in which they led to 'widespread complaints about a decline of moral standards in Britain during and immediately after the war' and that 'the arrival of peace was attended by fresh fears', regarding, for example, 'female emancipation': signified 'from cocktails to jazz, cinema, lipstick, face powder and bobbed hair' which supposedly 'threatened … the population'.[37] This contrast between moral complaints, which of course were made only by certain sectors of society (typically middle-class men), and women's experience of modernity, is an important line of enquiry throughout the book. It analyses this animosity towards the 'new woman' of the 1920s, and evaluates to what extent it can be viewed as an expression of trauma.[38]

In addition to the trauma of the war, the ongoing developments of post-war modernity are regarded as a further source of anxiety. As Chapter 1 establishes, modern, everyday life was often described as 'violent' by a range of sources, including modernist literature and fashion magazines such as *Vogue*.[39] One aim of this book is to uncover why modern life was perceived in this way, particularly within fashion. Whilst this violence of interwar modernity has not been explicitly studied, particularly not in relation to fashion, several writers have made associations between mass modernity and a sense of anxiety, including Andreas Huyssen, who has associated male fears of mass modernity with fears of women.[40] This phenomenon is identified within this book as particularly relevant to fashion. Elizabeth Wilson has built upon this link between women and modernity, in *Adorned in Dreams: Fashion and Modernity*: 'the colliding dynamism, the thirst for change and the heightened sensation that characterize the city societies particularly of modern industrial capitalism go to make up this 'modernity', and the hysteria and exaggeration of fashion well express it'.[41] It presents a comprehensive argument on the connections between fashion and modernity, which this book draws upon, and relates explicitly to the specific context of violence in the interwar years for the first time. These ideas are also addressed, for example, by Christopher Breward and Caroline Evans's edited collection, *Fashion and Modernity* (London: Berg, 2005), which includes a notable study on mannequins, 1900–25. Wilson's *Sphinx and the City: Urban Life, the Control of Disorder, and Women,* while presenting different aims to this book, contains important crossovers, through its examination of women's place in the city, including London, Paris and New York. Here, Wilson expressed that:

> the city, a place of growing threat and paranoia to men, might be a place of liberation for women. The city offers women freedom …. On the one hand it makes necessary routinized rituals … but despite its crowds and the mass nature of its life … at every turn the city dweller is also offered the opposite – pleasure, deviation, disruption.[42]

This book builds upon this argument, and examines the place of women both as representative of male anxiety, and as disruptive of the status quo, finding pleasure as well as threat within the modern, post-First World War city.

One fashion designer in particular enabled women to take on this independence within a pressured environment. While a range of designers including Madeleine Vionnet and Elizabeth Hawes are considered within this book, the designer who explored the themes under consideration most explicitly was Elsa Schiaparelli. Her designs during this period reveal a deep engagement with the visual culture and various social contexts that surrounded them, which have yet to be thoroughly acknowledged by existing literature. One publication which has begun to fill this gap is Dilys Blum's comprehensive *Shocking! The Art and Fashion of Elsa Schiaparelli* (New Haven: Yale University Press, 2003), which thoroughly established the complexities of Schiaparelli's insight and engagement with the art world. Blum commented that 'Schiaparelli's influence on the Surrealist community has yet to be fully acknowledged or documented,' a fact which remains true, and one which this book intends to contribute towards.[43] Through critically engaging with and explicitly contextualizing Schiaparelli's work and frequent engagement with Surrealist artists during the interwar period, this book provides new insights, both on Schiaparelli and Surrealism, and also on the period itself, through exposing Schiaparelli's own response to and participation within it. Whilst she was an important figure within Parisian couture, she can also be classed as the 'other' herself. She described feeling like an outsider in her biography, *Shocking Life*, which she linked to both her Italian nationality, and what she perceived as her unconventional appearance.[44] Her innovative approach to design and artistic collaborations also differed from convention, and altogether this enabled an alternative and even subversive view. In this way, she and the Surrealists she collaborated with were able to present a new form of empowered femininity despite, or because, of the turbulent historical context.

This offers a new interpretation of Surrealism itself, which has been accused of violating the female body through its artworks.[45] This book engages with arguments presented by later publications, such as Katharine Conley, *Automatic Woman: The Representation of Woman in Surrealism* (Nebraska: University of Nebraska Press, 1996) and Alyce Mahon, *Surrealism and the Politics of Eros, 1938–1968* (London: Thames and Hudson, 2005), which have questioned this. Conley has clarified, for example, that 'Surrealism as a movement … was not unremittingly misogynist, as has sometimes been suggested'.[46] Using the viewpoint expressed within writings released by the Surrealists themselves, this book asserts that women and femininity represented an alternative, an escape, to the rational, masculine causes of the First World War. In this way, women were crucial to the Surrealist pursuit of the 'marvellous'. However, in order to bring about the shock necessary to force people to question their lives, and society, and to subvert the status quo, women were sometimes seemingly objectified or violated in artworks. It is from this standpoint that this book considers violence, particularly of a sexual nature, towards women in Surrealism.

Certain further publications are of particular relevance due to their studies on the way in which trauma is represented in fashion. Rebecca Arnold's important demonstration of fashion's ability to embody, reflect and promote the complex emotions, fears and dreams of society in *Fashion, Desire and Anxiety: Image and Morality in the Twentieth Century* (London: I.B. Tauris, 2001), through an examination of material from the 1970s to the beginning of the twenty-first century, is a stance that this book explores during the interwar years. Furthermore, she relates this specifically to violence within 1990s fashion design: 'violence has been used as both aggressive confrontation with the flawed nature of capitalism … and as a means to assert glamorised visions of power for the alienated'.[47] This book builds upon the connections Arnold made between fashion, society and morality and explores them in different contexts. Caroline Evans's *Fashion at the Edge: Spectacle, Modernity and Deathliness* (New Haven and London: Yale University Press, 2003) has similarly illuminated ways in which late-1990s fashion has engaged with societal anxieties, including darker areas such as death. Furthermore, her article 'Masks, Mirrors and Mannequins: Elsa Schiaparelli and the Decentred Subject' applies psychoanalytical theory to Schiaparelli's designs, which resonates with this book's attention to psychoanalysis and fashion at large.[48] Indeed, Elizabeth Wilson identified the rich potential of the relationship between fashion and psychoanalysis in 1985:

> Fashion clearly does … tap the unconscious source of deep emotion, and at any rate is about more than surface. Fashion, in fact, is not unlike Freud's vision of the unconscious mind. This could contain mutually exclusive ideas with serenity; in it time was abolished, raging emotions were transformed into concrete images, and conflicts magically resolved by being metamorphosed into symbolic form.[49]

Despite this rich potential, these connections have been underexplored, with the notable exception of Alison Bancroft's *Fashion and Psychoanalysis: Styling the Self* (London: I.B. Tauris, 2012), which covers a broad range of themes and twentieth-century fashion. This book engages with aspects of this approach, and applies it to a narrower focus, in order to understand the impulses and manifestations of violence in French, British and American interwar fashion.

Structure

This book is constructed of four chapters, each based upon one aspect of physical and/or psychological violence. Chapter 1 explores forms of and connections to Assault; Chapter 2, Fragmentation, of both a literal and metaphorical nature; Chapter 3, Eroticism, which considers sexual violence; and Chapter 4, Absence, which examines deathliness. The chapter sequence begins, in Chapter 1, with an exploration of visual violence of the body and mind at large. The body is then physically broken down over the course of the book: fragmented within Chapter 2, reduced to a sum of fetishized parts in Chapter 3, and finally reaches the point of deathly disappearance in Chapter 4. As the book is organized thematically in this way, each chapter is roughly chronological within itself, including examples spanning the interwar years, and from all three cities. Through repeating the chronology in each chapter, the development of violence within fashion, and its significance and relation to the wider context is reinforced, and patterns emerge. In each case, violence tends to initially occur within fashion at an image-based level, such as advertising or editorial, towards the beginning of the period, before gradually building up to feature most prominently upon the body within fashion design from the mid-1930s onwards. In this way, each chapter traces why, as *Vogue* cautioned in 1927, 'no woman [could] afford to ignore the danger points in the path of chic'.[50]

1   Assault

Beauty doctoring: Advertising violence and femininity

'You are a beauty doctor, aren't you?'
The girl smiled.
'Yes, I suppose that's what I am called.'[1]

A young woman lies back on an immaculately made bed, with starched, white sheets. Her head is slightly raised, as she looks to another woman, who leans over whilst attending to her. This woman wears a smart, simple nurse's uniform, complete with a regulation hat. She smiles kindly as she carries out her work, caring for the reclining woman, who appears to be her patient. Both Figures 1.1 and 1.2, which were each produced in 1922, demonstrate this medical mise-en-scène. Despite their strong iconographic correlation, however, they originate from disparate contexts. Figure 1.1 is typical of early 1920s hospital scenes, and depicts a nurse attaching electro-cardiograph wires to a patient, photographed at the National Hospital for Diseases, London. Figure 1.2, on the other hand, was published as part of a beauty advertisement, for the skincare brand *Marinello*. Beneath the image lies bold, cursive text proclaiming: 'Learn how to develop your beauty type to its full charm.'[2] The caregiver, then, despite her appearance, is not a nurse, but, in fact, a 'beauty specialist'.[3] The reclining young woman, therefore, is not a patient in the medical sense, but a client, seeking, as the advertisement put it, 'complete loveliness'.[4] This advertisement was not alone in its adoption of medical scenes in order to sell beauty, and formed part of a growing trend towards a medical aesthetic in beauty advertisements produced in London, Paris and New York, and published by the fashion magazines of each city.

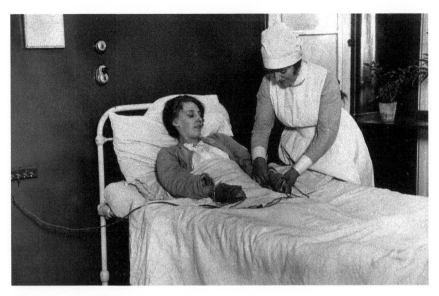

Figure 1.1 *Photograph, The National Hospital for Diseases of the Heart, London: a nurse attaches electrocardiograph wires to a patient in bed to record her heartbeat, c.1922. Wellcome Collection. Attribution 4.0 International (CC BY 4.0).*

Medicine was particularly associated with women during the war, and their roles as nurses were frequently propagated by wartime imagery, including Figure 1.3, a wartime poster which encouraged women to become nurses. Post-war beauty advertisements drew on this association between women and nursing; however, unlike wartime imagery, they depicted women as receivers rather than dispensers of care, as demonstrated by Figure 1.2. Here, the brand emphasized the advertisement's medical content through its setting, which includes a pristine sink, and a plethora of containers upon a shining surface. This detail creates depth and a comprehensive, believable sense of the space. Yet, as an illustration inserted within an advertisement, this sense of reality is confined. In this way, it is presented as a vision, a dreamlike image, enhanced by its undulating, as opposed to rigid, border. This dreamlike state connects to psychoanalysis, which fundamentally developed as a discipline during the early twentieth century. Dreams formed an integral part of the period's psychoanalytic theories, and the discipline's pioneer, Sigmund Freud, argued in *The Interpretation of Dreams* that 'the dream in its essence signifies the fulfillment of a wish'.[5] If commercial imagery presented dreamlike visions, it follows that their subject addressed a certain wish and offered the promise of its fulfilment. The vision-like image of medical attention within beauty advertising therefore suggests the fulfilment of a subconscious need for healing.

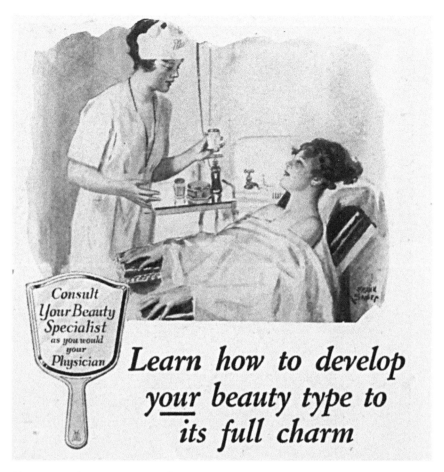

Consult
Your Beauty
Specialist
*as you would
your*
Physician

Learn how to develop your beauty type to its full charm

Figure 1.2 *Advertisement, Marinello, 1922.*

The widespread presence of this imagery within high-end fashion magazines indicates women's publications to be objects of dreamscape that commodified the resolution of trauma and fear, resulting from the recent assault of violence.[6] Gary Cross has pointed out in relation to the interwar years that 'ads [*sic*] linked material goods to immaterial longings, blending social, psychological, and physical needs indivisibly'.[7] Therefore, the presence of healing within advertisements indicates that it belonged to a 'longing' or 'need' that advertisers perceived women to have, which is what rendered it desirable and commercially viable. This was carried out upon an entirely subconscious level, which corresponded to contemporaneous theories of advertising, as advised by the French journal *Arts et Métiers Graphiques* in 1927:

Figure 1.3 *Albert Sterner, lithograph, We Need You, 1918.*

Publicity, like anything which falls under the senses, may be perceived in the state of waking, or on the contrary in the state of sleeping – during the hours where the spirit is passive, available for the impressions that are indifferent to it in appearance. – An idea is going to lodge itself in one of the folds of the brain, in one of its mysterious pockets, in the subconscious![8]

The process of advertising, psychoanalysis and the beauty advertisements that connected to it through their portrayal of medical imagery therefore all relied upon the unconscious state. In turn, the very war trauma commercialised by such medical imagery also resided upon a largely psychological, unconscious level.

It is no coincidence, then, that the beauty advertisers' dependence upon the subconscious coincided with psychoanalysis's rise in popularity and credibility during the post-First World War years. As Freud put it:

> This episode [of war] … has not been without importance for the spread of the knowledge of psycho-analysis. Many medical men, who had preciously held themselves aloof from psycho-analysis, have been brought into close touch with its theories through their service with the army compelling them to deal with the question of war neuroses.[9]

The war, with its physical and psychological assaults, was therefore a major factor for the growth of psychoanalysis, and for the increasingly positive reception it received within medical circles and the wider public alike, as its benefits for veterans, who suffered traumas such as shellshock, were realized. For example, according to Élisabeth Roudinesco, 'it might have been the sight of these men, with their missing limbs and dazed expressions, that made Jacques [Lacan] want to be a doctor'.[10] It was only through becoming a doctor that Lacan was able to practise psychoanalysis later, as training was only available through a medical career path, as Freud's mention of 'medical men' suggests. Furthermore, although psychoanalysis was refined by Freud in Vienna, its development after the war was closely connected to France, Britain and America. As Roudinesco has observed, the discipline in fact 'originated in France, for it could be traced back to the meeting of Freud and Charcot at the Salpêtrière'.[11] In Paris, a succession of psychoanalytic societies were established throughout the 1920s, including the *Evolution psychiatrique* in 1925, and the *Société psychanalytique de Paris* in 1926.[12] Similarly, the British psychoanalyst Ernest Jones wrote in December 1918: 'In both England and America [psychoanalysis] has made great progress of late … it arouses general interest in every circle … '.[13] Additionally, the discipline's post-war popularity can also be attributed to the first translations of major works, such as Freud's *The Ego and the Id*, published within London, Paris and New York at this time.

The beauty advertisements, in drawing on the subconscious through medical visions, therefore reflected the rise of psychoanalysis in the cities they were published in, and also reinforced the growing association between the fields of psychoanalysis and medicine. Moreover, psychoanalysis was one of the only fields

Assault

that documented female war trauma, which further links psychoanalysis with women and the advertisements that targeted them through the commercialization of such trauma. For example, the case that Lacan claimed was most crucial to his work on hysteria was the war-induced trauma of a female civilian.[14] Although hysteria had long been associated with women, and only recently re-classified as an illness of the mind rather than womb, it is telling that he highlighted this case above more widely documented cases of male shellshock.[15] Not only is this evidence for the existence of female war trauma, which the beauty advertisements indirectly addressed, but they did so through the use of psychoanalytic methods, which were themselves a recognized tactic of contemporary advertising. On this psychological level, residing trauma could be subconsciously recognized and restored, and the device through which advertisements played out, and commercialized, this form of restoration was through the medical healing of the human body.

Advertisements appeared within French, British and American fashion publications that specifically referred to healing. For example, in 1924, Viabella claimed that 'the care and cultivation of beauty is a specialist profession demanding expert knowledge of the ills to which beauty is heir and skill in corrective treatment'.[16] The advertisement, in deeming treatment to be necessary in this way, works on the same assumption as in Figure 1.2, that there was a form of damage in need of restoration. Similarly, another 1925 Marinello advertisement explicitly referred to 'destruction' as a problem.[17] Such advertisements highlighted, and created, forms of damage within women, and placed their products in the powerful position of being supposedly able to repair them. They both addressed and perpetuated trauma, through offering the tantalizing promise of a form of control and order to help make sense of the uncontrollable upheaval of the war. One 1927 Parisian beauty advertisement even boasted its ability to heal the '*défectuosités*' of '*les combats*', and claimed that its featured product had been used by Roman gladiators.[18] What the advertisements universally claimed to offer, therefore, was a solution to heal various forms of damage, through what was effectively an act of reparation, which would cure and restore women from psychological war trauma.

Post-war reparation took various forms, and in addition to the psychological reparation addressed by beauty advertisements, acts of social, political, cultural and economic reparation on a wider scale were also necessary. As Romy Golan has described, the French government set in motion a *rappel à l'ordre* (call to order), a 'political and cultural agenda ... largely aimed at repressing the trauma of war',[19] which entailed 'a collective ethos driven toward the restoration of what had been before the war'.[20] This involved programmes for national reconstruction, both collectively and individually. Britain too took restorative measures, and set up a Ministry of Reconstruction in 1917, which introduced an ambitious programme of reform in 1918, including health schemes and national mass housing.[21] Although America was more distant, Daniel Rodgers has written that at this time, 'American politics was peculiarly open to foreign models and imported ideas',[22] and it too felt the need for reparative policies. For example, in the field of rehabilitation, the physical reparation of the body, Beth Linker has written: 'the Allied and Central Powers instituted rehabilitation programs … Eventually … the United States adopted programs in rehabilitation, too, in order to help their own war injured recover'.[23] The United States' well-known post-war period of isolation also involved an element of self-protection, of turning inwards as one collective, cohesive body. What these policies share, directly and indirectly, is a move towards restoration and healing in recovering from the war.

This reparation on a macrocosmic level was also played out through microcosms. Melanie Klein began to formulate her psychoanalytic theory of reparation from *c*.1921, concurrently to the above policies. She claimed that when an infant's wish is not attended to, they become consumed with destructive phantasies towards their mother. In order to progress from this, and begin developing their ego, they must enter the 'depressive position', when they are 'faced with … guilt and despair … [and] the wish to restore and recreate' their mother.[24] Essentially, they begin to consider others as well as themselves. She defined reparation as 'controlling destructiveness and repairing and restoring damage done',[25] which also applies precisely to the acts of reparation undergone by Britain, France and America following the war, which reveals the widespread extent to which reparation occurred.

According to Klein, reparation occurs throughout life and is 'the basis of the ego's capacity to maintain love and relationships through conflicts and difficulties'.[26] She asserted that this 'is also the basis for creative activities',[27] such as art, which is 'rooted in the infant's wish to restore and recreate his lost happiness … '.[28] It is interesting, then, that the drive towards post-war recovery in British, French and American government also took place within the concurrent art of each country, another way in which macrocosmic policies were both reflected and constructed on a microcosmic scale. Jay Winter describes this phenomenon as a 'backward gaze'[29] conducted by 'so many writers, artists, politicians, soldiers, and everyday families in this period' alike.[30] Indeed, despite pre-war abstraction, many artists returned to traditional scenes and to classicism, attracted by its apparent unscarred wholeness. Pablo Picasso's figurative *The Source*, 1921, for example, is a noticeable departure from his previous Cubism, and displays classical ideals. While the return to order was most explicit in French policy, and responding art movements such as Purism arguably most pronounced in France (where Picasso was based), its reflection in art spread across Europe. In England, for example, Roger Fry, Wyndham Lewis and David Bomberg have all been associated with a return to order.[31] Several American artists displayed similar tendencies, including Lyonel Feininger, who painted heavily romanticized, nostalgic city scenes due to being 'enraged with the sights and sounds of New York'.[32] Certainly, the comparative lack of visual representation of the life-changing monstrosities of war within each country is striking. Art moved, then, through various methods towards a clean, whole body; something which, in offering medicalized, sterile visions of care and healing, beauty advertisements also achieved. Governmental policies, art and beauty advertising all served to stave off trauma in this way. Staving trauma was the motive behind Klein's model of psychoanalytic reparation, and she directly linked art with this. All three phenomena reacted to the war's trauma through reparation, in the same way an infant controls destruction according to Klein.

Through offering images of clean, whole bodies, beauty advertisements took part in this collective, reparative drive, and presented their products as able to fix and heal bodily damages. This strongly evokes the role of the doctor. Pertinently, Viabella claimed to possess 'expert knowledge of the ills' in order to administer 'corrective treatment', which is in fact an apt description of the role of a medical doctor. Indeed, the same advertisement unhesitatingly used the term 'Beauty Doctor' in place of 'beauty specialist', and similarly equated beauty practitioners with their medical 'equivalent', cautioning: 'Choose your Beauty Doctor .... As you choose your medical attendant.'[33] Using the phrase 'medical attendant' in place of the more traditional 'doctor' reserved the gravitas associated with the term 'doctor' exclusively for beauty. Marinello [Figure 1.2] had made a similar association: 'consult your beauty specialist as you would your physician.'[34] This marks a distinct shift in references to medical practitioners within beauty advertising. As late as 1918, advertisements occasionally proffered quotes from particular medical doctors to vindicate their products, such as Northam Warren Corporation in *Vogue*, July 1918. The later examples, however, present themselves as replacing the very doctors whose endorsement they had previously sought.[35]

This corresponded with the wider public's changing attitude towards medicine as a result of the war. While the military fatalities of the war were unprecedented, they were dwarfed by casualties: approaching 4 million, over 1.5 million and almost 250,000 troops survived with wounds, injuries and sickness in the French, British and American forces, respectively. This had a significant impact on medical treatment, and in 1919, the Director-General of the British Army Medical Service reflected:

great improvements have been made in many directions … the advance … has been very marked. Thousands of limbs and lives are now saved which, at the commencement of the war, would have been regarded as irretrievably lost.[36]

This sense of progress impacted beauty advertisements: by portraying medicine in this positive light, and adopting a medical theme, they could share the favourable associations of wartime medical advances. Therefore, medical attention, which had been a question of survival during the war, was now being presented as a capitalist object to incite desire and be consumed. This commercialization of subconscious trauma and the desires it provoked, through the visual and textual presentation of beauty practitioners as doctors, again recalls Freud as it offered the enticing prospect of wish-fulfilment.

Furthermore, beauty advertisements even claimed that their practitioners held powers that outreached their medical equivalents. Marinello [Figure 1.2], for example, claimed to 'make an expert diagnosis of your beauty needs and scientifically bestow the supreme gift of beauty upon you.'[37] In addition to aligning their power with that of medical doctors, beauty advertisers took this much further, and presented this power as omniscient and omnipotent, a claim that it could not fulfil in practice. This was even recognized in literature: in Florence Warden's 1920 novel, *The Beauty Doctor*, for example, two women were recruited for their 'pretty face[s]'[38] by a beauty practitioner, who told customers they had been 'perfect wreck[s]'[39] until 'treated'[40] by her. The trainees deemed this 'nonsense',[41] and marvelled at the deceptive nature of beauty treatments, such as 'hair washing' which 'seemed … oddly like hair dyeing',[42] and even answered 'yes'[43] when asked, 'you are a fraud, of course?'[44] Nonetheless, despite this awareness, they continued to practice as 'beauty doctors'.

In over-exaggerating their authority in this way, beauty advertisements fell into a fallacy of modernity, which Michel Foucault outlined in *The Birth of the Clinic*. Here, he dismissed society's expectation, and belief, in doctors' ability to 'totally and definitively cure'[45] all as mere 'day-dreaming',[46] a choice of language that once more conjures Freudian wish-fulfilment. Instead, he argued, society's unrealistic expectation of doctors is merely one of the many false myths perpetuated by modernity. Therefore, the beauty advertisements' self-imposed powers, in order to promote their services, can also be seen as a fallacy of modernity. The doctor was a positive trope upon which to draw, and offered the enticing combination of hope, cures and proven, extensive knowledge with which to administer them. This constructed a concept of seductively achievable beauty, and an impression of certainty and safety, which was crucial in comparison to the danger of the recent war.

However, violence and instability did not end with the war, and post-war modernity itself created further uncertainties, which *Vogue* described as 'the violence and ferment of the life to-day'.[47] Gilbert Guilleminault recounted hedonism as a direct result of the war, and commented that 'on the 11th of November [1918] an era of sheer madness opened up for the French'.[48] Similarly, in 1920, *Vogue* declared '… like New York, [Paris's] image is the image of ultra-modern civilization, luxurious, careless, violent …',[49] and Sally Alexander has described the 'atmosphere of constant anxiety'[50] that pervaded post-war London. Beauty advertisements commodified female war trauma through psychoanalytic means, but could they continue to target the war's residual effects?

The war had a significant impact on women's independence, opening up more opportunities and creating a notable sense of freedom.[51] However, this simultaneously brought them into contact with the violence of modern life: more and more women – particularly those who were younger and single – entered the city, pursuing work and entertainment alike.[52] Not only was their independent presence in the city relatively new, but cities were the very epicentre of frenzied, violent, post-war modernity. The particular demands of 1920s beauty compounded this experience, by heightening feelings of exposure. Fashion revealed more bodily contours, and exposed more flesh, than ever before. And cosmetics, which were only recently available on a mass-produced, easily obtained level, had been associated with prostitution up until the First World War.[53] Post-war modernity therefore brought increased scrutiny and anxiety for women.

Beauty advertisements aligned themselves with these changes, emphatically declaring themselves as modern. For example, Viabella singled out the 'modern resources and modern equipment'[54] needed in order to achieve beauty, and Helena Rubinstein sympathized that 'woman is a very busy individual … struggling to attain even a mediocre complexion or to maintain her good complexion at its best'.[55] Conveniently, she asserted her own 'scientific beauty-preparations' as antidotes of 'unerring efficiency' to combat this chaotic existence. Other beauty manufacturers similarly used projections of clinical efficiency in order to advertise. A 1924 Elizabeth Arden advertisement also linked modernity and science, enthusing that 'the modern science of Elizabeth Arden brings sure and natural beauty to every woman'.[56] Its use of both 'modern science' and nature to entice women is somewhat oxymoronic, and reveals a conflict between previous methods of advertising beauty, which appealed to nature and natural beauty, and the clinical post-war approach.[57] In 1926 Madame Theux even referred to the 'études biologiques' apparently undertaken in the development and production of her hair care products, and presented an advertisement in the style of a scientific research report.[58]

This adoption of science shows beauty advertisers' desire to increase expectations of reliability and results, which would offer the crucial, comforting notion of certainty after the war, and present a coping mechanism for women for the frenzied modernity that followed. It was also important in establishing the international beauty industry's reputation, considering its relative infancy in terms of mass-consumerization: product sales, for example, doubled from 1919 to 1929.[59] This appears to be the first time in which the definitively modern phenomenon of (pseudo)scientific beauty advertising appeared to any significant extent. Moreover, de Certeau has described the way in which ' … scientific work (*scientificité*) has given itself its own proper and appropriate places through rational projects capable of determining their procedures',[60] which offers an apt description of the technique used by these beauty advertisements. De Certeau, like the advertisements themselves, connected this strongly with modernity, and argued that the 'remainder'[61] of anything non-scientific 'has become what we call culture. This cleavage organizes modernity'.[62] Traditionally, beauty would fall under the 'remainder', in the category of culture. However, by aligning itself with science, it created its own credibility and entered modernity. This appropriation of medicine, science and modernity contributed to the advertisements' restorative attempts, via psychoanalytic means, to heal, or commodify, women's trauma and anxieties provoked by the war, and the chaos of the cities that they subsequently faced.

On one level, the advertisements fulfilled a subconscious fantasy of healing women. Yet in doing so, they also presented women as requiring 'correction', as explicitly stated by Viabella.[63] Indeed, while the 'violence' of exposure in the metropolitan city was represented as at once dizzying and horrifying for women within *Vogue*, their newfound freedom was also perceived with alarm by wider society. The kinds of women buying newly available beauty consumables correlated with those feared by conservative voices as the 'new woman': young, single, supposedly seeking hedonism above marriage and motherhood. Fears towards this 'new woman' developed over the period and were present within popular culture. For example, Victor Marguerite's 1922 novel, *La Garçonne*, which fictionalized the 1920s 'New Woman'[64] was banned in France, and comments such as 'these aren't young girls! There are no more young girls!'[65] were rife in the press. Similar reactions occurred in British and American fiction. One character in British author Norman Douglas's novel, *South Wind* (originally published in 1917 and reprinted throughout the 1920s) expressed 'alarm' for 'he did not altogether approve of the New Woman',[66] and American writer Zane Grey included the line 'I'm not taking into consideration the new-woman species' in his 1923 novel and later film, *The Call of the Canyon*, lamenting that 'modern girls' were unable to 'make

[use] of education' due to 'their surplus energy'.[67] These concerns can be associated with the wider call to order: during the war, gender roles became somewhat confused, and as Amy Lyford has written,

> It was key [for the call to order] that the new, postwar society would not differ much from the old, particularly in terms of relations between the sexes. Many hoped that men and women alike would return to their prewar social roles, with women at home and men in the fields or in the factory.[68]

Furthermore, in 1924, Jacques Boulanger claimed 'the *femme moderne* is above all a creation of the war',[69] and as Mary Louise Roberts has argued, 'the modern woman provided a way of talking about the war's more general trauma'.[70] In the same way, beauty advertisements were also a means for trauma.

On one hand, beauty imagery that visually placed these women under medical attention, and used projections of scientific infallibility and omnipotence, can be seen as soothing trauma and anxiety generated from the war and the devastating losses suffered as a result of the 1918 flu pandemic. Yet at the same time, traces of the wider anxiety towards and criticism of women and their changing roles in society were also present within cosmetics advertisements, particularly as depictions of scientific, medical intervention intensified as the 1920s progressed.

For example, in 1927, Elizabeth Arden published an advertisement featuring a photograph by Baron De Meyer, which, barring the model's makeup, closely resembled a hospital operation.[71] Indeed, the model wore modest, oversized and simply cut clothing that was more akin to a hospital gown than contemporary styles, jarring with her fashionably applied cosmetics. Her face was bound with white, bandage-like cloth, as she lay back on a bed, which feasibly resembled either a beauty treatment bed or a hospital equivalent. A pair of hands came towards her. One hand gripped the model's head, in a firmer manner than typical within beauty treatments. The other gripped a thin, sharp implement, poised by the model's face, as if about to be deployed. This mise-en-scène was not uncommon, and similar set-ups appeared within several contemporaneous advertisements: medical-style bandages regularly appeared wrapped around models' faces. In a 1928 example by Contouré Laboratories, for example, a model, whose head was also wrapped in a bandage-like cloth, sank back onto a white bed. Her face was expressionless, whilst an unidentified stranger's hand held a syringe-like appliance to her face, which was larger in length than her head.[72] The depicted scenes within beauty imagery progressed, therefore, from light, smiling, healing medical care, to full-blown operative, surgical, invasive treatment. They presented the notion that women could, and should, be radically altered or 'corrected' through beauty: a situation that, when involving imposing implements in close proximity to the skin, by mysterious, non-medical operators, was wrought with potential violence, and the threat of assault.

Violence was also a major aspect of the call to order, which as Lyford has asserted, depended on the very violence that it attempted to forget.[73] However, the manifestation of violence that grew in relation to medicalized visions of beauty went beyond this. One of the 'legacies of the First World War'[74] was the rise of fascism, which although most active in Austria, Germany, Hungary, Romania, France and Italy, was widely reported by the British, French and American media, and spawned both fascist and anti-fascist movements and sentiments in each country.[75] For example, in 1925, Duncan Aikman expressed fears about the danger of fascism in an article entitled 'American Fascism'.[76] Together, as Philip Morgan has commented, this 'affected the political "mood" of the post-war years in Europe', and America, as a whole.[77] The ideology celebrated and perpetuated violence, and one way it did so was to transform violence from a destructive force into a healing one, through language and image. Benito Mussolini, for example, drew frequent connections between violence and surgery, and declared in 1925 that 'violence must be generous, chivalric and surgical'.[78] By using the medical metaphor of surgery, violence is justified as necessary, healing and efficient, as opposed to unwanted, harmful and destructive. Whilst beauty advertisements such as the aforementioned examples by Elizabeth Arden and Contouré Laboratories were clearly not part of the fascist discourse, they too used the same metaphor within the same timeframe, and presented invasive, unnecessary surgery as necessary and beneficial. This parallel was at times very precise: the potential violence of Elizabeth Arden's 1927 advertisement was largely created by a scalpel-like tool that hovered ominously close to the model's face. Similarly, in 1922, Mussolini had asserted 'it is necessary … to use the scalpel inexorably to take away everything parasitic, harmful and suffocating …'.[79] Whilst he was referring to Italian governmental offices, his use of metaphor is indicative of rising tension within the Western political scene. This permeated various areas of culture and even extended to beauty advertisements. The scalpel's presence within a seemingly incongruous beauty advertisement suggests that something equally 'parasitic, harmful and suffocating' still lingered within women by 1928. On one level, constructing surgical scenes within advertisements continued beauty's increasing engagement with modernity, implying efficiency and productivity. Yet paradoxically, their very necessity disclosed lurking, 'parasitic' trauma, both in terms of unresolved war wounds, the further onslaught of modern life for women and wider society's alarm towards this. They also presented an image of violent correction and latent assault. Whilst the First World War was over, anxiety was not, and the rise of fascist regimes was a seed of violence that would only grow.[80]

In the immediate post-war years, then, beauty advertisements engaged with women's experiences of suffering, appealing to notions of wounds on a psychological level. They presented the enticing image of peaceful care, healing and wholeness, and through doing so, participated within the wider return to order, which despite having definitively taken place in France, also disseminated into Britain and America. This took place on both a governmental and cultural scale, and Klein's contemporary theorization of reparation links all three methods of healing – governmental, artistic and through beauty – as attempts to restore damage and stave off trauma. The beauty industry, which was in a process of establishment, offered reassurance and armour for women against recent and ongoing uncertainty and anxiety, of the flu pandemic, war and the assault of the modern city that ensued alike. Yet this image of comfort was not always what it seemed. New tendencies to over-assert the medicinal and scientific nature of beauty products, falsely align the industry with the increasingly positive reputations of medicine and psychoanalysis, and cunning attempts to work psychoanalytically all disaccorded with the infancy of the industry and the formulations it produced. This turned women's anxieties into products to be consumed, and aligned with contemporary criticism towards women, which itself can be understood as stemming from wider societal trauma. In doing so, the advertisements implied that women's superficial appearance required correction, ultimately insinuating that their natural state, which had previously been idealized as a beauty aspiration, was no longer desirable nor acceptable. By the end of the 1920s, this even included 'correction' of a violent nature, with the depicted implication of physical assault.

Colour: The assault of modernity

In 1923, the *Gazette du Bon Ton* employed 'un professur de "couleurisme"' to provide advice for an article entitled 'Couleurs Dangereuses et Vertueuses' [Figure 1.4]. Set upon a solid background of vivid, mustard yellow, the text and accompanying line drawing, both printed in strong black, created a stark contrast, and subsequently jarring visual sensation for the reader. Could this uncomfortable viewing be an example of the danger of colour referred to by the article? Can colour perform an assault on the senses in this way? If this explains the *Gazette du Bon Ton*'s reference to danger, what, then, associates colour with the journal's second description, 'virtuous'?[81] Such ideas on colour were not obscure, and in fact appeared over a range of contemporary media, particularly the fashion press. Two years later, in

Figure 1.4 *Gazette Du Bon Ton, No. 5, 1923.*

1925, for example, *Vogue* mused that 'there is … a touch of the soldier's swagger … of flaunting danger … in red hats'.[82] It proposed, then, that colours have an ability to project characteristics. In this case, the characteristics were associated with military violence, closely connected to the recent experience of the war.

Certainly, where beauty is concerned, colour was loaded with meaning. Before the war, the visible use of makeup and cosmetics still harboured traditional associations with questionable virtues. Afterwards, as Aileen Ribeiro has pointed out, cosmetics 'largely' but 'not completely' became 'free from association with immorality and sexual temptation'.[83] Gradually, makeup became more accepted, and even celebrated, and the quintessential style of the high 1920s was a celebration of its own artificiality. However, during the earlier years of the decade, the sphere of cosmetics still harboured questions of morality. In high fashion magazines, key selling points for advertising products included the traits of being 'natural' and 'undetectable'. For example, in a 1922 advertisement, *Bourjois* praised French women for their 'universally admired … faces [which] never show a trace of powder'.[84] Published in British and American titles, it urged its readers to adopt this sensibility and emphasized the brand's French origins by advising its name should be 'pronounced Bourge-wah', connecting them with the brand and its heritage. It exhorted:

> it is not the cheek that glows with the red of the nose, nor the skin that has the
> wax-like pallor of the lily. The two must be mingled in a hue that is delicate,

modest, natural. And therein lies the secret of Bourjois' … Java Face Powder. Designed to please the critical eyes of women … Java is, before all else, natural.[85]

If only natural and unnoticeable colour 'pleased women's eyes', what could be said of a more unnatural and explicit usage?

As Kathy Peiss has described, the wealthiest patrons of cosmetics sought, and were shown by cunning shop assistants, 'high-priced or imported brands with light scent and natural tints'.[86] Certainly, women within this stratum remarked on the vulgarity of explicit colour, and one Thompson shop assistant commented: 'I thought it was extremely vulgar to go around with "varnish" on the nails'.[87] On the other hand, other socio-economic groups, for example, 'Jewish flappers', usually bought 'deep red or orange lipstick made by Angelus', according to a *Walgreen's* shop assistant.[88] There is clear evidence here of prejudice: choices in cosmetics, as determined by colour, were perceived in relation to, and even as the determinant of, class. So, the way in which women wore, or chose not to wear, colour on their faces had significant implications on the way their status was perceived. Explicit colour signified a less advantaged social status, such as that belonging to an entertainer or immigrant, whilst a paler, more subdued usage evoked privilege and the old-world, aristocratic value historically attributed to pale skin. This subjected women to several conflicts. Moral values regarding makeup were rapidly shifting, yet not homogeneously enough to make them entirely innocuous. Moreover, consuming such products made assertions about one's position within society, and the results were inescapably displayed on one's face. The acts of buying and wearing makeup were fraught with pressure.

Furthermore, colour itself contained intricacies of meaning that extended beyond the quantity of usage, which had the potential to further compound such feelings. Jean Baudrillard concurred with the contemporary commentators above, that 'colours have psychological and moral overtones … Tradition confines colour to its own parochial meanings and draws the strictest of boundary-lines about them'.[89] Specifically, he added that this occurs 'even in the freer ceremony of fashion'.[90] Moreover, despite the differing context of his *System of Objects* to the fashionable speculations of the 1920s discussed thus far, he confirmed that 'muted tones', such as black and white, are most 'chic' by their very nature of showing 'repression', by displaying restraint. The same attitude had been promoted by *Vogue* in 1925, when it advised that 'grey is as ladylike a colour as exists … Men … really prefer circumspection of conduct and costume on the part of the ladies of their world'.[91] For both Baudrillard and the magazine, therefore, subtlety equalled a refined elegance. Did loud colour therefore equate to the opposite of elegance: brashness, in both appearance and perceptions? This array of associations rendered the act of getting dressed to be charged with uncertainty and necessitated careful consideration.

This was further complicated by a sense of contradiction that began to appear within the spectacular realm of advertising. For example, in 1922, Dorin of Paris advertised their beauty 'preparations' alongside a full-page, full-colour illustration [Figure 1.5].[92] It depicts an artist's palette, with rouge in the place of paint. Their colours range from natural pinks to decidedly less natural blues and oranges.

Figure 1.5 *Advertisement, Dorin of Paris, 1922.*

In the centre of this colourful cosmetic array is the contented face of a heavily made-up woman, depicted with expressive brushstrokes as if by the hand of an artist, using Dorin cosmetics as a medium. Such imagery was successful enough to be repeated in a further version of the advertisement during the same year, with another woman depicted in the same painterly way. In 1920, Rigaud had made comparable use of pots of rouge as a visual basis for advertising. However, although Figure 1.6 features a long line of pots, open to reveal their colour, the colours here are based around more traditional shades of pink. Furthermore, although a young woman is depicted actively applying such products, and clearly wears rouge on her lips and cheeks, it is noticeable rather than overt. The difference only two years later with Dorin's equivalent was that by presenting makeup as a direct metaphor for paint the message was transmitted that cosmetics could (and should) be creatively enjoyed, and that fashionability necessitated women playing the role of an artist, to make lavish use of cosmetics as paint. This further confronted moral and social implications of colour, promoting women to actively engage with colour, despite its recent negative associations.

Colour had also received newfound interest during the late-nineteenth century, when 'a renewed prestige of color'[93] emerged amongst artists and writers. Previously, colour had been dismissed by figures such as Descartes due to its dependence on the 'uncertain workings of the fallible human eye', but as this uncertainty transitioned towards certainty, 'chemists like E. M. Chevreul investigated color with scientific precision'.[94] By the 1870s, this interest began to emerge within painting, and the Impressionist school drew on developments produced by Delacroix, Turner and Courbet's triumph of colour over form. However, the colours used were 'often juxtaposed rather than smoothly blended',[95] which art historians, such as Martin Jay, have described as a 'violent decentering'[96] of the Western art historical canon's traditional preferences. This forbears the violence associated with colour thirty years later, in the mid-interwar period.

By encouraging women to become artists through cosmetics, as the advertisements discussed above began to, they too could create juxtapositions: a practice which was referred to within interwar fashion magazines. Marya Mannes wrote, for example, that 'Paris is dizzy with contrasts ... outwardly streamline; inwardly 1890'.[97] Not only did she reveal the 'contrasts' that abounded visual life, but she specifically linked this to the time and place of the Impressionists, when colours and contrasts had triumphed. She also alluded to the same 'violent decentering' as Jay, by stating that the effect of such contrasts was dizziness. Such associations were frequent: *Vogue*, for example, commented on 'contrasts' as 'violent', which was usually deemed an 'unfortunate' occurrence.[98] One example given of such misfortune was orange and purple: a combination again described as 'violent'.[99] Stark colour contrasts, then, forcefully entered into the period's

Figure 1.6 *Advertisement, Rigaud, 1920.*

sartorial vocabulary, and their aesthetic effects were perceived 'violently' by the fashion press. Additionally, this continued a 'violent decentering' that had begun thirty years previously.

This labelling of contrasting colour as violent correlates to the biological process of perceiving colour.

When the eye perceives a colour that jars, it is a source of strain: a sensation increased further by the opposition between two colours of this sort. During the 1920s, a succession of manuals on the mechanics of vision were published, developing from nineteenth-century advancements. In 1924, Sir John Herbert Parsons published an *Introduction to the Study of Colour Vision*, which comprehensively described the way in which perceiving colour involves 'stimulation of a retinal area … followed at a certain interval by sensations, potential or kinetic, of an opposite nature, a phenomenon known as "succedaneous" or "successive contrast."'[100] Excessive 'brightness' or 'contrast' would therefore over-stimulate these mechanisms, leading to potential strain. Violent effects could therefore be brought about through vision. Importantly, women could employ, and empower themselves with, this effect, by adopting it into their visual, fashionable appearance.

The association between violence and colour was not restricted to jarring contrasts, and also extended to individual colours. The *Gazette du Bon Ton* pinpointed this oddity in 1923, in its aforementioned article on virtuous and dangerous colour. Rather than being inanimate and therefore unmistakably 'virtuous', or devoid of meaning, the so-called expert on 'colourism' professed that colours have a deep inner meaning ('signification intime'): some delight ('ravissent'), and others can drive one to madness ('à la folie').[101] Similarly, two years later, *Vogue* described 'certain shades' as being able to 'scream at one'.[102] One colour in particular continually emerged within this context: as *Vogue* put it in another 1925 article, 'red [i]s the most violent colour'.[103] Yet another article published the same year offered a detailed explanation:

> Red … [is] like the sound of a trumpet, for among colours it is more than apt to take the high note of authority … soldiers were once all glorious with it and still preserve it in cap bands, tabs, and ribands … it warns and dominates in a fierce and powerful way … think of the tide of it there is inside us, too; full beating and fiery … human beings are slyly inclined to red, even if they do not hear it screaming … there is no year when it can not be felt throbbing somewhere in the dark and all ready to flash out again.[104]

Here, powerful and specific associations are given to the colour, including its relation to blood and therefore, seemingly human nature. The colour is presented as beyond fashion due to this power: its magnetic draw supposedly compels human nature towards it, regardless of the 'year' or season in fashion terms. The connection with soldiers conjures images of violent, catastrophic, yet noble battle scenes, due to the mention of 'glorious', and reverence evidenced towards military dress. Such couplings, of course, had particular resonance for the date it was written, six years after the end of the First World War. The implications of the conflict were far from resolved, and even in 1928, a further three years later, its impact continued to be lamented by the fashion media: 'war, revolution and economic disaster have made things violent', wrote *Vogue*.[105] Nevertheless, the link between the colour red and military violence was a lasting one, and in 1937, Adrian Stokes described 'glaring pillar boxes' as having 'entered into companionship with the red, and with each other, like soldiers who make a solid pile of their (red) hats to prove their amity, the distinctiveness of each as brother'.[106] Whilst Stokes wrote on the eve of the Second World War, a sense of anxiety and foreboding had already been suggested by the similar associations made by *Vogue* in 1928. Despite their precision, and reference to a very specific form of violence, Stokes and *Vogue* experienced red in near-identical manners, which strengthens both the notion of a universal colour perception, and the relationship between colour and violence at large.

Vision has often been associated with modernity and considered to be at the top of the hierarchy of the senses in Western society. Freud proposed that civilization itself is 'a consequence of man's raising himself from the ground, of his assumption of an upright gait'.[107] To him, the basis of modern, functioning human civilization was the 'transformation of importance from smell to sight'.[108] Smell was associated with animals on all fours, and sight with humans, suggesting evolution towards logic and rationality. However, on the 'phantasmagoric, often gas-induced haze'[109] of the frontline, sight could not be depended upon for survival, and as Jay has elaborated, 'when all that the soldier could see was the sky above and the mud below, the traditional reliance on visual evidence for survival could no longer be easily maintained.'[110]

These experiences began to emerge within art and writing, through works by figures who had endured them directly during the war, including Georges Bataille and André Breton. The wounded eye surfaced as a frequently occurring symbol, from Luis Buñuel and Salvador Dali's 1928 film, *Un Chien Andalou*, which graphically split open an eye with a razor, to Bataille's 1928 novel, *The Story of the Eye*, the plot of which subjected the eye to a tirade of graphic abuse.[111] Although different in approach, these examples are typical of the Surrealist visual and literary attitude towards the eye and vision at this time. By assaulting the eye, and removing it from its privileged position of elevation, it was therefore brought back into contact with the 'baser' human instincts that Freud had described civilization, modernity and vision as moving away from.

This 'violent interrogation of vision',[112] as Jay has coined it, has further implications on the notion of violence in colour. A range of sources proposed an active relationship between the viewer of colour, and colour itself. For example, *Vogue* stated that 'there is something about a flaming spot of colour that few females can resist … There is a certain something about red which gives confidence.'[113] Not only does viewing colour produce a wealth of associated imagery, but the article insinuated, therefore, that these associations, when adopted and worn on the body (whether through clothing, or on the face through cosmetics) transferred onto the wearer, and were able to invoke a change in psychological state. In this case, the author argued that this could be positive. However, the article warned that it is not for 'the timid … nobody should go about looking meek in violent colours.'[114] One's internal state could be reflected, or created, through external colour. Yet it was presented as a fashion object, which must not clash with any other element of one's appearance, and instead contribute to a harmonious, sartorial whole, like any other accessory. Maurice Merleau-Ponty's later theorization of the *Phenemology of Perception*, 1945, closely concurs with this process. He argued that 'to look at an object is to inhabit it, and from this habitation to grasp all things in terms of the aspect which they present to it'.[115] For him, perception is bodily in its very nature: the self is not separate from the world it perceives, but rather, the two enter into a dynamic dialogue of exchange. If the two could mutually affect and alter each other in this way, the dual experience of colour is further confirmed. It became a source that could be both a passive attack (through inadvertently coming into contact with it), and a source of active infliction (through employing it directly, and therefore gaining from its psychological overtones and projections).

The mid-1920s shift in beauty advertising, from recommending a natural appearance, to promoting overt colour, continued into the 1930s, and placed the implications of colour onto a wider and increasingly relevant scale. By 1931, for example, Elizabeth Arden produced an advertisement which boldly announced, in capitals, 'THE TRIUMPH OF COLOR IN MAKE-UP'[116] as its headline, accompanied by a suitably colourful illustration depicting a woman at her dressing table, wearing prominent pink blusher, red lipstick, and dark, blue eyeshadow, behind a large array of products, which supposedly had been lavishly used to construct her appearance. Rather than cautioning that cosmetics must match, or enhance, one's natural complexion, the brand instead offered the enticing option of 'a new complexion … to match every gown', reassuring potential customers 'you can wear any of them', which contrasted previous advertisements' warnings using hair and skin tones to strictly dictate what was permissible to wear.[117] Another advertisement by the brand of the same year furthered this message, with a title asking 'WHAT MAKE-UP are you wearing with the NEW COLORS?', supported by text which questioned: 'you don't expect to wear your green beads with every sports frock or carry your pink chiffon hankie with every evening gown. Why, then, expect make-up to do justice to every costume?'[118] Women were encouraged, in the name of fashion, to attain the very ideals that had previously been warned against, and which had harboured potentially damaging associations. Overt colour – which had only recently been slurred – was now presented as attractive and aspirational. Not only was colour perceived violently, but it led to a violent assault to what had previously been considered good taste.

This surge in women being (successfully) encouraged to adopt, an increasingly wider array of colour in their cosmetics took place amidst the Great Depression. Despite considerable hardship suffered internationally, including both France and the UK as well as the United States, and drastically decreased production, the sales of cosmetics in fact steadily rose during the 1930s, and comparatively, the industry did not experience the negative impact as deeply as many others.[119] This trend of increased beauty product sales during periods of wider economic difficulty has been popularly dubbed 'the lipstick effect', and has endured to the present day.[120] Whilst colour was being aggressively promoted within beauty advertisements, purchasing cosmetics could also have an uplifting effect psychologically: they were more attainable to purchase than other luxurious items, and in this case, such overt colour also physically brightened the face. This further reinforced the transformative qualities of colour, and its ability to alter the disposition of both its wearer and their onlooker.

Colour was also becoming more commonplace within everyday life, in wider culture as well as makeup. The 1920s saw an increase in colour in magazine publishing, and while black-and-white advertisements were still published during the 1930s, this became infrequent. Furthermore, as Charles Tepperman has described, 'in 1928 … color photography was still a rarity in commercial movie theatres … that year, Kodak introduced their Kodacolor process' which allowed amateurs to pursue colour in film, which 'produced a new aesthetic terrain'.[121] This created a further avenue, within the decade, in which colour became more ubiquitous. These changes, in the increasing occurrence of colour, were further cemented during the early 1930s, when colour films, although rare, began to appear commercially as well as in amateur endeavours. They were accessible to women through cinema-going, which, as Bryony Dixon has noted, was particularly receptive and appealing to women of the era.[122] Technological developments created further avenues through which women were exposed to colour. This brought with it the range of effects discussed, many of which connected directly to violence, in both bio-mechanical terms and psychological effects. Modernity was being created, and was experienced, through vision, which opened up the beholder to vulnerability from colour.

This influx of colour also appeared within the fashion world. Sonia Delaunay, for example, saw 'color as the skin of the world', and bold colour contrasts influenced her fashion design and artistic output alike.[123] This was part of a growing receptiveness towards an area ripe with new effects, experimentation and advancement. Matilda McQuaid has described the way in which 'it was color alone that created the virtual movement in [Delauney's] work, reflecting the age of modernity and its technological innovations – electric streetlights, airplanes, cars, and industrial machinery – which inspired her artistically'.[124] Colour, and therefore vision, was therefore strongly related to modernity. Indeed, the advancements of modernity itself, such as colour film and photography, disseminated to culturally active women through magazines and the cinema, for example, re-generated uses of, and attitudes towards colour, so much so that it infiltrated fashion design itself. This way, it not only became part of women's surroundings in modern life, but it also inhabited their bodies, cloaking them with a persona of specific effects.

As colour increasingly entered everyday life within the modern city, post-war implications upon women exaggerated their exposure to it. As more and more women entered the metropolis after the War, with newfound independence and relish, they spent more time in the very epicentres of colour's newfound omnipresence. Their contact with colour was instated from multiple sides: passively, in the form of the cultural changes that led to a bombardment of colour, and through being frequently active in areas most exposed to such developments. This brought women into heightened contact, therefore, with a form of potential violence and trauma, both physically in the mechanisms of vision, and metaphorically, through the vivid and violent contemporary colour associations that were circulated.

Around the same time, Jacques Lacan was beginning to theorize the gaze. In a seminar on 'The Split between the Eye and the Gaze', he emphasized the anxiety that occurs when one realizes that, in addition to being able to look, one is also a visible object, that can be looked back at: 'I see from only one point, but in my existence I am looked at from all sides.'[125] Furthermore, he related this specifically to women: 'The spectacle of the world, in this sense, appears to us as all-seeing … this all-seeing aspect is to be found in … a woman who knows that she is being looked at.'[126] For interwar women, being more exposed and present within the city heightened this sensation of a world that permanently watches those who frequent it. This permanent burning of the gaze was compounded by the combined assault of colour and modernity: colour became more prevalent and was perceived more violently with modernity, which itself was linked with vision. The eye, therefore, was under attack from all angles, both physically, when forced to confront the biologically aggressive impact of colour, and metaphorically, in terms of the written and visual attack on vision. In addition, women were being encouraged, for the first time, to incorporate such effects within their appearance, through fashion and beauty, despite preceding advice to the contrary.

This turbulence and uncertainty were reflected in several accounts of female experiences of modernity. In 1935, for example, Princess Marthe Bibesco described the act of a woman treading city pavements as 'a flight, a transport, a call to violence'.[127] She continued to ask: 'What are they fighting against? Who is the invisible enemy they are hurling this defiance at?'[128] Referring not to increasing militarization, the rise of fascism, socialist rebellion, or any other considerable threats of the early twentieth century, she described the seemingly simple, humble act of walking on a New York City street. Here, even 'the air of New York lashes women, making them walk erect'.[129] This sense of violent assault evoked, such as city air 'lashing' women, accords with the violence of the gaze and visual assault of colour, and the moral anxieties and contradictions provoked as a result.

As colour continued to rise in popularity and usage, this violence became present even within the very advertisements that promoted it. The same year, Savage produced a lipstick advertisement that starkly emphasized colour. It depicted a woman's head and shoulders, with whitened hair and skin, resembling classical statuary. Whilst classicism was a fashionable reference, its purpose was to emphasize the woman's (already emphatic) makeup application, with bold blue eyeshadow, vivid coral blush and blood-red lipstick. And this visual abundance did not relent: the main advantage proposed by the advertisement was that it 'actually stays on all day … or ALL NIGHT'.[130] The brand's unconventional name, which adjoined every product name, such as 'Savage Lipstick' and 'Savage Rouge', furthered its potentially threatening associations. The effects of this could be dangerous by the brand's own admittance: another of its advertisements, also produced in 1935, prominently labels its own 'hues' as 'maddening'.[131] While the adjective may have expressed intensity, 'maddening' could clearly also describe the experience of women, as their independence was countered by an assortment of visual bombardment under the experience of modernity.

As unfavourable moral associations of colour in appearance were shed, women could appropriate colour. This was a way to embrace fashion and fun, but also a means to return the gaze, and combat the visually assaulting experience of the modern, post-war city, which was increasingly filled with colour, owing to developments in both visual technologies and fashion. The very perception of this colour was perceived as violent biologically, evoking a sensation of physical assault, and furthermore, associations of colour were frequently and directly linked with violence and the recent traumatic events of the war. These effects created a disorientating assault to the sense of vision, as experiences of colour in everyday life dramatically increased. At the same time, an attack on the sense of sight within culture was a way to 'violently disturb … the corrupted, habitual vision of everyday life', and therefore the modes of operation that had theoretically led to the war and its long-lasting, residual trauma.[132] For women, too, appropriating and reflecting back colour, representative of modernity and possible violence on several levels, was a way of owning the gaze. It could respond to trauma, shield from conflicting and troubling messages, and meet the growing demands of modernity, which were all increased by colour. As one 1928 *Vogue* article expressed, fashion could reveal 'character' and a 'desire for freedom', either by 'being too violent or not violent enough'.[133] This reflected fashion's simultaneous expression of, and effect on, the psyche, and the way violent tropes could be reappropriated to gain power and independence. At the same time, there was a fine line between 'too' much or 'not … enough', representing the confliction felt by the magazine's female readership as a result of shifting and opposing societal expectations. This continued throughout the interwar period, and in 1936, *Vogue* confirmed: 'and on it goes, this insistent clamour for violent colour against black'.[134]

Fighting back: Elsa Schiaparelli

Elegant lines of cream cotton in a corded weave fall gracefully from neatly pleated shoulders, to an elegant mid-calf level [Figure 1.7]. Weighty folds give a sense of high quality, stylish comfort and ease. A well-placed collar, finished to confident, flattering points, sets off the ensemble with assurance. However, strategically placed pockets begin to raise questions about the conformity of this fashionable piece. Their raised position evokes hunting jackets, and the flaps are fully functional, deepening this sense of sturdy practicality. Elsa Schiaparelli was by no means the first designer to take influence from violent pursuits by c.1933, when she produced this piece. Such crossovers had occurred centuries previously, but particularly peaked with the onset of the First World War. For example, in October 1914, just as the conflict had begun, the national British newspaper *The Manchester Guardian* wrote that 'one is decidedly struck with the tendency to adopt – or rather adapt – several military styles', and it specifically referenced 'coats and capes', much like Schiaparelli's later version, as especially receptive to this.[135] However, Schiaparelli exaggerated this tendency to a new level. Whilst two lines of buttons stand strikingly down the centre, in a conventional, double-breasted style, the buttons themselves are far from conventional. From a distance, they appear to be uniform pieces of moulded brass, yet upon closer inspection, it becomes apparent they

Figure 1.7 *Elsa Schiaparelli, Coat with Bullet Casing Buttons, c.1933. Metropolitan Museum of Art, New York.*

have been modelled to resemble convincing bullet casings, evoking the potential power and violence of the perceived bullet within.

Bullets were not the only objects that Schiaparelli employed in order to subvert norms and expectations, to question and counter conventionality and add a frisson of fun. Nevertheless, in other collections, such objects took more innocuous forms, such as shells or lips. The seemingly sudden, and adamantly explicit introduction of violence onto an otherwise traditional coat, then, makes a deliberate statement. On one hand, she characteristically played with, and carefully exaggerated, the already implicit elements of hunting within the coat. This went beyond traditional military influences, and created a cunning, knowing dialogue.

Yet, on the other hand, developments in the international scene were beginning to deteriorate, and this sudden exaggeration, on a very specific theme, resonates precisely and hauntingly. In January that year, Adolf Hitler was appointed chancellor of Germany. While the consequences of this could not be fully appreciated at the time, other concurrent and consequent events pointed towards an unfavourable outcome, including the Reichstag Fire, completion of the first concentration camp, setting up of the Gestapo secret police, the officialization of Hitler's dictatorship and the legalization of eugenic sterilization. Whilst the locus and biggest impact of such happenings were in Germany, their implications were to affect the wider international scene. For example, during the same year, the Four Power Pact was signed between Germany, France, Britain and Italy, which, according to contemporary sources in Britain and France, such as the (British-published) *International Press Correspondence,* provoked 'uneasiness' and 'watchfulness' despite having been conceived by Mussolini supposedly to promote the opposite.[136] Furthermore, on 12th August that year, Winston Churchill gave a public speech warning that Germany was rearming, and emphasized the danger this posed.[137] This plethora of disquieting events, of which the above are but a selection, was reported widely across Europe and America. Their occurrence within the same year as the production of Schiaparelli's coat, due to their ubiquity, seems unlikely to be a coincidence. Rather, by escalating military crossover in dress to this scale, in much the same way as political events were escalating, Schiaparelli made a direct comment upon them through her design.

The context of this comment, of course, was manifested in dress, and thereby upon the body of the wearer. In this light, the placement of the bullets has particular resonance. Contrasting the coat's pale wheat hue in dark brass, they form two strong, direct lines, running from either side of the wearer's neck and down the torso. Their placement is assertive, unapologetic and unmistakable. What is the implication of an overtly military object being so purposefully placed in this way? On one hand, removing bullets from their usual context, and placing them, quite literally, onto the body brought the wearer into physical contact with (potential) violence. However, the consequences were not necessarily negative or passive. As established in the previous section of this chapter, women's presence was increasing within the modern city, bringing with it the gaze from all angles, and colour – with its myriad associations of violence – both contributed to and combatted this. Beholding a woman wearing Schiaparelli's coat took this even further. Whilst the main body of the coat is more unassuming, the bullets serve to confound, and shock, the viewer, upon realization of their form, especially if they had not been identified at first sight. Whilst they bring the wearer into contact with objects of potential physical assault, they also arm her. Furthermore, in relation to the escalating turbulence of events in 1933, the presence of the bullet cases served as a walking reminder of further violence looming.

Such anxiety continued to mount, and in 1936, civil war broke out in Spain, which would emanate unrest into Europe and America. Although America remained neutral, it was all too aware of its implications. For instance, in 1939, *Life* magazine would comment on its impact, that it had been 'a testing ground for the tools of battle … a dress rehearsal for the next World War … ', and described the 'lessons' that 'the world's general staffs learned' as a result.[138] Also in 1939, Benjamin Munn Ziegler commented that the 'Spanish "civil" war ha[d] rocked a none too stable world precariously to and fro', which again emphasized the repercussions it had outside of Spain, and highlighted the widespread existing tension of the time, which the civil war only served to heighten.[139]

The same year, Schiaparelli produced a pair of evening gloves, currently in the Palais Galliera's collection, Paris. They were by no means her first, and appeared within a collection that featured hands as a large theme; however, they differed considerably from their precursors and peers. Whilst other examples played with coloured fingernails and animal skins, this pair took a more sombre approach. Produced in black calf velvet, the gloves are elegant, dark and refined. Yet at the end of each finger is a gilded false nail in gold. On one hand, this queried notions of the body and its boundaries, re-defining the relationship between the body and dress: fingernails are expected to lie beneath the fabric of a glove, so externalizing them is a form of subversion. Yet by producing the 'nails' in a material that does not attempt to appear natural or realistic, and is defiantly un-living and metallic, a connection can be drawn from the golden, metallic tones that the bullets of the bullet casing coat also shared. Whilst the gloves are not directly associated with violence, they are charged with its potential. Indeed, just as there is a deliberate lack of attempt to mimic the natural fingernail in colour or texture, the nail shape itself is much more akin to claws, pointed and curved, than the average human nail. The sharp point equips the wearer with the potential power to wreak physical assault and devastation at whim. Conceptually, this provided a sense of control that was opposite to the increasing destabilization in Europe, and its repercussions in America.

Two years later, Schiaparelli re-visited this theme in a ring design. It was composed of three separate parts, designed to be worn on the same finger, with a capped piece at the end, and two broad, flat rings to be worn along the length. Together, they covered almost the entire length of the finger, with gaps between sections allowing the finger joints to move. This, in conjunction with its tough construction materials, of metal and diamond, lent a distinctly armour-like quality to the ring. Building on this connotation of battle, the capped piece at the tip of the finger was sharply pointed, resembling a destructive weapon, much like the claw gloves above. The ring therefore created a shield around a body part that is typically exposed, and also equipped it with the potential to inflict violence. Indeed, the design was reminiscent of a knuckle duster, which was known by Schiaparelli's contemporary audience as a real weapon rather than fashion accessory. For example, in 1921 *The Saturday Review* had referred its use during the First World War: '... the armies on the Western Front had gone to earth within a few yards of each other, and the fighting was of so close a kind that even fists, clubs and knuckle-dusters came into play'.[140] This was direct reference to weaponry was also poignant at a time when the Spanish civil war, and its affects within other countries, had continued for two years, and would persist until 1939. Designed for her wealthy, fashionable, female clients, wearing the ring offered a dual sense of protection and power, and figuratively armed them to be able to face the disquietude of the day. In addition to providing comfort on a political level, this was important in the context of the city, where the modern women who patronized Schiaparelli faced ubiquitous criticism through social commentary,[141] and an assault of colour, which this could create a barrier against.

Again in 1938, Schiaparelli produced her Tear Dress, which also employed tropes of concealment and exposure, on a larger scale (pictured to the left in Figure 1.8). It appeared within her Circus collection, but decidedly differed from its accompanying garments, which in theme took after the collection's title. Originally pale blue, and now faded to an off-white hue, the dress is an elegant ensemble, carefully skimming and flattering the contours of the body, and crowned with a flowing, matching veil. Breaking up this smooth surface, however, is a pattern composed of dark pink and purple abstract, splattered shapes, each mirrored by a small black and pink design below. They deliberately take the form of *trompe-l'oeil* tears or rips, with the lower half of each shape resembling a piece of hanging, torn fabric. This is a clear act of (artistic) assault, with imagined violence having been inflicted in order to impose the rips, and the wearer therefore seeming to have experienced a considerably traumatic event. In the veil, the rips have been further exaggerated, and produced through physical cuts. This ripping was received by the current fashion establishment with particular controversy. Despite widespread coverage of the Circus collection as a

Figure 1.8 *Peter King, photograph, Display of French Fashions featuring Elsa Schiaparelli's 1938 Tear Dress and 1927 Cravat Jumper, Victoria and Albert Museum, London, 1971.*

whole, the dress received relatively little attention, and was not reported by any French publication, despite Schiaparelli's stature.

Whilst the tears were original and shocking in the context of dress, similarities had appeared shortly beforehand within art. Schiaparelli worked on the piece in conjunction with Salvador Dali, who designed the print. It has close parallels with several of his paintings, produced slightly earlier, including *Necrophiliac Springtime*, and *Three Young Surrealist Women Holding in Their Arms the Skins of an Orchestra*, which Schiaparelli owned, both 1936. In the former, a woman stands before an oneiric background, wearing a long, white gown, which clings to her contours before flaring out slightly towards the feet. Whilst her head is composed entirely of flowers – which would form the basis of another interaction between Dali and Schiaparelli in her *Shocking* perfume bottles the following year – what is pertinent here is that rips cut up the long sleeves, adding to material's grimy quality. Clear slashes of exposed flesh appear through the shredded material, adding a sense of horror. Furthermore, this dark motif is subtly repeated along the main body of the dress, and could represent tears, dirt, shadow or a combination. The trope is more explicit in *Three Young Surrealist Women ...*, where three women are sheathed in similarly tight-fitting, full-length and full-sleeved gowns. In the central figure's gown, clear slashes and rips similarly expose her flesh, in the same diagonal manner as the previous painting. Both pieces viscerally make the association between flesh and dress clear through the medium of painting, emphasized by the surrealistic and haunting settings. When translated onto tangible, physical dress through Schiaparelli's 1938 dress, this oscillation became embodied and real, and as Caroline Evans has suggested, Schiaparelli's tears may go beyond suggesting torn textiles, and even suggest violently torn flesh.[142]

Strong similarities can be found in several Surrealist works, including those by Leonor Fini, who similarly depicted women wearing ripped clothing at the time. In her 1938 *Self Portrait with a Scorpion*, for example, she stares directly out of the canvas, her eyebrow fiercely arched, her gaze direct, and her hand defiantly on her hip. This displays her forearm and elbow, above each of which is a large slash in her clothing. The holes are made more prominent by the fact that elsewhere, her clothing is modest to an exaggerated extent: full sleeved and coming up to the base of the neck. The shoulders are particularly pronounced with ruffled material, very much in vein of Schiaparelli's contemporaneous designs. Seemingly in order to heighten this sense of enclosure, two extra folds are present in the chest region, and excess material gathers in the sleeves. In contrast, the two patches of pale skin appear even more exposed and overt. Like Schiaparelli's tears, these are assertively cut, though in Fini's elbow, loose threads can just be seen, emphasizing the violence of the action necessary to produce such an effect. Yet Fini heightened this further in an even more aggressive move. She wears only one glove, in an incongruous grey shade, compared to the warm tones of the remainder of the outfit. Furthermore, it is neatly and deliberately folded up at the base, revealing not just her wrist, but the venomous, predatory tail of a scorpion. This charged, potential violence illuminates the rest of the piece, and the red under-shirt becomes a gaping slash, fraught with the violent connotations of red explored in the previous section. Despite the ravaging that has taken place on her dress, and the imminent danger enclosed within disconcertingly close proximity to her hand, her cool gaze speaks volumes. It asserts power and control, even in the face of the greatest adversity. Her compromising position could easily translate to victimization, but the way she carries herself communicates the opposite: it is the viewer, not her, being assaulted.

Can the same be said of Schiaparelli's Tear Dress, considering the similarities in design at play? Like Fini's ensemble, the wearer of the Tear Dress is surprisingly enclosed; the piece is unexpectedly modest. While the gown is strapless, it is full length and not overly low cut. Furthermore, the veil, whilst slightly sheer, provides additional coverage. In addition, it was presented with a pair of long gloves which covered most of the arm. The immediate impression for an onlooker is of exposed skin, yet this is trumped upon realization that, upon the body, the tears are merely a clever trick of design. The flesh tone of the gloves works in conjunction with this, appearing nude from a distance but in actual fact protecting the skin. Therefore, the outfit initially creates an impression of vulnerability, and violation, yet poses a concealed attack upon the viewer, through being in actual fact unexpectedly intact. Palmer White has, in other contexts of Schiaparelli's oeuvre, described what he deemed her 'hard chic' aesthetic as able to 'protect … the New Woman from counter-attacks by the male'.[143] In this context, not only does the dress rebound any predatory male visual advances, but it also provides protection on a greater scale: it becomes armour, directly taking on any feminine vulnerabilities and wholeheartedly rebuking them.

By this stage, Euro-American developments had intensified considerably. Nazism escalated, and in 1938 Hitler took full, singular control of the German military, and German troops occupied Austria, which led to a Europe-wide crisis. The British Ambassador to Germany attempted to pacify relations, with an agreement not to use warfare to change African borders in exchange for power, but this was refused. Alliances were made (and turned down) among several countries should war strike, including a confirmation from France that it would aid Czechoslovakia if Germany invaded, and a refusal on Britain's part that it would not side with the USSR. Despite reassurances to the contrary after the Munich agreement between Britain, France, Germany and Italy, the moves made were clearly building up to the outbreak of war.[144] Alongside this, the ongoing Spanish Civil War, as Richard Martin has highlighted, made it clear that 'Fascism was spreading throughout Europe'.[145] He directly related this to Schiaparelli's Tear Dress, asserting that 'references to shattered glass and rent fabric would have held strong implications for both the political and visual worlds'.[146] This is certainly valid, and the same can be said of its links to the wider, and similarly threatening happenings. It embodied mounting fear and anxiety, and played out the potential destruction that was around the corner. Not only were pressure and anxiety prevalent in the nucleus of the modern city, but here newspaper headlines and cinema newsreels were a constant reminder of oncoming danger. Highlighting this, and placing the potential violent effects of such danger upon the body was a way to take ownership, power and protection – a way to prepare.

At the beginning of this chapter, it was established that the assault and trauma of the war, in addition to the flu pandemic, infiltrated many aspects of social and political life, and had a lasting impact. This was commonly played out in relation to women, exposing them to vulnerability, and even the violent potential of direct and dangerous assault within beauty advertising. As times and priorities transitioned, this impact did not slacken; rather, it was augmented by the shifting scope of modernity. New experiences could bring both exhilaration and additional senses of assault. A resurgence in the appearance of colour had a wealth of effects: in addition to developing cultural and technological pursuits, it bombarded women with conflicting principles and growing anxiety. Nevertheless, whilst colour had violent effects upon the beholder, as reported by a range of contemporary sources, this did not equate to a one-sided assault. By incorporating the very colour that chaotically surrounded them into their appearance, women could create a shielding, deflecting coping mechanism. Schiaparelli further extended this effect, by deliberately drawing upon women's trauma and notions of vulnerability, and turning them into cunning modes of attack, incorporating tropes of violence. Over the course of the interwar period, women's representation and experiences were transformed. They began with vulnerability, which led to a sense of reparation, and then a two-folded dialogue with both the problems and delights of modernity. Finally, at a critical time before the outbreak of an arguably even more destructive war, Schiaparelli's designs became a fused embodiment of these issues. The mounting trauma many women suffered throughout the interwar period could be combatted by fashion that had its own imagined potential to inflict physical assault, offering an assuaging form of metaphorical defence.

2 Fragmentation

Dividing the mind and body

In 1921, the *Gazette du Bon Ton* published an article on a current trend for narrow ribbons. The accompanying image, Figure 2.1, was designed to show *'quelques dessins nouveaux et leurs applications'*: showcasing and demonstrating potential ways to wear them.[1] It featured a surrealistic composition, with oversized ribbons cascading from the top left corner, overlapped by floating faces, and phantom poles bearing wearer-less hats. In only one case does a face appear entirely intact. The others retain various states and combinations of completion: the eyes are missing in all, while one has a solitary pair of eyebrows, and in another, lips appear alone. Together, an unsettling sense of blankness is invoked, an imaginary dystopia when facial features are unnecessary and interchangeable.

Why was the female face fragmented so dramatically upon the pages of a fashion magazine at this time? As a result of the First World War, the phenomenon of physical fragmentation had become increasingly interwoven into everyday lived experience. The previous chapter explored the radical catalyst that the war became in advancing medical progress, and one such practice was amputation. Over 1.25 million French, British and American men lost a part of their body during the conflict of the First World War. French amputees made up around 1 million of this number, British 250,000 and American 3000. They were left with a painful physical and emotional reminder of horrors undergone, and a lifelong loss that could never be restored.

While this physical trauma occurred directly upon the male body, the wider public was also affected, and came into contact with this suffering on an individual, private, family basis, and also through contact with the public on the street. Jim Wolveridge, for example, remarked upon the ubiquity of wartime amputation in London: 'there was a Mr Jordan who'd lost his right arm, my old man who'd been gassed, and the man at the top of the street who was so badly shell-shocked he

Figure 2.1 *Gazette Du Bon Ton, No. 10, 1921.*

couldn't walk without help. And there were always lots of one-armed and one-legged old sweats begging in the streets.'[2] Women made similar observations, including Caroline Playne who described the returning soldiers whom she saw in Brighton: 'hundreds of men on crutches going about in groups, many having lost one leg, many others both legs, caused sickness and horror. The maiming of masses of strong, young men thus brought home was appalling.'[3] Joanna Bourke has perceptively described a dichotomy in the public's reception towards injured soldiers. On one hand, there was a 'sentimentalization of the war-wounded during the war and in the early 1920s', when 'public rhetoric judged soldiers' mutilations to be 'badges of their courage, the hall-mark of their glorious service, their proof of patriotism", which supposedly even meant that 'women were particularly fond of falling in love with the wounded'.[4] However, in practice, 'prejudice flourished'.[5] For example, in 1916, *The Times* wrote about the 'curious belief, widely entertained among women, that deformities were inherited'.[6] This attitude also appeared within literature: in Henry Adams's *Democracy: An American Novel* (1925), a female protagonist, Madeleine, was perturbed for a fellow character, Mr Carrington, an ex-soldier with an amputated leg, because she was 'certain no woman will ever marry him if he looks like that'.[7]

This chapter aims to explore the impact of this newfound presence of limblessness within everyday life, and the reverberations felt within society, which were expressed in a range of artworks and literature. It will consider how the prevalence of amputation, which was present to the greatest extent ever seen upon the male body,[8] connected to the newfound appearance of fragmentation within fashion magazines, and how this affected perceptions of the female body, beauty and fashion at large.

The facial fragmentation in the *Gazette Du Bon* was one of myriad examples. In the same issue of the publication, for instance, another article used heads to illustrate an article on Scotland, and depicted uniform, doll-like face and neck entities, each wearing a different form of tartan. In 1924, *Vogue* promoted an explicitly positive perspective on fragmentation, and extolled the fragment's virtues in an article entitled 'The Lure of the Little',[9] claiming that 'the little thing always has the effect of a fragment'[10] which is 'more obviously perfect than the large'.[11] A fragment, a piece of a whole, was valued more highly than the larger gestalt. The *Gazette Du Bon Ton*'s and *Vogue*'s articles were part of a new wave of coverage of and supportive sentiments towards fragmentation, which had an impact upon perceptions of the (largely female) body.

This prevalence of fragmentation in fashion magazines, which at this point in the early 1920s, often focused upon the head and face, was parallel to changing perceptions of the mind and body itself. Psychoanalysis had advanced at a fast pace in order to address the consequences of the war, and one aspect that emerged as a result was the notion of body image. Paul Ferdinand Schilder first presented this concept in *The Image and Appearance of the Human Body*. Although it was published in 1935, his findings were based directly on his work with amputee soldiers after the war. Schilder wrote that 'when a leg has been amputated, a phantom appears; the individual still feels his leg and has a vivid impression that it is still there. He may also forget about his loss and fall down. This phantom, this animated image of the leg, is the expression of bodily schema.'[12] This led him to develop what he was to deem 'body image': a term that has become heavily associated with fashion, that was in fact born out of the war. He defined it as '… the picture of our own body which we form in our mind, that is to say the way in which the body appears to ourselves …'.[13] He proffered that whilst sensations are given to us in multiple ways and from multiple places, such as 'from the muscles',[14] body image entails a combination of both the lived, physical experience of the body, and its mental perception.[15]

According to Schilder's theorization, even when missing limbs, the mind could still 'feel' them, and the body remained intact and whole in this way, mentally, through body image. Schilder therefore developed the concept of a united body existing within the mind, even when it was not physically 'whole'. The fragmentation within the *Gazette Du Bon Ton* during the early 1920s, which focussed on the face and head, therefore carried out the very opposite function: they decisively severed the head from its body, and therefore made a separation between body and mind. Similarly, instead of making strides towards wholeness, *Vogue* explicitly praised the fragment itself.

This opposed contemporary conceptions of the role of the image in psychology. In 1936, Jacques Lacan first formally presented his theory of the Mirror Stage, which introduced the notion of the fragmented body as central to human experience.[16] Lacan's theory was developed from work carried out during the earlier interwar years, such as Paul Guillaume's 1925 *L'Imitation chez l'enfant*, and Henri Wallon's 1931 article, 'Comment se développe chez l'enfant la notion de corps proper'.[17] Lacan expressed that from birth, humans experience their bodies and existence in a state of fragmentation, which he compared to the mangled bodies painted by Hieronymus Bosch. It is only when an infant first identifies with its own reflection in a mirror, that it recognizes itself as 'I' and becomes whole,[18] forming the 'mirror stage'. For Lacan, the recognized mirror reflection represents 'the visual Gestalt of the human form, coherent, erect, and masterful, promises stability, unity, and wholeness …'.[19] This suggests that when a body part is missing, it becomes incoherent, weak and unstable. However, building on Schilder's definition of body image, Lacan claimed that 'the identification with this visual Gestalt allows the body image to serve as a defensive mask, concealing the aboriginal state of fragmentation and the experience of bodily fragmentation that may re-emerge under stress'.[20]

Therefore, within everyday life, the perception of oneself is held together by a sense of 'wholeness' that resides in the realm of images, initially formed in the mirror. However, the memory of the fundamental fragmentation of humanity, according to Lacan, continues to haunt the ego, and is manifested in 'images of castration, emasculation, mutilation, dismemberment, dislocation, evisceration, devouring, bursting open of the body'[21] which 'torment mankind'.[22] Furthermore, at times of particular stress, the original 'experience of bodily fragmentation'[23] re-emerges. Not only did Lacan suggest, then, that the state of fragmentation never truly disappears, but he also linked this with violence: when 'the subject experiences [this primitive] anxiety associated with bodily fragmentation',[24] he added, the 'integrity of the body image is attacked or threatened',[25] leading to 'an impulse to aggression'.[26]

The war itself was a profound example of a period of stress, and therefore had the potential to instil such anxiety, aggression and ultimately a breakdown of body image from whole to fragmented. That the war in fact caused this eruption of violence, and literal mutilation and fragmentation of the body, only served to intensify the fragmentary effects that Lacan theorized. It is notable, then, that after the war, the attitude towards the face, body and wholeness changed upon the pages of fashion magazines. Theoretically, the pages of a fashion magazine promote the same image-based ideal as the Lacanian whole body as conceived in the mirror stage. With polished images, and carefully considered text, they are a platform upon which aspirational values can be elegantly laid out, working towards the creation of an ideal, if only in the realm of images. Before the war, in 1913 for instance, *Vogue* declared that 'the very essence' of the 'well-gowned woman of to-day' depended upon 'the utter obviousness of the whole'.[27] The image that accompanied this article included illustrations of various ensembles arranged across the page, and in each one, the entire figure of the wearer is visible, from head to foot. Even when articles focused only upon accessories, there was a tendency to avoid fragmenting the body. For example, on 15 March 1912, *Vogue* described new ruff and veil styles, but rather than fragmenting body parts to display new accessory trends, as the *Gazette Du Bon Ton* later did, it instead depicted the collars alone, and featured a full-length photograph of a fully clothed model. The post-war trend towards commonly fragmenting the body as in the *Gazette*, and praising the fragment above the whole in *Vogue,* therefore represented a shift in attitude towards the body. This accorded with Lacan's notion of the fragmented body: a significant, horrific event caused the image-based whole body, as preferred before the war, to viscerally rupture. Rather than creating perfected unity, as is the possible scope of a fashion publication, the post-war fashion features instead were testament to the after-effects of violence, which was evident through fragmentation. This was a form of transposed violence, now made visible at a level of representation.

At the same time, other efforts were made towards restoring wholeness. Certainly, the state of fragmentation happened on a societal, as well as individual, level. In France in particular, and Britain and America to a lesser extent, images of wholeness pervaded after the war within national governmental imagery. The whole body, 'whose restored wholeness functioned on an explicit level as an antidote to the traumatic memory'[28] was especially called upon in this light. In particular, this was played out through the image of women, such as Figure 2.2, a

Figure 2.2 *Poster, Crédit Français, c.1920.*

poster for the Crédit Français. Here, a strong and healthy woman, wearing modest, traditional garb, and carrying a rustic and plentiful bundle of wheat, promotes values of health, stability, fertility and wholeness. Therefore, the breakdown of the female body within fashion magazines served as a challenge this nationalistic appropriation of the whole female body.

This fragmentation of the female body in fashion, particularly of the head, became more and more intense over the course of the 1920s. In 1928, *Vogue* Paris featured Figure 2.3, an illustration by Cecil Beaton. It portrays a woman languishing on a chaise-longue, luxuriously dressed in an evening gown and abundant jewellery, with carefully applied makeup. Her left arm extends out before her, as if to check her makeup in a mirror before heading to an evening soiree. Despite the overall ambience of elegance, the image contains a jarring element: in her hand is not a mirror, as might be reasonably expected, but instead a dismembered head.

The presence of a woman with a disembodied head recalls the biblical figure of Salome. According to the New Testament, Salome served the head of John the Baptist upon a platter, and accordingly, the image of a fragmented head within Christian culture became associated with the apparent dangers of female seductiveness and superficiality.[29] These moral implications of a link between fragmentation, femininity and violence continued to be pertinent for women into the post-First World War context, when film versions of the Salome narrative were produced in 1918 by William Fox, and in 1923 by Charles Bryant.[30] Beaton's image therefore appeared to acknowledge – and challenge – continuing anxiety

Figure 2.3 *Cecil Beaton, illustration, Vogue Paris, 1928 © Cecil Beaton/Vogue Paris.*

towards modern women. It invoked a clear reference to Salome, yet presented the fragmented head as an asset, rather than source of shame. Indeed, the depicted woman coolly contemplates it, in the same way one might ponder over an accessory, or critique an aspect of one's appearance, as if it were a reflection. This suggests a knowing exposition of the process behind the Lacanian Mirror Stage. Moreover, by juxtaposing a whole, intact body with a duplicated fragment of the same head, Beaton's image simultaneously incorporated national and governmental strides towards wholeness, and also the new, radical, ruptured form of femininity that served to contest it.

This contrast was also reflective of Freudian post-war psychoanalysis. Sigmund Freud defined his seminal structure of the psyche itself in 'The Ego and the Id' in 1923, which requires a splitting or fragmentation of the self. He defined the id as being 'the dark, inaccessible part of our personality',[31] of which 'what little we know of it we have learned from our study of … dream-work'.[32] It is the instinctive, subconscious side of humanity. The ego develops out of the id, he claimed, and 'attempts to mediate between id and reality',[33] dealing in reason. The notion of the very essence of the (same) self being split or divided in this way is echoed in Beaton's illustration. Could the woman in her entirety be the sensible, mediating ego, trying to control the more subversive id? The expression of each 'face' in Beaton's illustration is calm, however the eyes of the right-hand face appear to be slightly more closed. This suggests that the right-hand face is more in touch with the unconscious, and could represent the id. The way that the left-hand face remains attached to the rest of the body, and holds out the second face for examination, suggests a degree of calculation, and that it deals in reason, meaning that it may relate to the ego. Indeed, it is the ego that regulates the id, keeping it in check and in accordance with society rather than with its base drives. Beaton's image therefore encapsulated the tensions that were being played out within society and expressed through the female body. He alluded to these divides in society, and in values: the traditional and mainstream versus the modern and avant-garde. Additionally, by explicitly illustrating a division between the head and body, he referenced the multiple new theories being worked on within psychoanalysis, by Schilder, Lacan and Freud. The image's parallels with the Freudian ego and id in particular reinforce the divide that can occur with one's own mind, suggesting an instability of and fragmentation within the individual self, as well as within society at large.

Fragmented modernity in the city

As the 1920s progressed, the anxieties of the First World War, and its impact upon attitudes towards the body and mind, were further contended with post-war modernity itself, which was also experienced fragmentarily. Modernist writers, including James Joyce and T. S. Eliot, reflected this sensation within puzzle-like texts containing disjointed imagery, which were sometimes released episodically, adding to their fragmentary nature. Joyce's *Ullyses*, for example, was first published in its entirety in 1922, but had been serialized from 1918.[34] Here, he described bustling city life: 'cityful passing away, other cityful coming, passing away too: other coming on, passing on. Houses, lines of houses, streets, miles of pavements, piled up bricks, stones. Changing hands.'[35] Indeed, many Modernist plots were located in the city, portraying the constant ebb and flow of traffic, people and images. In T. S. Eliot's *The Wasteland*, 1922, for example, the following verse appeared:

Unreal City,
Under the brown fog of a winter dawn,
A crowd flowed over London Bridge, so many,
I had not thought death had undone so many.
Sighs, short and infrequent, were exhaled,
And each man fixed his eyes before his feet.
Flowed up the hill and down King William Street … [36]

Each author evoked a strong sense of frustration, fatigue and disconnection with city life. This created a literary fragmented city, where modern anxieties were created and concentrated.

It had already been established that the cumulative effect of navigating these rapidly changing – and often violent – images could lead to particular psychological anxieties. In 1903, Georg Simmel had remarked that city life bombarded the occupant with fragmentation: 'rapid telescoping of changing images, pronounced differences within what is grasped at a single glance, and the unexpectedness of violent stimuli'.[37] He related these experiences to a form of city-induced anxiety:

… to the extent that the metropolis creates these psychological conditions –
with every crossing of the street, with the tempo and multiplicity of economic,
occupational and social life – it creates the sensory foundations of mental life.[38]

By the early 1920s, these effects were only amplified. The violence of the war and its prolonged effects were met with a rapidly increasing influx of people, images and technological innovations, experienced at greater speed than ever before. In 1920, Barbara Low described this as 'the pressure of what is called Civilization' which was 'too extreme, too rapid in its action'. [39] This experience of life as a vast influx of images and experiences meant that each one could only be experienced fleetingly, as a fragment, developing a sense of fragmentation that contributed to modern anxiety.

Contemporary literature widely emphasized the 'helpless woe' and 'brutality', that this could create, to use Virginia Woolf's phrasing. Indeed, her 1925 novel, *Mrs Dalloway*, described the harrowing city experience of one character, Septimus Warren Smith:

> Vans roared past him; brutality blared out on placards; men were trapped in mines; women burnt alive; and once a maimed file of lunatics being exercised or displayed for the diversion of the populace (who laughed aloud), ambled and nodded and grinned past him ... each half apologetically, yet triumphantly, inflicting his helpless woe.[40]

These traumas did not exist solely in the literary and psychoanalytic city but were representative of reality. Numbers of those living and working in the city and nearby suburbs soared, as society became increasingly urbanized.[41] This was the site where modernity was played out in full, where images rapidly changed as one traversed the street.

One demonstrative example is the newspaper industry, which proliferated dramatically within America, Britain and France alike during the 1920s. In America, 27 million readers regularly read newspapers in 1920, and this increased rapidly over the decade, with almost 40 million readers by 1930. In Britain, newspaper circulation almost doubled from 1920 to 1939, and in France, both general and specialized newspapers and magazines vastly increased in titles and circulation.[42] Fashion was also affected: *Vogue* Paris launched in 1920, and its circulation in all three countries almost doubled over the 1920s.[43] The fast, flicked pages, containing juxtaposed items, contributed to the new abundance of imagery.

On one hand, these rapid changes and mass increases triggered anxiety, as theorized by Simmel and reflected within Modernist literature. On the other hand, they could also be seen as representing modernity and progress, with the city itself as a locus. This notion was also expressed within literature. For example, John Dos Passos wrote, in his *Manhattan Transfer*, 'we are caught up ... on a great wave ... of expansion and progress'.[44] Indeed, at a mainstream level, authorities in Britain, France and America explicitly emphasized notions of efficiency and speed. During the 1920s, for example, London Transport employed prominent artists to produce a range of posters in order to promote the efficiency, speed and therefore modernity of the underground. Horace Taylor produced a design in 1924 that featured three escalators, filled to maximum capacity with a colourful range of city dwellers. Its large number of jostling bodies evoked the busyness of city life, while graphic stripes denoting escalators suggested modern efficiency in containing and processing them. This occurred to such an extent that people were encouraged to be machine-like, as in Alan Rogers' 1930 London Transport poster design, which promoted 'speed' both through its typography and inclusion of a figure drawing a bow and arrow. Similar values were disseminated in America and France. Karen Lucic has described the way in which American modernists also expressed speed and efficiency through 'exploiting the image of the machine' after the war, often depicting 'images of urban America … especially views of New York City'.[45] C.R.W. Nevinson's *The Soul of the Soulless City*, 1920, is a representative example of this phenomenon [Figure 2.4]. Its frame is filled with soaring skyscrapers, cropped off the canvas to suggest endless height, and its train tracks, leading directly into the buildings, dramatically conjure modern efficiency and speed, its critical title placing the machine firmly at the centre of modern life. In Paris, these concerns were discussed in avant-garde groups, and Le Corbusier wrote in *The Decorative art of Today*, 1925: 'the machine brings shining before us disks, spheres, the cylinders of polished steel, polished more highly *than we have ever seen before* …'[46] Modernity and modernism during the 1920s were inextricably linked to the machine: an association that reflects the dehumanizing effects of modern city life. Its constant stream of conflicting, crowded signs led to an existence so fragmentary that only machines could navigate it without anxiety. The pace of modern life rapidly quickened, and the traditions and rituals that previously steered everyday existence were dissolved.

A range of competing forces were therefore at play, bringing both progress and tension. For Susan Stanford Freidman, the culmination of these developments was the very 'starting point of modernism'.[47] While this brought 'new technologies and methods',[48] these led to the 'experience of fragmentation and disintegration', ultimately instigating 'the crisis of belief that pervades twentieth-century culture'.[49] Therefore, the dichotomy between fragmentation and wholeness that pervaded within wartime amputation, post-war psychology and propaganda, and modern city life altogether led to an unsettling, disrupted sense of existence.

Contemporary writers have explored the effects of this onset of mass modernity upon women. For example, Andreas Huyssen has argued that 'certain forms of mass culture, with their obsession with gendered violence are more of a threat to women than to men. After all, it has always been men rather than women who have had real control over the productions of mass culture.'[50] In 1925, F. Scott Fitzgerald conveyed this feeling of vulnerability, when he described Daisy in *The Great Gatsby* as a 'girl whose disembodied face floated along the dark cornices and blinding signs of New York at night'.[51] This phantasmic image strongly evokes the fragmentation that appeared within fashion magazines and psychoanalysis

Figure 2.4 *C.R.W. Nevinson, The Soul of The Soulless City, 1920.*

alike, and places it directly upon city streets, which are perceived as violent or threatening. The image was so central to the novel that it was represented upon the original jacket cover by Francis Cugat [Figure 2.5]. Here, fragmented, faceless,

Figure 2.5 *Francis Cugat, book cover, F. Scott Fitzgerald, The Great Gatsby (New York: Charles Scribner's Sons, 1925).*

female features are drawn on a deep blue background, as if floating in the night sky. They recall the *Gazette du Bon Ton*'s earlier fragmented features upon the fashion page. The eyes, eyebrows and lips are also carefully lined and painted to show the thick, fashionable makeup styles of the period, in much the same way as Beaton made up his aforementioned 1928 illustration. Fragmentation is inextricably linked with the emblem of a fashionable woman. Here, the bottom of the page is lit up in a blaze of bright colours in the foreground, depicting a cityscape as if it were alight, demonstrating their 'blinding' nature that Fitzgerald described. As well as conjuring a sense of the violence of colour established in the previous chapter, it directly associates the mental and physical violence of fragmentation with the city as an explicit locus. Indeed, a crystal blue tear falls from one of the eyes, about to drop onto the colourful chaos of the city below.

Beauty, art and the isolated eye

Modernity's relationship with fragmentation also impacted beauty marketing. The centre of fragmentation – the city – was frequently associated with women's makeup, and became a frequent reference within beauty advice. Elizabeth Burris-Meyer declared that 'the city women were the first to take up the use of cosmetics during the early 1920s.'[52] Makeup was firmly associated with the city, and specifically eye makeup was deemed most crucial in this regard: in 1922, *Emily Post's Etiquette* advised readers to wear 'eye makeup if you live in the city'.[53] Clear associations were made between the eye and the city, and women were advised that it was appropriate to adorn their eyes in order to navigate it. Whilst the products and exemplifiers of modernity, such as newspapers, explicitly competed for the eye of the beholder, women, who were both beholden and beholders themselves, were instructed to emphasize their eyes, particularly within the context of the violently fast-paced, image-fuelled city, where modern developments were most concentrated.

The eye was similarly emphasized within the makeup trends of the high 1920s, which heavily exaggerated and outlined them. Eyebrows were thinly plucked or removed entirely, and drawn back in a thin, curved line. The eyes were emphasized further through curling the eyelashes: the 'Kurlash' eyelash curler was first produced in 1923 by William Beldue. One of the most popular innovations of the decade was mascara. While it had existed before in pan form, usually for stage and film makeup, more and more companies began to produce their own variation, in a range of forms including cake, wax and liquid. Maybelline, for instance, after launching in 1916 as Maybell Laboratories, developed its mascara formulas during the 1920s. A 1920 advertisement for 'Lash-Brow-Ine', a balm that claimed to enhance the growth of eyelashes and eyebrows, declared that 'Beautiful Eyelashes and Eyebrows Make Beautiful Eyes – Beautiful Eyes Make a Beautiful Face',[54] singling out the eyes as being fundamental to beauty. By using cosmetics to highlight, open and exaggerate the eyes, including outlining them thickly with dark eyeliner, they were effectively separated and fragmented from the rest of the face.

A later Maybelline advertisement demonstrated this fashionable, fragmented aesthetic in 1923 (Figure 2.6). Featuring Clara Bow, it immediately captures the attention of its viewer, with her cropped face carefully presented according to the trends of the day, complete with shiny, bobbed hair and a long beaded necklace. Her low, precisely cut fringe deliberately and expertly draws attention to her large, wide eyes, which are framed further by carefully darkened, separated and elongated eyelashes, with prominent eyebrows echoing their shape. With a great contrast between the whites of the eyes and the darkness of the makeup, they are an arresting centre point to the advertisement. All aspects of Bow's appearance have been styled by the brand to place focus upon her eyes. The text concurs the strong visual message, promising 'eyes that charm',[55] and draws on the cinematographic heritage of eye makeup: 'even the most beautiful actresses of the stage and screen now realise that "MAYBELLINE" is the most important aid to beauty'.[56] Again, the eyes are given the highest priority within a beauty regime, further separating them from the remainder of the face and body, and perpetuating fragmentation. Therefore, not only were fragmented images of the female face produced upon the published page, but marketers also instructed women to create this style upon their own faces, by defining their eyes according to this beauty trend.

This message was universal across brands: careful application of eye makeup could create 'a spirit of mischief, a "come hither"' look', as a 1925 advertisement for Winx Waterproof Mascara declared.[57] It included an illustrated woman with wide-set eyes, lavishly framed with dark eyeliner, elegantly elongated eyelashes, and a carefully controlled, tapered eyebrow. Rosy pink rouge created a flattering flush below the eyes, again drawing attention towards them. The advertisement also mentioned 'an upward glance' as being another attractive outcome of using (its advertised) cosmetic preparations for the eyes.[58] This related the eyes with emotion, conveying flirtatious movements such as fluttering the eyelashes. Connecting movement with the eye indicated a usage of the modernist tropes of movement, efficiency and speed. What's more, the prescribed movements described, such as 'an upward glance' further recalls the newspaper industry, and its careful consideration of, and appeal to, the eye's movements, and also the contrived expressions of film actors. The advertisement, therefore, further linked women with developments in modernity, and advocated a machine aesthetic.

This connection to modernity, expressivity and performance was reflected and strengthened within the packaging of eye makeup itself. Inside the upper lid of

Figure 2.6 *Advertisement, Maybelline, c.1920–3.*

Maybelline mascara boxes (which were depicted in the bottom left-hand corner of its 1923 advertisement [Figure 2.6]), a photograph was inserted of the actress Mildred Davis's eyes. The box's rectangular shape crops her face, so only her eyes, glancing upwards, are visible, her lashes carefully darkened, lifted and separated. This mounting of a photograph within cosmetic packaging was novel, and made an explicit link to film, as well as emulating the photographs placed within the text of newspaper spreads. The effect was as if Davis's photograph had been lifted from a media publication and affixed to the mascara lid.

This echoed the techniques of contemporary photo-montagists and collagists, who cut images from printed media, and placed them into a new context. Collage was popular within the pre-war Dada movement, and continued to become an increasingly popular medium during the 1920s. The medium itself involves the selection and physical cutting of various existing visual materials. Not only was diverse imagery juxtaposed together, but it was also physically removed from its original context, creating an entirely new one through slicing and splicing. The medium itself, then, demands explicit and violent fragmentation upon a material level. Indeed, Elza Adamowicz has commented on the 'overt display of fragmentation' within Dada and Surrealist collage of the 1920s and 1930s.[59]

It was in 1919 that Max Ernst first considered the medium of collage, through looking at an illustrated catalogue, and he went on to produce myriad collages and photomontages.[60] Looking back on this discovery, he described the 'irritating',[61] visceral effect that the images had upon his own eyes as he observed them, which reinforces the jarring visual effects of colour and modernity discussed in Chapter 1. He even felt that through the act of collage, *banales pages de publicité* could expose *plus secrets désirs*,[62] exposing the subconscious. Yet Maybelline's mascara packaging demonstrated that, sometimes, the desires and anxieties of society could also be revealed in quotidian, commercial sources, which could perform the same revelatory act of fragmentation.

This reading of collage as revelatory of private thoughts has become a primary interpretation of the medium within contemporary art historical literature. Critics such as Elza Adamowicz and J. H. Matthews have analysed Surrealist collage in particular as a method, much like automatic writing, for 'tapping the resources of the unconscious mind … generat[ing] a flow of multiple, contradictory images'.[63] This process could therefore generate disconnected, fragmented, juxtaposed imagery, which reflected the frantic pace and experience of modern city life discussed above. Also, as a semi-conscious action, with the artist holding back on conscious thinking in order to allow a form of automatism to flow, it led to 'the expression of the fragmented inner voice',[64] and further revealed the fragmentation and disembodiment of an individual's inner psychic world whilst navigating societal changes.

Ernst's singling out of the eyes and vision within the fragmentation of collage was also a focus that his Surrealist peers explored. Man Ray's *Object to Be Destroyed,* for example, was originally made in 1923, although later remade in several variations, including a 1933 example using Lee Miller's eye. It made direct links between the eye, imagery, fragmentation and violence. Using a paperclip, Man Ray affixed a picture of an eye, again, cut from a photograph, as if a collage, to the arm of a metronome. As the metronome ticked, the eye moved from side to side, as though watching. He explained that the ticking noise was a background to his painting activities: 'the faster it went, the faster I painted; and if the metronome stopped then I knew I had painted too long, I was repeating myself, my painting was no good and I would destroy it'.[65] Attaching the eye 'create[d] the sensation of being watched as I painted' as 'a painter needs an audience'. The piece therefore used the notion of destruction to represent the anxiety caused by the simultaneous sensation of watching and being watched. It might be bearable for some time, but eventually it leads to violent feelings of destruction. Man Ray's work connects newfound, metropolitan-based anxieties with the eye, and the violence of fragmentation. The eye also appeared severed and isolated in many other Surrealist oeuvres, from René Magritte's *The False Mirror,* 1928 to Claude Cahun's *Object,* 1936. Therefore, in both art and beauty trends, the eye was being highlighted and fragmented, marking it as a central symbol of modernity. It was both a vessel through which the stresses of modernity could reach the psyche, and a tool through which to steer it, and emit one's own piercing observations.

Another of Man Ray's works, *Tears,* a photograph produced in 1930–2, also explored the eye and closely connected it to contemporary themes of collage, fragmentation and beauty. It bore a striking resemblance to the image of Davis inserted into Maybelline's mascara box. Man Ray worked as a commercial fashion photographer in addition to his artistic pursuits, and this piece links the art and fashion industries. In both Man Ray and Maybelline's cases, each black-and-white, high-resolution photograph was cropped to a pair of female eyes, which gaze upward. This focus upon the eyes is aided further by the heavy application of mascara to the eyelashes, each one dark, thick and elongated, with the product visibly clumping in excess within each one. A deliberate upward glance in each photograph not only showcased the models' makeup, but it also once more emphasized movement, connecting it to the concerns regarding the eye, and the idolization of the machine, discussed above. Man Ray added glass beads to represent tears within his piece. They mimiced and highlighted the false emotions that are conveyed through acting, such as those Davis herself portrayed. Simultaneously, they were also highly fabricated and aestheticized, with radiance, clarity and a perfectly spherical composition, as a further glamorous adornment to a woman's face, strictly related to the eye. Nevertheless, they were fundamentally evocative of sorrow, capturing the experience of the fashionable young woman, traversing the burgeoning metropolises of London, Paris and New York, with exhilaration and exhaustion alike. The images each suggested that women could better equip themselves to face these sources of anxiety by scrupulously following beauty ideals, and making-up their eyes. In Maybelline's photograph, Davis portrays defiance. Yet Man Ray's piece, evocative of a film still itself, was so similar that, with the addition of glass tears to Davis's face, the same sorrow would be portrayed. Man Ray highlighted the falsehood of the emotions conveyed through acting, yet also suggested that these sentiments could be harboured by real women, beneath their scrupulously put together, armour-like appearance, with eyes defiantly accentuated through makeup, in accordance with contemporary demands.

These traits remained a prime concern during the 1930s, and Cecil Beaton explored them within his 1937 *Greta Garbo*. This mixed media piece, of another star, featured a photograph of the actress's face, tightly cropped and cut out, which he placed onto a painterly background. Juxtaposed on top, and surrounding her face, were four pairs of the actress's eyes, in photographic and artistically sketched form. Each set was again cropped, and presented as a fragment, within a stylized mask shape. In each pair, the eyes have a different position and therefore expression, from staring openly to seductive. The multiplicity of the pairs of eyes within the piece conjures a sensation of the gaze on a mass scale: multiple pairs of eyes watching. Certainly, actresses such as Greta Garbo had a profusion of observers. However, Beaton's collage incorporated illustrations as well as Garbo's photograph, which recalled the illustrations within women's magazines and advertisements. Similarly, the cropping of the photographed eyes overlaid upon Garbo's face invited close focus towards the sultry, fashionable eyeliner, mascara and eyebrow pencil that her eyes had been made up with, a demonstration as clear as within a beauty feature or advertisement. This inclusion of multiple forms of media suggested that everyday women were also under the scrutiny of multiple onlookers. This was emphasized by dark, expressive, painterly brushstrokes that formed the background, evoking movement and mass crowds.

In the collage, each pair of eyes, in addition to displaying different makeup styles, glances in various ways: from eyelids semi-closed, to looking up or away, but in one case, they directly meet the gaze of the onlooker. This reminds the viewer that, while women could be an object of scrutiny, they could also actively engage with their own observing gaze. Just as they could both be 'attacked' by the visual violence of colour, they could also project it themselves to 'fight back'. The use of eye makeup, and attitudes expressed towards it during this period from the mid-1920s to the mid-1930s worked in conjunction with this sensation of a dynamic dual dialogue, based on vision. Wearing a range of fashionable makeup styles could also provide the means necessary to return the gaze, and could perform

Fragmentation

as another tool to equip women for modern life. Rather than be vulnerable to a fragmented lifestyle, eye makeup offered a tool of comfort and armour.

Far from remaining an avant-garde exercise, these considerations continued to significantly influence creative considerations within fashion magazine editorials by the mid-1930s. *Harper's Bazaar* UK, for example, produced an unusual piece on Nathalie Paley, a Russian aristocrat and celebrity, in 1934. Instead of showcasing traditional portraiture, they 'noticed separately her eyes, mouth, hands, ears, hair … from these scattered observations we … formed our impression of her'.[66] The article presented several photographs, all tightly cropped to focus on one particular, fragmented aspect of her appearance. The opening image featured her cropped eye, staring determinedly ahead, set off by a thin, drawn-in eyebrow, and lashings of mascara. Over the following pages, her appearance continued to be presented in fragmented shots, conducting what the magazine termed, in the piece's title, an 'Anatomy'. This conveyed a clinical designation of the body and its potential dissection.

This creative editorial decision signifies fragmentation in fashion's continued and increased momentum. The eye in particular was singled out and fragmented, both literally in collage, and suggestively, through contemporary demands of makeup. Yet by enhancing its status through layers of makeup, and physically multiplying it through layers of images, its effects, and power, could be magnified. If feminine fashionability and glamour, as expressed through the eye, had become associated with the anxieties provoked by modern, city life, then multiplying the eye could recover what was lost through violent fragmentation. Intensifying the gaze in this way could reflect anxiety away from observed subject, and onto the observer.

The classical versus fragmented body

The fast-paced modernity that led to the simultaneous progress, anxiety and fragmentation over the 1920s and into the mid-1930s did not relent during the latter part of the 1930s. Rather, the economic depression and increasing political instability served to compound anxiety, and contribute further to changing attitudes, which continued to be explored through representations of women. In the face of this relentless unease and unsteadiness, a new aesthetic began to gain favour across Europe and America. Ideals of classicism began to permeate society and culture, from political imagery and ideology, to fashion, art and design. They were revealed through a visual language that favoured principles such as balance, proportion and wholeness, which directly contrasted the instability and fragmentation that had been caused both by the aftermath of the First World War and by developments within modern life. Referring to classicism conjured a sense of order amongst present-day upheaval, and could serve as an idealistic antidote to restore fragmentation. These convictions appeared within imagery of the female body. Nevertheless, dissenting forays into fragmentation continued to appear in relation to women, particularly those produced by Surrealist artists and Elsa Schiaparelli. This led to opposing perceptions of the female figure: classical and whole versus fragmented.

New developments within fashion design were one avenue in which this new, classical aesthetic manifested itself. Madame Grès and Madeleine Vionnet, for example, favoured classically inspired draping, and the bias cut, which involved cutting on the diagonal which would follow the body's contours and enhance the drapery. Vionnet's design process involved her working directly onto the female body itself, requiring clever and careful consideration and use of fabrics, shaped directly onto the living form. Vionnet embraced new fabrics and techniques, at the forefront of modernity, yet used them in such a way that demonstrated remarkable craftsmanship, and remained 'consciously classical and timeless', as Caroline Evans and Minna Thornton have described.[67] The way in which these designs were disseminated furthered this deliberate, core classicism, such as Figure 2.7, a 1933 photograph by George Hoyningen-Huene. The model's halterneck dress deftly contours her torso before cascading into flowing lines of fabric, which explicitly related to the straight lines of the column which she poses against. With her hair slicked back smoothly, the styling emphasizes the sculptural qualities of the dress, as if she too were carved from stone.

These changes in fashion coincided with developments in art. During the 1930s, the sculptor, Frank Dobson, studied ancient art in the British museum, and this interest was strongly reflected in his work. His *Torso,* 1933, for example, used a simplified form and flowing lines to produce an homage to the torso in Portland stone. Its elegant simplicity and proportions reflected the new cultural tendency to favour classicism, taking inspiration from the natural, naked, female form, which he studied from life. These ideals were aptly expressed through the vehicle of statuary, centred around the torso, appeared widely throughout the decade.[68]

Slightly later, in 1933–4, Dobson produced another work, which focused on the torso of the naked female form, once more missing arms, and part of its legs. In this case, modern dress was incorporated into his classical aesthetic. The body, although depicted as naked, was slightly idealized, as if it were wearing garments: the natural curve between the waist and hips was smoothed slightly, and the breasts prominently pushed out. There was less definition of natural features, and the muscle tone, navel and naturalistic fullness of the thighs, which had all been

Figure 2.7 *George Hoyningen-Huene, photograph, Crêpe Evening Dress by Madeleine Vionnet, Vogue Paris, December 1930.*

present within the previous piece, were diminished. It makes sense, then, that the sculpture, of painted composition and plywood, was in fact commissioned by C. Douglas Stephenson on behalf of the Charnaux Patent Corset Company, and was entitled *Charnaux Venus*. Although appearing naked, the piece was clearly intended to resemble the body as if wearing a corset produced by the company. This was also evidenced by smoothed facial features and slicked hair, which recalled current beauty trends, such as dark lips and lacquered hair, which, hardened and set close to the head, in itself evoked statuary. It is evident, then, that whilst the classical aesthetic suggested naturalness, there was in fact considerable manipulation of the body required in order to achieve it.

In March 1934, Curtis Moffat photographed Dobson posing with four versions of this torso-based sculpture. In this case, the statues each wore a selection of lingerie products, produced by Charnaux. While the presence of statuary torsos within the photograph was a clear reference to classicism, here, other factors competed with the usual connotations of tradition, purity and wholeness. The de-limbed nature of the torso was emphasized above wholeness: only enough of the body necessary to display the advertised products remained. The British actress Jeanne de Casalis, whose father owned Charnaux, stood in the centre of the statue-mannequins, alongside their creator, Dobson. Her appearance, laden in layers of luxurious furs, contrasted the undressed, unliving nature of the mannequins. Nevertheless, there was similarity in the profile of the faces, and the outline of the hair, which suggested that underneath the woman's glamorous appearance, similar garments were helping to shape it. In classical imagery, the appearance of the torso usually serves to suggest harmonious ideals. However, here the body part appeared to be more radicalized. Not only did de Casalis, in her living, whole form, highlight the statuary torsos' fragmented nature, but the statues also modelled the very undergarments that were necessary to mould the female body (including de Casalis') into an accepted form according to convention. The use of smoothing, shaping undergarments, such as those made by Charnaux, could help to promote control and discipline, in the face of uncontrollable adversity. Yet streamlining the body came at the expense of discomfort and constriction beneath the contoured body. Exposing the process in the photograph ripped away the glossy layer of streamlined fashion, and revealed the rigorous process underneath. Discarding the limbs in this way, due to being necessary to the purpose at hand, also suggests a violent, fragmentary attitude towards the body, that only deepened as the decade wore on.

Adolf Hitler and Benito Mussolini were concurrently using classical statuary to promote their fascist ideals within propaganda. In a 1935 speech, Hitler declared that 'each politically historical epoch searches in its art for the link with a period of [an] equally heroic past. Greeks and Romans suddenly stand close to Teutons'.[69] This was particularly evident on the occasion of the 1936 Summer Olympics in Berlin. Hitler seized this as an opportunity to promote the Nazi party, and heavily used imagery to associate it with ancient Greece, where the Olympic Games had begun. This was reflected by the stadium, pageantry, and even in the official

Fragmentation

poster selected for the games, by Franz Würbel. It depicted a golden, wreathed victor outstretching a muscular arm, as if he were an ancient statue. Additionally, Olympic statues were erected in Berlin that were designed to represent the 'ideal' body, further evoking classical statuary, with muscular, idealized bodies that were uncompromisingly whole. While Hitler drew upon ancient Greek imagery, Mussolini manipulated the heritage of ancient Rome to promote his own fascist party. He commissioned an exhibition dedicated to *Romanità* itself, for example, which opened in September 1937. Here, historical events were juxtaposed with present ones, directly linking ancient Roman victories with present fascist activities. For example, extracts of a speech that Mussolini had made on 9th May, 1936, were hung above Roman busts, and onto the pedestal of a statue of Victory, the Roman goddess.[70]

This appropriation of the Classical body was also taken up by Salvador Dali. In 1936, amidst the height of the Nazi and fascist adoptions of classicism, he produced his *Venus de Milo with Drawers*. By inserting five drawers within this epitome of the classical, balanced, beautiful body, he took the current taste for classicism, which had become a dominant force in art, fashion and even politics, and disrupted and interrupted it. He deliberately toyed with and mocked these contemporary usages of classical values, for example through six mink pompons that adorn the head and each drawer of the piece, adding a level of shock and absurdity. Moreover, they also express sensuality, with their tactile material, playing up to Venus's status as the goddess of love, and also invoke texture and dress. Venus's depicted dress, carefully draped around her lower half, was similar to the kinds of materials that present-day women were fashionably wearing upon their bodies. Not only, then, did Dali mock and highlight the cynicism that existed behind many modern references to classical imagery, but he also further related it to femininity, and incorporated dress.

It is perhaps unsurprising, then, that he would collaborate so successfully with Elsa Schiaparelli, or that their joint work would go on to explore these boundaries. At around the same time, the pair incorporated these ideas within Schiaparelli's boutique, Schiap, which she had opened shortly beforehand in 1935. They dyed an oversized bear in Schiaparelli's signature shocking pink, which brought vivid colour dissonance and the violent visionary effects this brought with it, as established in Chapter 1. Dali carved drawers within its stomach, which were used to display jewellery, brutally cutting the body open, and dividing its stomach into (re-)moveable fragments. While the body was an animal's, it was placed within the female realm of a fashion boutique (which itself was female-owned), and this association of femininity is reinforced by the use of Schiaparelli's shocking pink. This dramatic act of fragmentation also had psychological implications. Drawing on classicism as well as contemporary psychoanalysis, Dali stated that 'the only difference between the immortal Greece and contemporary times is Sigmund Freud, who discovered that the human body, purely platonic at the Greece epoch, nowadays, is full of secret drawers that only psychoanalysis is capable of opening'.[71] The anthropomorphic bear, then, signified the depth and variety of layers within the human mind that psychoanalysis could unravel. In the context of Schiaparelli's boutique, the fragmented bear-cum-chest of drawers suggested that fashion too could unlock, and display, aspects of the self.

The duo would take this one stage further, directly into dress design itself, and in 1936, Schiaparelli produced women's skirt suits that also had drawers in the form of horizontal pockets, with metal drawer handles. They were pictured in the 15th September edition of *Vogue* that year, with a photograph by Cecil Beaton of two models wearing the suits [Figure 2.8]. The caption described: 'That famous surrealist, Salvador Dali, inspired Schiaparelli to put pockets like bureau drawers on her suits', and the feature included a past line drawing of Dali's, in white upon black.[72] It appeared to be a study for his 1936 painting, *Anthropomorphic Cabinet*, in which a woman lays on her side, again in a traditional, languishing, classical pose, with drawers dividing her upper body.

While contemporaneous manifestations of the classical body constructed a sense of wholeness, Dali and Schiaparelli's fragmentation of it through drawers exposed the superficiality of this.

While they may appear wholesome, this was superficial, and really based on considerable constriction and manipulation: both of facts, for example in Mussolini's conveniently edited version of Roman history, to the physical contortion of the body required to achieve the pure, ideal lines of the classical body, as revealed by Dobson with Charnaux. Dali and Schiaparelli therefore interrupted and exposed this process through fragmentation. The drawers represented the idiosyncrasies and intricacies of the human mind itself, which could be 'opened' through psychoanalysis, as Dali expressed in his statement above.

This role is altered when applied to fashionable clothing, published in a women's magazine. *Vogue* described the drawer-pockets more light-heartedly, as 'individual imaginative quirks' with a 'touch of Surrealism'.[73] Moreover, when worn upon the real body of a woman, the drawer-pockets take on further meaning. Indeed, whilst some of the drawer-pockets did function as pockets, and could contain personal items in the role of a 'drawer', others were false and merely decorative. This suggests an element of control: only the (female) wearer could know which were the 'real' drawers, and what they contained. Schiaparelli produced another variation of the theme also in 1936, her Bureau Drawers Coat, with a dark, knee-length coat adorned with eight pockets also in the style of drawers, with ringed metal

Figure 2.8 *Cecil Beaton, photograph, Bureau Drawer Skirt Suits by Elsa Schiaparelli, 1936.*

handles. With a similar mix of functioning and decorative-only pockets, the wearer was bestowed by the garment with a similar sense of control. The coat enclosed her body with a shielding cocoon, covering from her chin to her wrists, and past her knees. She was presented as a woman with her own personal and complex facets, which she alone could control whether to keep locked or to expose. It was a coat that could be slipped over any outfit, to create a personal form of armour. This accords with Palmer White's reading of Schiaparelli's day wear, which he described as 'hard chic … [with] a militant, masculine quality', and a 'hard, highly individual femininity' that would 'protect the New Women from counter-attacks by the male'.[74] This worked in conjunction with the fragmentation and emphasis of the eye discussed earlier in this chapter, as a means to confound onlookers. Together, these ideas also relate to two concepts discussed in Chapter 1: the use of colour as a visually violent counter-attack, and Schiaparelli's own garments that presented the threat of physical violence.

However, this psychological (and physical, considering the garments' enveloping of the body) sense of comfort did not negate the inherent violence necessary within the concept of fragmenting the physical body. The violent viscerality of this concept is particularly well-represented by Hans Bellmer's *Dolls*, produced around the same time, *c.*1933–7: a series of sculptures and photographs that feature the violent dismemberment and re-arranging of a female mannequin or doll, leaving them as a mere sum of body parts. The production of the first 'doll' coincided with the year in which Hitler first rose to power in Germany, which has been read by art historians as an intentional protest.[75] Bellmer himself stated that 'if the origin of my work is scandalous, it is because for me, the world is a scandal'.[76] Such explicit fragmentation of the female form can indeed be interpreted as a violent protest towards extreme politics, by breaking down the apparent wholeness and purity that they perpetuated through classicism. Other critics have interpreted the *Dolls* as a literal embodiment of the Freudian concept of castration;[77] however, the near-total fragmentation of the (female) body also makes an important statement in regards to Dali and Schiaparelli's concurrent explorations of the subject, in the context of the modern experience. Indeed, as Hal Foster has written, 'in his erotic manipulation of the dolls [Bellmer] explores a destructive impulse that is also self-destructive'.[78] Rather than representing a male fantasy, or a sexual corruption of a childhood emblem, the dolls can be seen to instead represent the subject himself or herself. Ruth Ronen has argued that 'the horror in the threat of disintegration that the doll embodies is the most desired state, a source of immense attraction, since it marks the return of the subject to the state that eludes the safe outlines of the self, where subject and external objects are undifferentiated'.[79] Rather than being mere objects of sadism, the dolls instead become objects of identification. This accords with Lacan's view on masochism: he wrote that 'the position of the perverse masochist is the desire to reduce himself to this nothing that is the good, to this thing that is treated like an object, to this slave whom one trades back and forth and whom one shares'.[80] They express, then, the ultimate end of fragmentation: nothingness. In this way, as Rosalind Krauss has argued, the *Doll* imagery 'produce[s] the image of what one fears, in order to protect oneself from what one fears – this is the strategic achievement of anxiety, which arms the subject, in advance, against the onslaught of trauma, the blow that takes one by surprise'.[81] While initially, fragmentation of the female form is easily interpreted as a violent attack, it also serves, then, as another form of psychological protection. The subject is in fact safe: when reduced to 'nothing' in Lacanian terms, the state of inertia at the beginning of life, before pain is perceived, instead it is the spectator that takes on the horror and anxiety of the image. This further contributes to Dali and Schiaparelli's drawers within the female body: while they present considerable fragmentation, they also serve to safeguard the wearer, leaving only the onlooker to be affected.

This physical fragmentation of the female form continued to pervade Surrealist art, and Roland Penrose's *Real Woman*, 1937, for example, featured the same disfigured, fragmented torso that Bellmer reduced many of his *Dolls* to. In the same year, Schiaparelli presented her own direct and explicitly violent exploration of the theme, with her fifth perfume bottle, *Shocking*. It represented a sharp change from her previous models which had followed more traditional formats, such as 'S' which launched in 1928 with a simple, spherical bottle with a pearlized stopper. In the case of *Shocking,* however, its title was an accurate description of its bottle: it took the form of a naked, fragmented, female torso.

While a fleshy, voluptuous shape contrasted by cold, hard material is a description applicable to an artificial mannequin, classical sculpture or the *Shocking* bottle alike, Schiaparelli's version represented an abrupt, violent de-construction of the female form. She deliberately signified an overflowing vitality bursting out, through constructing the bottle stop as a wreath of flowers. This signified a clear link to concurrent Surrealist endeavours, by juxtaposing traditional references and creating new meanings, which also separated her torso from mainstream endeavours, and injected violence. This was increased in usage: lifting off the flowered lid to apply the perfume exposed a cut-off neck, rendering it to be ghastly. As Elizabeth Wilson has stated, fashion 'always hide[s] a wound'.[82] Schiaparelli inverted these terms, by forcing users to continually carry out the act of beheading the dummy, and expose what would be, if it *were* real, a gaping wound. By revealing this horror, she invoked similar shock tactics to the Surrealists. Not only did this separate their work from the status quo, which promoted rationality through the classical, whole body, but by carrying out the act themselves in a masochistic manner, they could be protected from any sadist onlooker, and reflect the anxiety back onto them. In Schiaparelli's case, this could be carried out literally: her customers sprayed the scent directly onto their own bodies, which enveloped them in a protective cocoon, much like the Desk Suit and Bureau Drawer Coat. The perfume, a traditionally glamorous and feminine object, also acts as an invisible celebration of feminine vitality, represented by the flowers erupting from the top of the bottle, surrounding the 'wound' where the neck is missing. This sense of unrelenting life and vigour further served to oppose the cold, hard and calculated appropriations of the classical body in mainstream imagery. This sense of life and viscerality was again evident in several concurrent Surrealist works, such as Marcel Jean's *Horoscope,* also 1937, a dressmakers' dummy painted with an elaborate, colourful rib cage, effectively transforming it into a fragmented torso, with the inner body bursting out.

This Surrealist stance on fragmentation, which often used the emblem of a torso, even became reflected within more mainstream outlets. The violence of these explorations, and their significance to human drives, did go on to influence the commercial world, within which a Surrealistic aesthetic became popular during the mid-later years of the decade.[83] In March 1938, for example, *Harper's Bazaar* used the repeated shape of the torso as a bold cover design. Not only was the torso itself de-limbed, but an abstract black-and-white pattern across each one made the very torsos appear to be fragmented and in pieces. One single cropped eye appeared in the middle of this configuration. It depicted more than simply a reader's observation of the coming fashions, as the headline declared, but also emphasized the way in which fragmented modernity was experienced visually. While the mainstream response was to combat this with a revival of classicism, and to favour balance and proportion, violence and fragmentation prevailed, as powerfully demonstrated by Surrealist activity, including Schiaparelli's fashion output. Whether knowingly or not, *Harper Bazaar*'s striking cover boldly depicted this very process.

These considerations began to affect the portrayal of and attitudes towards real bodies. In August 1938, British *Vogue* published an article entitled 'The Slender Truth', composed of slimming advice. This exemplified the control and discipline of the body advocated by contemporaneous strivings towards balance and classicism. The article detailed five different methods: dieting, exercise, massage, wax baths and sweating, and corseting. This reveals the effort and, in some cases, even pain, necessary behind achieving the favoured, fashionable appearance. The article even mentioned certain kinds of exercises as being 'violent', 'which may strain your heart'.[84] It demonstrated the way in which dress was perceived as having a crucial role in attaining the idealized classic form: 'a good corset can work wonders in the way of moulding and controlling too-lavish curves … it's firm, solid truth', explained the article.[85] Yet there was little 'truth' if such 'moulding and controlling' of the body was required.

Perhaps most representative of the piece's values, however, was a full-page photograph that accompanied it. Shot in black and white, with soft light, it depicted another nude female torso, with linen cascading from her arm, invoking classicism once more. Her limbs were again severed explicitly, with only stumps of the arms and neck remaining, and the legs cropped out of shot. Viewed in isolation, it could be an artistic, classical interpretation. Viewed alongside the accompanying article on the opposite page, though, the way in which they were intended to be consumed it has disturbing consequences. It suggested that, like the grotesque dismemberment in the photograph, the body can be vastly manipulated, even if this involved violent means.

These ideas had already been grappled with in art and photography, such as André Kertész in his *Distortion #86,* 1933, which explored the lengths that body manipulation could reach, with a fragmented female nude that bears striking visual similarities to *Vogue*'s later version. In particular, Jean Cocteau's avant-garde film, *Le sang d'un poète,* 1930, connected violence, fragmentation and femininity. Here, model, artist and muse Lee Miller was transformed into a classical white statue, her fragmented arms ending in explicit stumps. In the film, the statue initially appeared as a mere object, but it was given life and anthropomorphized when the male protagonist, an artist, placed a sketch of fragmented lips over its mouth. Throughout the film, various images of fragmentation, such as a spinning human head constructed from wire, appear. However, one scene pertinently links the protection of Lacanian masochism and disintegration[86] with Lacan's Mirror Stage. A solitary arm appears and hands the artist a gun. With the spinning wire head behind him, he shoots his own head. However, instead of dying, the fragmented head again appears in isolation, followed by a solitary mirror which fills the frame. The still living artist bursts from it. Then, in an act of aggression, he proceeds to smash the statuary Miller with a mallet, chipping away at her stone body, until it lies in pieces upon the floor. As with Bellmer's *Dolls,* fragmentation is carried out to its fullest extent, to total obliteration. The presence of the mirror recalls its function in Lacan's Mirror Stage: to symbolize the act of uniting the fragmented body upon a superficial, image-based plane. Reducing the statuary Miller to pieces recedes her to a state of inertia before the realization of the Mirror Stage, where pain is not perceived. Instead, the artist who inflicted this ultimate act of fragmentation and the viewers are the receptors of the horror.[87]

As the 1930s progressed, these values had seeped into, and influenced, commercial fashion and the ideology it disseminated. Violence towards and manipulation of the body became more and more explicit within mainstream media as the decade drew to a close, and the threat of a Second World War became clear. In 1938, for example, *Vogue* published an illustration by Edouard Benito, depicting evening gown designs by Chanel and Schiaparelli [Figure 2.9]. The setting was indicated, by a tower in the background, as being the prestigious

Figure 2.9 *Edouard Benito, illustration, Vogue, July 1938. Eduardo Garcia Benito, Vogue* © *Conde Nast.*

and fashionable Place Vendôme, however it had been isolated from the city, and instead transformed into a barren, oneiric background. The model wearing Chanel faces the viewer, whilst Schiaparelli's model faces into the distance, allowing a front and back view, similar to traditional fashion plates. However, neither of the models had heads attached to their body: instead, their necks ended in amputated stumps, and they raised a floating, severed head up in the air with their arms. This pose recalled the classical imagery of the 1936 Olympics, as if they were victors holding their prize. But instead, Benito subverted this association, and presented a sinister version, where heads become removable accessories. Indeed, an additional head lay alone on the ground, cast in shadow, as if it were redundant and had been tossed aside.

Furthermore, in 1939, the fashion journal, *Pinpoints*, published a large, vivid image, Figure 2.10. Its black line drawing was contrasted with a stark yellow background, immediately conjuring the violence of vision that was discussed within Chapter 1. Yet there was also explicit violence imbued throughout the subject matter. It echoed Schiaparelli's *Shocking*, with the presence of a limbless torso in the form of a dressmaker's dummy. Yet here, the severed limbs are present, and despite being markedly unattached to the body, the fragmented arms rise above the neck, as though still attached. In addition, the doll also seems to have a head, held between the floating arms, which appear to be in the process of coolly and detachedly interchanging it, recalling Beaton's 1928 illustration. Indeed, a further head rests placidly on the chair. With eyes peacefully closed upon each of the faces, they are presented as interchangeable accessories of the body. The doctrines of a malleable body, strictly moulded to meet the confines of modernity, culminated in this violent manipulation, decidedly linked to fashion, which was a perpetrator of many of these demands. Its Surrealistic references provide a shock tactic, to momentarily distract the beholder from everyday reality, and to perhaps ponder the absurdity of some of its demands.

Despite the wide onset of classicism throughout politics, art and fashion during the 1930s, violence and fragmentation prevailed in response to rapid and unsettling changes. After the war, reunion and wholeness were striven for on a macrocosmic level and continued to be perpetuated by governmental propaganda and mainstream media, which turned to wholesome and classical tropes in order to promote this, which in turn often featured manipulation of the female form. However, tension and anxiety remained, and were further compounded by the bombardment of modernity, particularly in the city. This was counteracted by avant-garde artists, Schiaparelli, and certain fashion publications through the use of fragmentation, which disrupted, interrupted and broke down the classical body. They resisted and fought against superficial wholeness, and instead bolstered fragmentation, which was carried out to various extremes upon the body. This offered several means of protection, comfort and rebellion for women: from the figurative annihilation of possible pain in certain Surrealist images, to the empowering gaze that multiple makeup styles provided upon the

Figure 2.10 *Illustration, Pinpoints, 1939.*

face itself. As the threat of a second conflict became ever more ominous, the shock tactics used to prove the point increased alongside it. This also marked a rebellion against strongly right-wing ideals, such as fascism, which also took on classicized tropes to serve their own purposes. During the 1930s, therefore, classicism and wholeness versus Surrealism and fragmentation emerged as two intertwining, yet opposing threads, each responding to the onset of a harsh modernity and reality. The (female) body was a crucial battleground upon which these tensions were played out.

3 Eroticism

Exploring eroticism

Within French, British and American media and literature, the morality of women came under frequent verbal and written attack. Moreover, these attacks were frequently relayed through fashion. Many writers noted changes in fashion during the 1920s, and associated them with a perceived increase in immorality, which they attributed to the First World War. For example, William Bolitho, looking back in 1930, described 'short skirts' and 'bobbed hair' as demonstrative of 1920s excess, which he blamed upon the generation's restlessness after the 'stupid and rough time of all after-war'.[1] Similarly, Walter G. Muirheid claimed that 'every big war has brought a reaction in reckless dress',[2] and even F. Scott Fitzgerald interpreted of the 1920s that 'something had to be done with all the nervous energy stored up and unexpended in the War'.[3] The overt and visual nature of female fashion made it a conspicuous target for criticism, as opposed to the less distinguishable presence of trauma. Moral criticism towards women and fashion could in this way stand as an outlet for residing collective anxieties in a newly unstable world, where they could be notionally expressed and appeased.

During the following years, women's fashion and morality remained closely linked. For example, in May 1921, the lead article within the New York *Literary Digest* posed the question 'Is the Younger Generation in Peril?'[4] The basis of such 'peril', of course, was changes in fashion, which resulted in a sudden explosion of exposed necks, décolletages, arms and legs. The effects of such changes were still being related to morality in 1926, when Hugh Kennedy claimed that current fashions would have been considered as 'nakedness' during preceding years.[5] Kennedy was attempting to emphasize his outrage by appraising contemporary fashion through the moral lens of the past. Whilst it would not have been considered decent previously, the revelation of more inches of skin had become more widespread due to its presence within the fashionable silhouette of the high 1920s, demonstrating fashion's role in defining acceptable perimeters of the body and its display. Kennedy bemoaned that 'the lack of morality is not in the nakedness but in the shame, and the shame grows less day by day'.[6] Therefore, he did not merely criticize physical exposition, but the lack of modesty and decorum that he felt it entailed. Once more in 1927, these ideas were even expressed by Pope Pius XI, who spoke of 'an increased immodesty in women's fashions'.[7] This demonstrates the large and international extent to which these 'concerns' towards women's fashion were debated and expressed. Furthermore, there were many attempts elsewhere to, as Angela Latham has put it, 'measur[e] … modesty by the yard',[8] and twenty-one states in America, for example, attempted to pass laws to limit aspects of female fashion, such as skirt length. The official restrictions on female fashion were therefore linked to the semblance of controlling morals. Indeed, also during 1927, the *Literary Digest* claimed a strong link between the 'decay of morals and the downfall of nations'[9] and the 'terrible potentialities'[10] of fashion.

For women, this wide-ranging 'outrage' presented a source of conflict and possible anxiety, as authoritative figures condemned the very styles that they were instructed to wear by the fashion industry. In Figure 3.1, for example, Marion Morehouse's arms, neck and décolletage are entirely bare. Her pale skin is highlighted by the contrast with a black Chanel dress, whose sequins serve to draw further attention to the revelation of her exposed skin, and un-corseted shape, and its knee-length hemline reveals her calves in sheer stockings. Her hair, drawn into a neat bun at the nape of her neck, ensures that the maximum amount of skin is displayed, and she looks purposefully to the side, so that the viewers' eyes may roam her appearance freely and undisturbed. For the many social commentators exemplified above, photographs such as this were supposedly obscene. Yet it appeared within *Vogue*, a reputable high fashion magazine, in 1926, and was taken by prominent photographer, Edward Steichen. This represents the tension embroiled within the female image during the 1920s, the dichotomy that it signified, between fashionable, modern and advancing, and sinful and shameful.

More recently, several theorists have proffered arguments to explain femininity within society of the period. Angela Latham, for example, has described female fashion at this time as 'the defining morality of the nation itself'.[11] Certainly, every aspect of a woman's appearance was an object to be assessed, and a potential entryway into deeper revelations of the collective psyche. Furthermore, writing in broader terms, Susan R. Bordo has asserted that 'the body is not only a text of culture. It is also a practical, direct locus of social control'.[12] During the 1920s, this occurred in a demonstrable way. The female body was the site where both cultural and social changes were played out, and upon which intimate subconscious

Figure 3.1 *Edward Steichen, photograph, Marion Morehouse Wearing a Chanel Dress, 1926 © The Estate of Edward Steichen/ARS, NY and DACS, London 2021.*

thoughts, desires and fears mingled and were exposed. On one hand, more choices in fashion, and the ability to reveal the body could represent freedom and autonomy, yet on the other, the female body served as a political and social vessel of morality, or lack thereof. The female body, fashion and sexuality became a platform for cleansing war and modernity-induced trauma under the guise of morality.

This association between fashion and sex prevailed and was considered widely during the period. In 1921, for example, Mary Alden Hopkins questioned

'Do Women Dress for Men?'. She emphasized the importance of dress in feminine identity: 'votes and jobs and citizenship have not lessened for women one jot the importance of clothes. Because women find them important, because they are an expression of her sex, her clothes are her second self'.[13] Hopkins interviewed several psychologists within her article, some of whom went even further. In addition to clothes being an expression of the female sex, as Hopkins herself asserted, Dr F. J. Richards, for example, proclaimed that women have a 'surplus of sex energy',[14] which could be contained through channelling into fashionable matters, and without this channelling, it 'might otherwise do actual harm'.[15] This opinion builds on Freud's assertion that 'sexual repression leads to neurosis'.[16] However, for Freud, this was a fundamental psychological model for both sexes. Richards' relation of this specifically to women and fashion suggests his uncertainty and fear towards female sexuality, and the mention of its 'actual harm' suggests that he believed this power to be latent within women. The postulation that this apparent power should be directed into fashion was a further way in which traditionalist fears could be comforted, and the existing, conservative status quo preserved, despite rapid advances in women's autonomy, which were reflected and added to by changing, modern fashions.

However, the fact that female sexuality was formally recognized was a radical development in itself, and as Maria LaPlace has noted, 'by the 20s there was an ambivalent acknowledgment of the existence and even legitimacy of female sexuality', for the first time.[17] The academization of sex grew rapidly from the early 1920s. Several conditions made this possible. Firstly, in 1922, new court rulings made it more difficult to censor, or lessen, sex within literature.[18] Secondly, during the early 1920s, new, younger publishers disseminated progressive ideas by European academics that had been deemed too subversive by established publishing houses, including Boni & Liveright, New York, who were the first American publishers of Freud. By the 1920s, Freud's major works were published and accessible in English and French, in addition to the original German, which meant that new psychological interpretations of sex and its importance could be read more widely. For example, as Margaret Anderson and Howard Taylor have noted, 'once Freud's writings were translated from German in the 1920s, they became the common language of sexuality among large segments of the public'.[19]

Publications on sex began to appear towards the end of the war, such as Marie Stope's 1918 *Married Love*, and continued with a quickened pace over the interwar period, with a plethora of examples published, including Theorodo Van de Velde's 1927 *Ideal Marriage*, and H. Havelock Ellis's *Psychology of Sex*, 1933. The ever-growing publications and popularity of psychoanalysis also played an important role within this, confirming sex as a subject worthy of academic attention.

Moreover, Freud in particular posited sexuality as a fundamental driving force of humanity. His developmental model of sexuality placed newfound importance upon this aspect of life. According to Freud, sexual expression begins in childhood and evolves over the entire lifetime, in levels of psychosexual development. He posed sexual energy, the libido, as the 'driving force behind all human endeavours, generating the tension and excited state that leads to creativity in artistic and intellectual expression'.[20] Furthermore, his interpretation of sex itself was intimately linked to violence and aggression, and he wrote in his *Three Essays on Sexuality* that:

> the sexuality of most male human beings contains … aggressiveness – a desire to subjugate; the biological significance of it seems to lie in the need for overcoming the resistance of the sexual object by means other than the process of wooing. Thus sadism would correspond to an aggressive component of the sexual instinct which has become independent and exaggerated.[21]

Not only was sex postulated as a fundamental aspect of human nature, but its nature was being explored. At the same time as Freud deemed aggressiveness an essential element of the male sex drive, images that exemplified this sexuality tinged with violence and violation appeared within art and literature.

These changes in attitude affected society at large and impacted the role of women. For example, in the 1922 edition of *Emily's Post,* one chapter was entitled 'The Chaperone and Other Conventions'.[22] However, by 1927, this had been revised to 'The Vanishing Chaperone and Other New Conventions'. Indeed, this reflected the dramatic changes in dating practices during the 1920s. Young people began to socialize and date potential partners outside the home and without chaperones, assisted by the increasing prevalence of technology, such as the car. Yet despite rates of pre-marital sex rapidly rising during the 1920s,[23] it was still frowned upon, and could ruin reputations. As Elizabeth Roberts has stated, 'private punishment and public humiliation' were not uncommon for women who became pregnant before marriage.[24] A complicated tension and conflict therefore brewed. On one hand, changes in society made the practical lives of some women easier, and the social waters freer for independent navigation. On the other hand, these improvements were intended to facilitate still pigeonholed roles of femininity. According to Judy Giles, the 'dominant discourses of medicine, science and psychology … posit[ed] a "modern" women [sic], freed from the restraints of Victorian repression', yet this 'apparently newly required robustness and common sense were to be at the service of marriage, housewifery and motherhood'.[25] Therefore, while previous repression was somewhat alleviated, it was expected that this would be redirected into feminine duty. Similarly, as Andrews has surmised, on the surface, 'interwar life for women revolved around duty, rigid boundaries, calmness'.[26] Therefore, women faced a conflict: societal practices regarding sex were loosening, and it had become newly accepted into the academic canon, yet it was still laced with condemnation. The moral code for women was no longer clear, and became contradictory and difficult to navigate, particularly for young, single women, who might be independent with a job in a shop or as a secretary, and who were, as Charles Eckert has explained, the target audience of modern marketers.[27]

One outlet through which individual desires could be explored in private and without condemnation was literature, which itself saw a sharp rise in eroticism during the 1920s. One genre that was particularly revealing is the woman's novel, which was frequently written by and for women.[28] As Nicola Beauman has analysed, 'the woman's novel between the wars reveals many overt and covert references to sex and sexuality', and furthermore, fashion played an important role within this, offering an early link between fashion and eroticism.[29] Indeed, as Andrews and Talbot have argued, they frequently included lengthy descriptions of dress that would 'not [have been] ... out of place in the pages of *Vogue*'.[30] The sensuality of fabric, which could be enjoyed both physically and visually, by the wearer and observer, points towards the erotic pleasure of the fantasy of fashion and consumption.

Elinor Glyn's 1922 novel, *The Man and the Maid*, is one such example. Nicholas, an injured male ex-soldier is convinced that 'no woman can feel emotion for [him]' due to his 'mutilated face ... and [amputated] leg from the right knee downwards', and the narrative is in diary-form, as he attempts to re-integrate into everyday life after the war.[31] With every woman Nicholas encounters comes a detailed description of her dress: one character, Coralie's, appearance is described as reliant on her 'entourage of beautiful things, the manicurist and the complexion specialist, the Reboux hats, and the Chanel clothes'.[32] He emphasizes the importance of his notion of fashion's role in society:

> Nina ... was looking ravishing in entirely new clothes ... Germans may be attacking Paris – Friends and relations may be dying in heaps, but women must have new clothes and fashion must have her say as to their shapes ... If there was nothing to relieve war and seriousness – all the nations would be raving lunatics by now.

He associates fashion with the trauma of the war, like the critics discussed above. However, in this context, a book written by a woman for women, this association is not expressed as a form of moral condemnation, but instead praises fashion for apparently preserving the sanity of nations within such a traumatic episode. In addition to comforting the strains of the war, he also consistently relates a fashionable appearance to sexual desire:

> They were so well dressed! … They wore elastic corsets, or none at all. They were well painted; cheeks of the new tint, rather apricot coloured – and magenta lips. They had arranged themselves … bringing out their gold looking-glasses and their lip grease and their powder – and the divorcée continued to endeavour to enthral my senses with her voluptuous half closing of the eyes, while she reddened her full mouth.[33, 34]

Fashion, in this case, is appreciated appraisingly, rather than being criticized as in the above examples. However, this association between fashion and sex eventually leads to sexual violence, such as rape:

> We rose from the table – And for a second she was so near to me the pent up desire of weeks mastered me and the tantalization of the morning overcame me so that a frantic temptation seized me – I *could not* resist it – I put out one arm while I steadied myself with the other by the back of a chair, and I drew her tiny body towards me, and pressed my lips to her Cupid's bow of a mouth – And Oh God the pleasure of it – right or wrong! She went dead white …[35]

Glyn explains this behaviour by writing that men are 'fools', only 'planning some fresh adventure for themselves, or how to secure some fresh benefit'.[36] Nicholas proclaims to his victim 'I am not a gentleman underneath – the civilization is mere veneer – and the *man* breaks through it – I have nothing to say – I was mad, that is all … perhaps some day you will know how you have been making me suffer lately.'[37] He asserts, then, that her fashionable appearance was a strong factor for the attack, which he felt unable to resist. Whilst the sexual content of the novel was therefore fused with violence, it did not function in the same way as the condemnation of the female sex and fashion discussed above. Indeed, contemporary reviews of the book praised its 'love affairs' which had 'just that touch of naughtiness which the suburbs look on with a frightened interest'.[38] Furthermore, Glyn, the author herself, frequently published articles in women's magazines. In *Nash's and Pall Mall Magazine*, October 1922, she wrote that the erotic elements of her novels, which she became known for, were

> often very much misunderstood … a number of people … buy a magazine, and they say, 'Here's an article by Elinor Glyn – it may be something spicy – I'll read

it.' Then they begin, and they skip sentences until their eyes light upon some passages which arrest attention, and which, perhaps, taken without their context, could wound the personal, or even national, vanity.[39]

This mention of the wounding of national vanity referred to the wider condemnation of women, fashion and morality discussed. Glyn opposed these stances, and instead proffered that men 'must be master because of his character before he will be obeyed by the modern girl', and that modern women enjoyed a range of fantasies: 'the place of a man in the eyes of each woman is where she personally wants him to be … on a pedestal … as an equal … as a slave … [or] in his arms as a lover!'[40] From her perspective, then, the sexual violence that sometimes appeared within her work could serve as a fantasy to be enjoyed by women. Contemporary reviewers agreed: 'there is an inexhaustible public for conventional love-stories … so that "Man and Maid," which is quite luscious and lovely, should sell readily.'[41] Therefore, on one hand, erotic literature offered a vessel for outraged moralists to vent their wartime trauma and modern tensions into. Yet on the other, it also offered an escapist outlet for women, a retreat not only from their own wartime trauma, but for the anxieties caused by their new, conflicted role in society, and the paradoxical place of fashion and sex within this.

Concurrently, avant-garde artists were also exploring fashion's links with sex and femininity and offered further aspects through which these fraught tensions surrounding fashion, eroticism and femininity could be worked through. Duchamp explored the matter with his appearances as Rrose Selavy, for example within three photographs taken by Man Ray from c.1920 to 1924. In Figure 3.2, Rrose wears a full coat, with a luxurious, sensual fur collar, and a brimmed, embroidered hat. Her face is fully made up with explicit cosmetics: heavy eyeshadow and eyeliner, darkly emphasized eyebrows, and bold lipstick creating a stylistic, feminine shape. Furthermore, Rrose deliberately poses in the style of a convincing, contemporary high fashion model: Duchamp had clearly studied contemporary fashion photography and magazines carefully. Rrose tilts her face to the side, and coyly raises a hand, evoking what was being produced contemporaneously in commercial fashion photography.

Prior to 1920, the use of photography within advertising was sporadic, and illustrations were more often found. However, during the 1920s, fashion photography became more commonplace. It is not without relevance that the first issue of French *Vogue* appeared on shelves in Paris, where Duchamp was living and working, and the edition was specifically named *Vogue* Paris. While illustrations were commonplace within the publication, the appearance of such magazines helped fashion photography to come into its own over the decade. Within Man

Figure 3.2 *Man Ray, Marcel Duchamp as Rrose Selavy, c.1920–4.*

Ray's photograph, Duchamp succeeds in deconstructing the eroticism of femininity within fashion photography upon the magazine page. By accurately recreating the style of and seduction within fashion photography, as a male artist rather than female fashion model, he exposed the artificiality and construction used to create the fashionable, feminine image. This worked to diffuse the contemporaneous criticism and sexualization of women's fashion: if it was exposed as artificial, then any attack towards women, or sexual violence caused by their fashionable appearance, could only then be superficial.

Rrose's next appearance would further conflate fashion, beauty and eroticism, and tinge them with subversion. In 1921, the same year that Chanel launched her first two fragrances, Marcel Duchamp and Man Ray together produced another semi-readymade, *Belle Haleine* – a Rigaud perfume bottle, to which they added a new label, and a picture of Duchamp as Rrose. Their re-interpretation of the bottle contained a wealth of characteristic puns, with deliberate eroticism. Firstly, the very name of the company, a traditional woman's name, *Belle Hélène* (beautiful Helen) has been subverted to 'beautiful breath'. This evokes great sensuality, of being close enough to somebody to see, taste or feel their breath, and suggests its caress on skin. The Surrealist duo built upon this through further wordplay. Upon first glance, the text on the bottle reads 'Eau de Violette'; however, they carefully re-arranged the letters to form 'Eau de Voilette', or veil water. Not only does the makeup of fragrance itself often contain deliberately animalistic and aphrodisiac notes, but in addition, the suggested notion of veiling is once more particularly sensual and potentially erotic. It conjures the idea of veiling, and therefore, unveiling, the body, presenting the body as something to be covered, uncovered and revealed at will, with the sensual slide of silk upon the skin. This idea resonates with the unveiling of the skin that 1920s fashion demanded, causing more skin to be shown than ever before, which provoked the controversy discussed. However, the act of applying perfume showers the body with an invisible mist, that envelops the skin, yet remains unseen by an observer. Therefore, it could act as a secret form of shielding, undetectably protecting the female wearer from an attacking gaze or criticism. While *Belle Haleine* was an art object, it nonetheless raised the association with women's quotidian perfume applications.

This emphasis of erotic potential came with a form of sexual violence. It is important to note the deliberate similarity of the French term for rape, *viol,* within the perfume title. Indeed, the term that would be expected, and is played on, is *eau de violette*, violet water, and the Surrealist subversion of simply two letters further adds to the piece's layers of eroticism, voyeurism and violation. Indeed, the term 'violation' itself is identical to the French term. Furthermore, interpreted in this light, where words contain multiple meanings, the word 'eau' contributes to these effects: while most obviously, it translates as water, when used in a perfume context, it also becomes, when spoken aloud, the exclamation 'oh!'.[42] This could denote pleasure, or surprise, and the idea of being startled during the private moment of applying perfume to the skin suggests the violation of intimacy, or an exclamation during an intimate moment. Duchamp purposefully intermingled the boundaries of private and public as a way to create a charged, voyeuristic eroticism, at a time when the acceptable boundaries of behaviour were ambiguous. This commented upon the violation of the female form that emerged within the growing sector of erotica, and emphasized its multi-faceted meaning, conflating threat with excitement, pleasure with pain. Furthermore, the use of a definitively female and glamorous object, the perfume bottle, linked this sexuality to fashion, similarly to the literary examples discussed.

In Duchamp's case, however, he highlighted the fetishization of the feminine by exposing its artificiality. This notion was concurrently explored within psychoanalysis, and in 1929, Joan Riviere produced a psychoanalytic theory which addressed such notions, 'Womanliness as a Masquerade'. She proposed that women's intellectual success represented a successful castration of her father's penis, and in behaving in an overtly feminine, sexualized and flirtatious way, she could attempt to avoid repercussions from such an act from the apparent father figures that she worked with. It is in this way, she decided, that: 'womanliness therefore could be assumed and worn as a mask, both to hide the possession of masculinity and to avert the reprisals expected if she was found to possess it.'[43] Therefore, she too proposed womanliness as something that is not innate, but purposefully constructed, using fashion and beauty as tools. The idea that womanliness can be easily acquired or shaken off suggests a certain superficiality of femininity itself, as though it is not a core trait, and must be constructed in order to be perceived. This was a crucial component of Duchamp's conflation of femininity, eroticism and sexuality in the above, and the trope through which he explored the contemporary contradictions that they were surrounded with.

Indeed, within mainstream media and culture, there was a conflict between simultaneous sexual liberation and repression. Whilst social boundaries were loosening, and there was a piqued interest in sex emerging within literature and society at large, at the same time women were seemingly punished for these changes through an upsurgence of sexual violence towards them within cultural works. This accorded with Freud's concurrent theorization of sexuality, which he asserted always contains aggression in the case of men. Underlying this attack was fear of the female sex, as an embodiment of rapid changes, anxieties and traumas, which was typically pinned onto the realm of fashion. This was subverted by both Duchamp and Riviere through breaking down the feminine, fashionable appearance, and destabilizing the traditional gender roles that the critical onslaught depended upon.

Fashion, femininity and fetishism

In 1921, the *Gazette Du Bon Ton* published an article entitled 'Doléances', illustrated with four large drawings [Figure 3.3], featuring women's figures from the waist down, wearing skirts. Despite the relatively early publication date, half of the women wear a skirt that is entirely transparent, revealing their undergarments beneath. Such a style was more commonly found in the theatre than in an affluent magazine, and was even criticized in this context. One anonymous writer in 1920 described theatre performance as follows:

> barefoot dancing with naked limbs being shown through transparent nets, abbreviated skirts, with flesh colored tights emphasizing the form and contour of the body by effective colored lights, are all a part of the nefarious business which escapes the ban under the guise of 'art."[44]

This aesthetic, in which the nakedness of bare limbs seemed to be enhanced and sexualized even further through the tease of transparent materials, was one of the reasons for which the theatre was reprimanded for indecency, and Billy Sunday

Figure 3.3 *Gazette Du Bon Ton, no. 9, 1921.*

claimed, for example: 'if you want obscenity you will find it in the theatre …'[45] That this transparency made its way onto the pages of a reputable fashion journal was therefore significant, and arguably had even more impact in this context. The couturière Chanel, for instance, cautioned in *Ladies' Home Journal:* 'Don't wear materials that [are] transparent … do not attract attention by such vulgar means …', which suggested that it had particularly provocative, and in her opinion, unacceptable, qualities.[46]

These elements of fantasy, sexualization, voyeurism and violation continued to appear within fashion magazines. In September 1933, *Harper's Bazaar* published a fashion spread on new synthetic materials. Entitled 'An X-Ray of Fashion', the garments featured were entirely transparent. It was not the first time that medical-style terms had been used within women's fashion magazines. Chapter 1 discussed the occurrence of the post-First World War 'beauty doctoring' aesthetic in women's cosmetic advertising, and Chapter 2 analysed the 'Photographic Anatomy' that the same magazine performed on Princess Paley the following year, in 1934. *Harper's Bazaar's* 1933 version, however, had a distinctly erotic slant, and advanced the *Gazette Du Bon Ton's* earlier suggestions of voyeurism, twelve years later. The x-ray concept implied that the models were passive to an active operator of the x-ray equipment (or camera). Rather than posing directly in undergarments, which would have had different, more deliberate associations, the notion of an x-ray suggested an unwarranted penetration of the outer surface of clothing, thereby gaining a glimpse of their underwear is to view something intended to be private. Moreover, in doing so, the reader was also turned into a voyeur through the simple act of turning the page and viewing the spread.

While on this basic level, the process was similar to that of readers viewing the *Gazette du Bon Ton's* 1921 version, as fashion had advanced over the decade in between, the reception and nature of the undergarments had developed. It was certainly a violation to see undergarments in the 1921 context, however, compared to *Harper's* 1930s version, much less flesh was revealed, and modesty was given through flowing petticoats. By 1933, the intimate viewing of underwear revealed even more of the model's body, as underwear had become more scant. *Women's Wear Daily*, for example, pointed out during the same year that 'many women prefer [this style of undergarment] to [the previous] corsets … they are made with brassiere tops, removable garters … and can be had in a variety of fabrics'.[47] Smooth lines, close to the body, with a wide range of available shapes, options and combinations were becoming increasingly popular, and 'greatly stimulated lingerie sales', as *Harper's* pointed out the following year.[48] Such options were fully displayed by *Bazaar's* 'X-Ray', which flouted the usual function of clothing, to cover the body, and once more instated the sexual fantasy of penetrating and seeing through clothing. Fashion magazines therefore significantly contributed to the sexually violating and voyeuristic imagery that confronted women through a range of everyday activities, and they started to become sexual voyeurs through images in fashion and film.

Such explorations of women, fashion and voyeurism also surfaced within commercial photography, such as Erwin Blumenfeld's 'Veiled Dancer', the same year as *Bazaar's* 'X-Ray'. The model posed on a plinth, extending her right arm outwards, allowing a veil to fall and drape elegantly. Its copious material encompasses her entire body, yet its transparency allows her shape to be glimpsed beneath. The light and shadows created swathe her body: the viewer cannot precisely determine her level of dress or nudity, which along with the contrasts of light and dark playfully invite the viewer to study the image, to pierce it with their gaze, in order to find out.

In the art world, Man Ray also explored these very elements of nudity, shadow, veiling and violating voyeurism within the same year, 1933, demonstrating the wide contexts in which these themes emerged. In a small series aptly titled *Erotique voilée,* he photographed fellow Surrealist artist Meret Oppenheim, and made a deliberate nod to an acknowledged form of Surrealist beauty, which, according to André Breton, must be 'convulsive or will not be at all'.[49] One way in which this could occur was through semiological, opposed categories, which together create a striking contrast to 'jolt' the viewer out of their everyday existence. The *erotique-voilée* was a definitive example of such a phenomenon, frequently listed by Breton, and John Roberts explains it as 'inorganic matter taking on the look of other things'.[50] Fittingly, Man Ray's representation was reproduced in the Surrealist journal, *Minotaure,* in May the following year, in order to illustrate an article by Breton on the subject of convulsive beauty.

In these images, Oppenheim posed behind the large wheel of a printing press, her hand and arm covered in black ink, which she raised to her head. The metal, mechanic, inorganic wheel juxtaposed the soft, sensual, living model, encompassing the ideals of convulsive beauty. While her modesty was minimally covered by strategic placement of the wheel's spikes and handles, the series is nevertheless charged with eroticism.

Not only did the nudity, sensual shadowing and elegant posing feature classic elements of erotic photography and cinematography, but furthermore, the handle of the wheel was knowingly placed in front of Oppenheim's body, as if a phallus. Moreover, there was deliberate violence within this eroticism. The spikes surrounding the press's edges were menacingly close to her naked skin, as if a torture machine, about to mutilate her. Jill Berk Jiminez has noted that Oppenheim 'smiles down at the machine', connoting 'a relationship like love', and argues that the 'violence is moderated and contained by the formal and erotic harmony of the juxtapositions'.[51]

However, her raised hand, whilst creating a graceful shape, also denotes weariness. Additionally, black ink was smeared upon her, appearing degrading, as if it had been placed forcefully. During the interwar period, Man Ray produced several examples of the female body trapped, usually by shadow, in order to create a veiled sexuality. Here, though, the shadows were joined by threatening metal spikes and the black ink, denoting aggression. Indeed, Man Ray also produced deliberately violent depictions of sexuality, such as his 1930 *Fetish* figure study, in which a near-naked woman was forcefully bound with strong black, sadomasochist-style straps, her breasts fully exposed and her body vulnerable to a potential oncoming attacker.

The sado-masochist style of dress featured recalled examples that the American photographer Charles Guyette was concurrently both photographing and selling. For example, his 1930s *Pony Series* of photographs featured a woman dressed with near identical accessories, of black straps containing her head, chin, waist, hips and wrists, which were 'controlled' by a woman in a carriage behind her, carrying a whip. Guyette advertised and sold similar photographs and accessories, which he discreetly advertised in *London Life,* 1934–5, by stating 'We have costume studies of all kinds. Lingerie, corsets, high heels, etc. Female boxers and wrestlers in action. Also other types.'[52] Guyette was inspired by Yva Richard in France, who similarly sold and photographed fetishwear during the 1930s.

As the name fetishwear suggests, these ways of presenting the female body had intrinsic connections to psychoanalysis, namely, Freud's theory of Fetishism. For Freud, a fetishized object can be used as 'a token of triumph over the [perceived] threat of castration and a safeguard against it'.[53] Most fetishes, he wrote, are objects from 'the last impression before the uncanny traumatic one',[54] for example, when a young boy first realizes that his mother does not have a penis. According to Freud, the object then becomes a psychological, sexual aid. The Surrealists were heavily inspired by this pioneering work. They believed that turning inwards, to one's personal interior, as psychoanalysis proposed to do, could unlock new secrets of existence to shake up society, and to counter what they perceived as the 'reign of logic' and masculinized 'absolute rationalism' that had led to the horrors of the First World War.[55] Many artists produced literal representations of Freudian theories, and Bellmer, for example, recreated the moment described within Fetishism through one of his dolls, *La Poupée*, 1935, which featured a pair of high-heeled shoes, as if seen by a young boy before observing what he perceived as 'castration'. These examples, which included mainstream and avant-garde, fashion and non-fashion sources, all demonstrate the intrinsic link between fetish, fashion and femininity.

In the Surrealist stance on the subject, the connection was pushed to the extreme, and suggested the fetishization of the female body itself. As Johanna Malt has explained, fetishism 'serve[s] as a vessel for the subject's projected desires and delusions',[56] and claims that 'Surrealist sculptural objects ... [can be] understood as fetishes in this sense'.[57] However, fetishism also offers a useful theoretical tool to unlock significances within the violation of the female body. Indeed, Freud's theory had only been publicly accessible shortly before many of the discussed works were produced. By reducing the female body to merely its sexual body parts, and/or by restricting its movement and agency, female sexuality becomes a malleable force, to please its viewer. The fact that many such works used deliberately artificial materials, or contrasted the living with the unliving, heightened and emphasized their fetishistic effects. Female sexuality becomes bound and contained, reduced simply to an unliving object, a fetish, a tool against sexual anxiety. In this way, a similar operation is carried out as in the filmic process discussed above: sexual violence and fetishization help to ease the threat of castration that, according to Freudian psychoanalysis, is inherently associated with femininity.

Furthermore, the Surrealist association of femininity with objects links to perhaps the most heavily fetishized objects of all: fashion garments, which the Surrealists duly explored. Indeed, in 1933, the Surrealist poet Tristan Tzara wrote an article on the sexualization of fashion: 'D'un certain automatisme du gout', again in *Minotaure*.[58] The article was illustrated once more by Man Ray, with photographs of couture hats, some of which were produced by Elsa Schiaparelli. Rather than being ordinary photographs of the accessories, however, he purposefully arranged them to resemble both male and female genitals. One shot, for example, captured a hat worn by a man. However, rather than being a standard portrait, the photograph was taken from above, so that only the hat and a suggestion of suited shoulders are shown. Through doing so, an unusual angle was revealed: the very top of the hat, in which a large fold dips into a crease, creating the hat's structure. Seen from this vantage point, however, it appeared to deliberately echo the vagina. As Mary Ann Doane has written, 'the female genitals are uncanny because they represent, for the male, the possibility of castration'.[59] According to Samuel Weber's reading of Freud's theory, the uncanny represents another defence against the threat of castration harboured by women, which Weber deems to be a 'crisis of perception and of phenomenality'.[60]

This postulates the hat or dress accessory, as another source of protection from castration, to be fetish object. Indeed, Freud himself deems the wearing of hats to be a 'phallic gesture'.[61] For Freud, the reality of dress is clothing, to be worn as part of normal apparel. But the unreal or fetish form of dress is, for the person possessing a fetish, an agent of sexual arousal. In Freud's work, as Tim Dant has articulated, 'the unreal object that arouses the fetishist indicates a perversion'.[62] Rather than being sexually stimulated by the usual object of desire, such as female genitalia, instead an unliving object becomes a substitute, due to the formative misconception of castration. Man Ray, like other Surrealists, knowingly flaunted this slippage between fashion, violence and sexuality. Fashion had become the site upon which to explore, contain and release post-war angst. Surrealist artists pushed this link to its extreme, and in doing so, demonstrated just how embedded within so many aspects of mainstream society it had become.

Indeed, Man Ray's photograph emphasizes the intense sexuality that can be found within an everyday object, within everyday life itself, including fashion, merely by changing one's vantage point slightly. This was suggestive of the Surrealist maxim that there is a 'constant unconscious production of sexual imagery throughout culture', as Rosalind Krauss has put it, including within the design of hats.[63] Furthermore, it reinforces the message that anybody can easily be a voyeur, with one slip of the eye, whether through choice or not. Not only is Man Ray's viewer forced to consider a quotidian object sexually, but this then alters their perception of wider life itself, which is potentially charged with similar possibilities. As Livingston has surmised, 'in his great photographs of the 1920s and 1930s, Man Ray succeeded in eroticising his objects, creating enduring poetic incarnations of surrealist's Sadist desire without violating his own classically grounded modernist aestheticism.'[64]

If the Surrealists emphasized the inherent sexuality within a range of everyday objects, then dress, with its intimate ties to the body, and its shaping, veiling and staging, is a prime example. As Benjamin stated, 'in fetishism, sex does away with the boundaries separating the organic world from the inorganic. Clothing and jewelry are its allies.'[65] Through fetishism, items of dress become sexualized objects, and fashion, with its ability to add an ideological layer and 'sex-appeal', as Benjamin put it, to dress, heightens this possibility even more.[66] By the mid-interwar years, the very female body as an entity became a fetish object itself, and was sexualized, violated and exploited.

Eroticizing the body

By the mid-1930s, these elements of eroticism and sexual violence became even more prevalent and made their way explicitly into conceptual fashion design itself. For example, transparent garments, which had been shocking and tantalizing when infrequently published in fashion magazines, became more commonplace. Elsa Schiaparelli, for example, played extensively with the new material, rhodophane, and *Vogue* featured her pale blue evening dress with a shimmering rhodophane apron, worn by Madame Vittorio Crespi, in January 1935. Clothing's most basic functionality, to cover and shield the body, was starting to give way, and by wearing new transparent fabrics, women were exposed to possible voyeurism and violation towards their own bodies. This trend was widely adopted, and rather than being popular for merely one season, resonated more deeply, and appeared within consumer and trade publications alike. In January 1937, *Women's Wear Daily*, for example, declared 'transparent frocks' to be 'an afternoon stimulant'.[67] Not only was the transparent trend becoming increasingly popular within both high and everyday fashion, but its classification as a 'stimulant' immediately suggests an arousal of the senses, and erotic potential. Similarly, in September 1937, *Vogue* casually described 'a transparent dinner dress'[68] within a report on new Paris fashions. Previously, the glimpses of the near-naked body that transparency allowed were a risqué rarity, but now, they were appearing within mainstream fashion.

Since the end of the First World War, the idealized body shape for women had been straight and streamlined. However, with the onset of the Great Depression, values towards appearance and the body became once again more conservative, and Rebecca Arnold has explained that such 'conventional gender construction was seen by some as offering an appropriate balm for the uncertainties of the period'.[69] A curvaceous silhouette began to become more fashionable once more, and lingerie evolved to meet this change. While the corset fell out of favour during the 1920s and early 1930s, and modern, interchangeable sets became more popular, by the mid-late years of the decade, lingerie began to return to an emphasis on wide hips, a tight waist, and emphasized bust. However, while such shapes returned, they did so in a very controlled manner, and were smoothly, tightly and purposefully contained – or emphasized – by lingerie. Corsets and girdles, albeit with new, modern and more comfortable materials and designs, once again became frequently bought and worn. Furthermore, bras began to be produced with very rigid constructions, and moulded the bust into a pronounced shape.

Vogue commented directly on these changes to the female shape within fashion, and firmly related them to wider contextual events. Looking back in 1939, Lesley Blanch commented:

> The last 24 years have seen woman describe a circle, from the stolid, ladylike, rather blowsy-looking pre-War beauty, through the urgent, uniformed War-days, to the hectic hotcha of the 'Twenties, cropped, plucked, and pickled in cocktails and nicotine. On she went, through the athletic, forthright, trousered, sun-worshipping 'Thirties, until … femininity dawned.[70]

Furthermore, the magazine decisively related these changes to a more eroticized appearance, declaring, after the shift, that 'sex mattered'.[71] Sex had become an explicitly favourable characteristic in fashion.

Figure 3.4 portrays an early example of this new image, a still from *Go West Young Man,* 1936. Here, the actress Mae West poses with a mirror, admiring her appearance. Her hourglass figure is displayed by her transparent sheath dress, which precisely covers her curves. Preserving her modesty are mere embroidered

Figure 3.4 *Film still, Mae West in Go West Young Man, dir. Henry Hathaway, 1936.*

Eroticism

99

flowers, which cluster over her pubic area, mimicking hair, and over her bust, which, as a glance between the gaps reveals, is enhanced by a moulded, pointed brassiere in nude satin. The gown softly flares out into a fishtail at her feet, which serves to emphasize further her hourglass proportions. She wears a sumptuous, soft white fur coat, unbuttoned, so that its rich, luxurious fabric serves to highlight her exposed skin. West became a popular and influential representation of this new, sexual femininity, and provides a useful case study to exemplify this transition, from a stoic, independent, and thin or masculinized female body, to a soft, curvaceous one which is intentionally seductive. She represents a more commercial and wider appeal than many of the examples considered in this book, tapping into the mass zeitgeist, yet she also had strong links with art and high fashion, as will be explored below. Her image was praised in the press: one journalist exclaimed that 'to see anyone so ... exaggeratedly alluring after years and years of flat chested, hipless ladies is by no means displeasing'.[72] Similarly, Elza Schallert in *Motion Picture Magazine* called her 'healthy and Amazonian ... the movie audiences have become curve conscious again – and Mae is leading the way ... she spells doom to the hollow-eyed, sunken-cheeked, flat-chested, hipless exponents of the neurotic', and Jim Timony wrote that she had 'the most beautiful and strongest feminine body in the world'.[73] These reactions occurred within the media and public alike, and as West's biographer, Jill Watts has recorded, her 'fan mail came from both men and women, and women sent not only letters of appreciation but also ones that asked for advice'.[74] These appraisals draw a distinction between West's voluptuousness, and the more angular bodyshape that had been fashionable previously, implicitly suggesting that the former was more healthy than the latter. West's studio emphasized this by frequently referring to her stamina and love of exercise.[75] However, no matter which bodyshape was popularly favoured, women could not escape commentary, criticism and tight control.

Like *Vogue,* West herself also related these changes towards the female figure to social, economic and political factors. For instance, she claimed that the typical 'flapper' look was the 'fault' of French designers, who created it by 'reacting first to World War One and later the Depression ... [and] pushed the lean and straight lines that forced women into an endless cycle of dieting'.[76] As a result, West had claimed that 'millions of women are undernourished and lack the vitality to wear ... fashion', which serves to highlight the discrepancy of self-enforced deprivation during a period where for many, this was an unescapable reality.[77] However, as economic figures started to pick up during the mid-1930s, West decreed that there was 'no need to diet anymore', and for her, the popularity of her figure marked 'a return to normal, the ladies' way of saying that the Depression is over'.[78]

Similarly, after Prohibition ended in America, Watts reported that West declared: 'now that beer is really back and we are all drinking it, why not wage a campaign for the return of the women's natural figure?'[79] For West, then, a curvaceous figure represented increased freedom and a less strict need for control, in terms of both managing one's own body, and navigating life in a changing wider context. She also strongly maintained a link between women's figures and the fashion that clothes them, and the broader social and economic considerations. However, such a body type was not necessarily natural or easy to attain for all women, particularly without controlling undergarments and strategic fashion, and therefore could be the source of further criticism and surveillance, both from others and herself.

West was not the only figure to relate changes in fashion to changes in the wider social and economic context in this way. *Vogue* commented in 1939 that 'the Great War left a race of nerve-shattered, disillusioned creatures, and that type, engendered by hardship and suffering, persisted and passed into beauty's currency. It was not de riguer to look innocent, or unravaged. Venus became a brittle, raffish goddess ... '[80] The author commented that this was a result of men becoming 'apathetic' as a result of hardship, and could therefore only judge beauty by 'weight, and youth', leading to the sexes being 'akin', and figures like 'skeletons count[ing] most. It came to pass that women were better killed than curved.'[81] Within this quotation, images of abject violence and deathliness are used to describe the more waifish figure that had been fashionable only a few years previously. After sustaining an economic depression, it was no longer desirable to appear unnaturally thin: instead, a curvier figure was desirable, and could represent an image of aspiration and of hope for prosperity. In this way, the female body was also thought of in terms of sex and procreation, with the emphasis on and eroticization of the bust and hips.

Similarly, the American designer, Elizabeth Hawes, also equated the return of the womanly figure with economic factors. She wrote in her book, *Fashion Is Spinach,* that 'it was the very obvious beginning of a return to prosperity which gave me time to have a flight of fancy, in the spring of 1935 ... '[82] Not only did this provide creative rejuvenation, but also resulted in practical benefits, and she noted that her 'customers began to order more clothes.'[83] In Hawes' case, the beginning of renewed prosperity allowed her business to pick up, as women started to have more freedom to make purchases once more. For West, the change in economic circumstance also allowed freedom of expression through, and a lifting of constraint upon, the body. However, in spite of this, it could be argued that West was in fact pioneering the return of a seemingly repressive framework for women, retreating back to the corseted, Victorian figure. However, West vehemently argued against such stances when raised, and she told *Vogue*, for instance that her corset was by no means restrictive, and did not 'bind' her figure. Whilst the corset functions to mould the shape of the body, it also provides support, and is not necessarily uncomfortable, as West confirmed. While *Vogue* concluded that West's image was 'an illusion', it also deemed this to be 'a healthier one for women' than the image that had been idealized previously.[84] In her own way, then, West used her body to fight convention and existing notions of desire. This subversive stance, while complicated, proved that dominant taste could be resisted.

In this way, West links the themes of women, sexuality, fashion and film.[85] West was widely praised within the contemporaneous media for bringing sex 'right out into the open' and celebrating it as 'beautiful'.[86] This opinion was representative of a wider one, and *Photoplay* magazine, for example, declared that 'sex is no tragedy. Nor should there be any sense of guilt attached to it. Sex is something to enjoy, something to laugh about. Certainly not a harmful, sinful thing.'[87] West helped to bring sex into, and to be normalized within, the public domain, and presented a model of healthy acceptance and indulgence. Whilst sex was very much an integral part of her public persona, it was not presented as shameful, and West herself later claimed 'I kid sex', referring to her humorous approach.[88] As a contemporary writer summarized, 'by signifying, she caricatured, parodied, and satirized sex, both undermining and underscoring the carnality she exuded … her sense of humour is her crowning attribute'.[89]

Another figure who similarly combined sex with humour was Elsa Schiaparelli, who worked with West on her costume design, beginning with *Every Day's a Holiday,* 1937. Schiaparelli adored West, who would also serve as a muse to several Surrealists,[90] because she 'brought back the frills and the curves and the pride of the feminine figure'.[91] This strong connection with Schiaparelli further underscores West's considerable significance to high fashion, as well as to Hollywood. Indeed, Schiaparelli strongly favoured and would go on to use the exaggerated feminine sexuality that she created for West within other designs. Not only was this ample womanliness duly reflected in her core design aesthetic, but it was also amplified. A typical Schiaparelli ensemble of the period featured a tightly nipped-in waist, emphasized hips and bust, and also frequently reinforced shoulders, to emphasize the hourglass silhouette exaggerated the feminine curves of a woman's body beyond their normal means. This was not the traditionally conservative and restricted femininity prevalent during the late nineteenth and early twentieth centuries. Schiaparelli built upon this previous hourglass, feminine ideal, by featuring classic elements, such as the emphasized bust and tight waist, but hyperbolizing them further, for example with prominent shoulder pads, the return of the bustle, and arrestingly bright versions of typically feminine colours, such as her 'shocking pink'. In this way, her enforcement and exaggeration of feminine traits in the body created a strong and assertive form of femininity, which took traditional traits and claimed them as their own. Therefore, her response to the fetishizing of the female body discussed in the previous sections is to critique it by re-fetishizing it herself.

Schiaparelli's enthusiastic approval of moulding the body was well documented within the fashion press. For example, in December 1937, *Women's Wear Daily* declared that 'Schiaparelli sees need for light but strong foundations', and that 'the thin woman is often more in need of corseting than the larger figure, for the proper silhouettes as defined in new fashions call for corseted figures'.[92] The magazine reported that Schiaparelli stated: 'many thin women do not realize the importance of a good foundation garment', and that most women should, and want to, wear lightweight, sheer foundation garments.[93] The entire Corsets & Brasseries section of this, and several surrounding, issues was comprehensively positive about the recent retail successes of corsets. Rather than restrict the body through previous, turn of the century means, however, Schiaparelli emphasized a new interpretation of heightened womanliness, making use of improved and more comfortable materials, to render the modern woman invincible: she could revive a traditionally desirable, womanly shape, but wear it in a comfortable manner, making use of modern advancements.

During the very same month, Schiaparelli designed her own line of 'foundation garments' for the first time, with the Formfit company, released on 16th December 1937, under a three-year arrangement. It boasted that 'every garment designed according to her ideas will bear a label "Approved – Schiaparelli – Paris"', and that it would 'help retailers solve the problem arising from the lag of perhaps six months between the new silhouette in the Parisian dress lines and the appearance of that silhouette in corsets. Under the new plan, this firm will be preparing its new line, while the same silhouette is being utilized by this couturière in the preparation of her spring showings.'[94] *Women's Wear Daily* pointed out in another article that women's fashion buyers called for 'rounder bustlines … in spring models', and that they were experiencing 'increasing customer calls for rounded lines'.[95] Schiaparelli's preference for a curvaceous figure, and the undergarments she put her name to with Formfit, was therefore part of a growing trend towards rounder lines in the feminine body, and their inseparability with a more eroticized fashion.

From the mid-1930s, Schiaparelli began to use 'falsies', breast pads inserted into the bust area to increase its appearance of fullness. This concept was immediately popular and became widely adopted and mimicked.[96] It picked up on the re-emergence of controlling underwear, such as the corset, girdle and pointed bra, and augmented them: whilst the former constructions could emphasize and control the natural breasts of their wearer, falsies, as their name suggested, exaggerated this further by augmenting the natural body. One of Schiaparelli's clients, Bettina Bergery, remarked that adding this invention to a dress was 'marvellous' and 'would give anyone a figure like Venus'.[97] This highlights fashion's transformative and constructive qualities, showing the way in which the appearance of femininity relied on careful external additions to the body.

Not only did Schiaparelli use falsies inside clothing, as a secret, private enhancement, she was also aware of their implications, inorganically creating an augmented body. In 1936, she produced dresses with padding applied in the bosom, but this time, sewn upon the surface of each breast, in a decorative, appliquéd style, known as the 'Falsies dress'. This augmented and drew attention to the breasts, but in this case, it did so knowingly and explicitly. It made public the private workings of a couture gown, and laid bare the construction of femininity, which became featured as an aesthetic element of the design. Her Falsies Dress comprised a simple black gown, its cut designed to skim over the wearer's curves in a precise manner, ending in ruching up to the neck. It had a modestly high neckline which contrasted two prominent circular patches over the breasts. Through this addition, the breasts were explicitly highlighted, yet the same time, remain hidden behind dark, textured material. She toyed with the spectator, by drawing their gaze in towards an erogenous zone, which was then confounded by being inaccessible. The perfect proportions of bust, waist and hips which Schiaparelli enthused over were simply highlighted by two thin lines of gold at the waist and hipline. She explicitly included all of the elements of traditional femininity that the mainstream demanded, yet ultimately contained and shielded them with the encompassing gown. Therefore, the gaze of an admiring viewer was caught off guard, as the eye was met by padding in place of the expected sexual object. The female wearer controlled her own sexuality, as a sexual *subject* rather than *object*. Earlier in the period, when pioneering erotic devices such as transparent materials first appeared within mainstream fashion, the erotic gaze was invited, and rewarded. However, with the Falsies Dress, the erotic gaze was still invited, but done so knowingly by the designer and wearer, safe in the knowledge that the viewer's eye caught by the emphasized breasts would in fact be met with nothing but the sight of padding.

Several of Schiaparelli's other designs during the end of the 1930s also drew attention to the erotic potential of the female form. For example, her 1937 collection featured 'suggestive brassiere-formed bodices', as *Vogue* described.[98] Within the magazine, the illustration of the dress was tellingly captioned 'sex appeal', and indeed, its tight fit on the contours of the body was far more clinging and revealing than the bias cut dresses that preceded it earlier in the decade. However, despite so much focus on a provocatively clinging cut, the body remained tightly undercover. Sexuality was worn as an external armour: it provided elements that may entice the male gaze, but used them as a weapon, for these very elements served to shield the body, and rebuff any potential visual violation.

In Autumn 1934, Schiaparelli had already produced an item with obvious erotic potential, an evening belt composed of a thick band of black silk, fastening with two interlocking hands. While it was another example of playful, Surrealistic aesthetic, and certainly relates to images of the hand within Surrealist oeuvre, here, its direct placement upon the body heightens its sexual nature. By wrapping it around the waist, the wearer is literally embraced by the belt, with hands placed firmly upon an intimate part of the body. The wearer would feel this embrace, and observers would see it. Schiaparelli repeated the motif in her Autumn 1937 collection, in a camel jacket adorned with embroidery based on a sketch by Surrealist artist, poet and filmmaker, Jean Cocteau. It depicted a woman, tipping her head back as if in ecstasy and sensually parting her lips, with her hand reaching around the waist of the wearer, in another embrace. Her long, full hair cascades down the right arm with thick strands of gleaming gold sequins. This abundance and decoration invite fetishization, for feminine hair is, as Ellis Havelock noted in 1927, a common erotic symbol.[99] Cocteau and Schiaparelli also collaborated on an evening coat for the Autumn 1937 collection, which again featured embroidered faces upon a jacket, with erotic overtones. This time, two faces appeared on the back of the coat, portrayed in simple, stylized lines, with only eyes and lips denoted. They turn towards each other with their lips puckered, as if about to lock into a kiss. The jacket captured this moment of charged sexual tension. The romance was furthered by a blanket of soft pink roses covering the top and shoulders of the jacket. In each case, Schiaparelli built layers of blatant sexuality, but in a way that protected the wearer from direct violation. By creating a fantastical scene of eroticism, as an image upon cloth, it is further removed from the body of the wearer herself. Furthermore, in choosing such a garment, the (typically female) wearer aligned herself with an active rather than the traditionally passive approach to sexuality, by carrying this image upon her body as she walks, displaying her autonomy. By knowingly participating in this layered and nuanced re-fetishization of the female body, she could control it.

This symbol of lips would become central to Schiaparelli, and also featured in another item of the same collection. Here, a sharp black suit is characterized by the bright, shining red lips that crown each pocket. In addition to adding a fun sense of personality to an otherwise smart suit, they are a clear avenue for eroticism. Situated at the opening of the pocket entails a clear sexual pun, and each time the pockets are used, the lips must be penetrated. Although a distinct and unique example, this tendency towards eroticism was part of a growing trend, and other designers featured similar elements, such as Mainbocher's veils adorned with lips.[100] Schiaparelli's suit was photographed for *L'Officiel* in October 1937 by Georges Saad, and the model's ensemble was completed with Schiaparelli's Shoe Hat, which also featured in the same collection, Figure 3.5. The nonsensicality

Figure 3.5 *Georges Saad, photograph, Skirt Suit and Shoe Hat by Elsa Schiaparelli, 1937.*

of the shoe's placement on the head is a reminder that Schiaparelli's stance on sexuality, like that of the Surrealists, could be playful as well as dark.

However, there are also deeper meanings prevalent. The shoe is bound up in sexual implications, such as the shift in posture it causes in the wearer, heightening her legs and causing her bust and bottom to protrude, and ultimately caging a sensitive body part. Indeed, as discussed, the high-heeled shoe, from which Schiaparelli's hat takes its direct form, is a common source of fetishism, as discussed by Freud in his 1919 article. By entirely displacing the shoe and inverting its position on the body, from bottom to top, Schiaparelli adds humour. She stops the shoe from being a mysterious, seductive item to be furtively glanced at, and instead places it in plain, unmissable sight, and by rotating it so that the heel protrudes upwards, its usual form is subverted. She uses humour to distort an element of feminine appearance that is typically sexualized by the male gaze and transforms the sexual into the absurd. This serves to re-fetishize a highly fetishized accessory.

Another designer who played a role in this new, deliberate, re-fetishized form of sexuality was Elizabeth Hawes, 'known for her outspoken feminist ideas and independent spirit', and a design aesthetic with 'unusually suggestive motifs',[101] as Reeder has described. Many of Hawes' designs c.1936–9 contained sensual, feminine features, such as 'the skirt with bustle fullness' that 'predominately featured in [her] fall collection' of 1937, as *Women's Wear Daily* reported, which they praised for 'injecting novelty'.[102] The publication deigned it 'the finest collection of her career' with 'a vitality and authority'.[103] The feature that was particularly complimented was the 'merging of geometry and moulding that produces bodices, shoulders and waistlines as smooth and cleanly curved as a glass bottle'.[104] Hawes took on nostalgic elements of the established womanly figure, and recreated them in modern ways. The magazine focused on the way Hawes' new designs deftly shaped the curves of a woman's body, in a similar commitment to traditional femininity as Schiaparelli. Indeed, it remarked on her 'fidelity to the wide skirts which she feels are more becoming to women, in which belief she reflects the preference of her own clients'.[105] Despite the focus on a hard, straight body in preceding years, fullness, softness and sensuality was now called for by both the fashion industry and the public that it provided for. Indeed, *Women's Wear Daily* specifically related 'the width of these skirts [which] by contrast creates for the moulded bodices and moulded … waistline' with the creation of a 'moulded feminine quality'.[106] Not only did Hawes create a feminine appearance, but she also shaped, enhanced and amplified conventionalized elements of feminine sensuality.

One of the most fitting examples of Hawes' stance on the new sexualized femininity is her "The Tarts" dress, 1937, with its explicitly sexualized title [Figure 3.6].

Figure 3.6 *Elizabeth Hawes, "The Tarts" Dress, 1937. Metropolitan Museum of Art, New York.*

According to the Brooklyn Museum, the dress was made to order in America, at a cost of $375. Contrary to its name, the dress as a whole is relatively modest, produced in dark green silk, with full length sleeves, a conservative mid-calf length, softly pleated skirt and a high neckline. However, this sombre background allows the appliqued design of the garment to be emphasized. A large, prominent red arrow divides the skirt in half with a bold red stripe, and culminates in an arrowhead that points directly towards the breasts. Similarly, on the reverse, another arrow, this one in royal purple, points towards the wearer's bottom. It unashamedly announces the position of two of the wearer's erogenous zones and draws attention to the sensuality of her body beneath the otherwise modest dress. While Schiaparelli's Falsies Dress augmented the breasts in black on black, here the violent colour contrast, in addition to the obvious meaning of the arrow as a device, draws the eye to a specific place. Schiaparelli, albeit in a muted palette, brought the eroticism of the body to the surface of clothing. Hawes, on the other hand, was knowingly leading viewers' attention to the existence of erotic zones, although they ironically remained hidden beneath fabric. Both designers, however, achieved a similar effect, by pointing towards the eroticism of the female body beneath clothing, but led the viewer into a playful, knowing trap, by advertising or emphasizing something that could not really be seen. Rather than being victims of violation, Hawes and Schiaparelli found a way to take control. This took the form of a critique of the sexualization of conventionalized femininity, through which they produced a modern form of empowered female sexuality.

Madeleine Vionnet's contemporaneous designs also drew upon these themes. Vionnet's creations depended upon a nuanced awareness and understanding of the female body, and she was known for radically cutting and draping on the bias, resulting in gowns that elegantly skimmed over bodily contours. Their simple lines belied the clever, complex constructions that Vionnet used to form her ensembles, typically based upon innovatively arranged geometric shapes. While Schiaparelli and Hawes (re-) fetishized the female body in an overt manner, Vionnet performed her own fetishization, but of other, less obvious, aspects of the female body, displaying a knowledge of its subtleties that only a lover would be expected to notice. In addition to this careful understanding of the body, and the high body confidence necessary to don her designs, Vionnet also participated with her period's fascination with feminine sexuality within fashion. Indeed, many of her designs display high sensual eroticism. Her Summer 1931 evening dress, for example, model 4336, comprised flesh-toned pink chiffon overlaid with black lace. The underlayer appeared as a second skin and created the illusion that the wearer was nude underneath the transparent lace: a shocking and daring combination at the time. Furthermore, she too highlighted the traditional feminine form, with a black belt drawing in the waist, emphasized by bold orange ornamentation. She would go on to repeat this eroticized illusion several times as the decade progressed.

Figure 3.7 *Illustration, Two Evening Dresses by Madeleine Vionnet, Vogue, 1936.*

For example, her 1936 dresses illustrated in Figure 3.7, also used transparent overlays above a closely fitting satin sheath. This time, the overlayer was composed of modernist horizontal lines, dissecting the female body, and showcasing it as a purposefully designed and created fabrication, rather than natural occurrence.

The various fetishizations and deconstructions presented by Schiaparelli, Hawes and Vionnet explored the violence and tension of the period by bringing eroticism and femininity to the surface, and critiquing concurrent fashion. They contrasted with and subverted the general trend at the time to invite the erotic gaze, in a one-way transaction. For example, in September 1937, *Vogue* provocatively titled an article on the new Paris collections 'Vogue's Eyeview of Paris Sex Appeal', one of the very first mentions of the phrase 'sex appeal' in the magazine's history. The article demonstrates the wide range of prominent designers who indulged in these ideals at the time, and the writer explicitly points out the sexualized nature of each garment. The author described 'Vionnet's innocent-looking, all-revealing Directoire, Mainbocher's and Paquin's seductive, come-hither veils …'[107] Even Chanel, who had famously designed for a straight, angular figure previously, produced 'full bosoms' and 'tiny waists at the Paris openings', with *Vogue* claiming that this 'influence[d] her whole Collection'.[108] Along with 'Molyneux's tempting décolletages' and 'slit skirts', the article concluded that 'the Paris Winter Collections resound with … anything that suggests allure …', and its summary of the recent collections urged women to aspire to 'seduction for evening; come-hither look, half revealing, half concealing lines; veiled eyes, romantic hats'.[109] Throughout the article, terms such as 'seduction' and 'temptation' were used, and 'sex appeal' frequently mentioned, with the recurrent assumption portrayed within the magazine that garments within these collections were designed for, and worn to attract men. Indeed, the writer deemed this aesthetic as 'inspiring clothes that men want to buy for women',[110] and provocatively decreed 'away with feminine independence. Back to charm and seductiveness'.[111] While at the beginning of the period, the male gaze was uninvited, and experienced as a visual violation, towards the end of the decade, then, this sexualized gaze was being actively encouraged through dress.

Fashion magazines continued to be concerned with the appreciation of men for the remainder of the decade. In *Vogue,* February 1939, for example, Jane Conway wrote an article entitled 'There's No Pleasing Them – MEN', in which she discussed the 'old' and 'insolvable problem' of dressing to please men.[112] She wrote that 'the machinations of the male mind – on the subject of women's clothes – have led me into some tortuous fence-straddling, jaundiced my eye, and befuddled my judgement'.[113] Significant physical and psychological discomfort, therefore, in adopting such uncomfortable clothing, was seen as necessary undertakings in the pursuit of appearing desirable. Four years beforehand, *Vogue* had interviewed men and published the results, and one questionnaire published in 1935 revealed that men preferred a 'soft', 'feminine' appearance, with garments 'showing the figure' or even being 'form-fitting', and 'sex appeal' was listed as a top requirement over terms such as 'style' or 'sweetness'.[114] This appeal to men remained consistent in women's fashion magazines, for both consumer and trade audiences: similarly, *Women's Wear Daily* reported later in September 1937 that 'men's preferences in women's fashions … have been played up by store after store this fall' making them 'softer, less severe'.[115] Furthermore, despite the liberating subtext of many of Mae West's statements, at the same time, there was a motive behind her particular stance, and a strong reason why it was ultimately not contested by the wider system around her: West's shape was knowingly appealing to men. While she always denounced 'binding' underwear, she nevertheless consistently advised that women highlight their curves with 'a little squeeze of the waist' in order to attract the 'roving eye' of men.[116] Although this came at a time when women's fashion had begun to diversify into sportswear and business suits, for example, in many strands, women's status once more assumed a more traditional role. *Vogue* confirmed that 'with this new role, came a new audience, and overwhelming, gratifying success. Woman is once more applauded, flirted, feted and flattered … a quality of ageless sex …'[117] Whilst there may have been less restriction and control exerted on the female body and sexuality, it was nevertheless subject to demands, and many figures within the fashion industry were happy to accommodate them. This traditional gender division harked to a comforting conservatism in the face of economic and political uncertainty. Whilst the economy had begun its slow recovery, political tensions were increasingly aggravated as the Second World War began to loom.

However, certain designers, such as Schiaparelli and Hawes, commented upon this spectrum, by deliberately using and exaggerating elements of it, to re-fetishize the fetishized. Even *Vogue* acknowledged this new form of femininity to be a 'role' based upon performativity, and Schiaparelli and Hawes used this distinction within their designs, protectively and assertively. The 'new breed' of femininity may have been pleasing to men's eyes, but clever and knowing design elements could ultimately rebuff this. Furthermore, even for a figure who seemed to participate wholeheartedly in these re-affirmed gender roles, such as West, this did not necessarily make women and femininity passive. Rather, as *Vogue* commented, West 'believe[d] in the Battle of the Sexes – and in being well equipped for the fray'.[118] Indeed, Watts has commented on the way in which for West, 'a sensual physique that excited men's passions was a woman's greatest weapon. Women could exert an extraordinary amount of power by appealing to what West believed was men's fatal flaw – their sex drive.'[119] Such language has inescapably violent overtones, pitting the sexes against each other in a battle setting, and, moreover, using a womanly appearance as a 'weapon'. A pleasing appearance might on one hand pander to a conservative and/or male audience, but adopting such an aesthetic knowingly could be a tool for survival, an armoury of defence and camouflage. Just as sex appeal could be used by a male audience to fetishize femininity and protect from castration anxiety, when women themselves built up their feminine appearance through dress, it could serve as protection to themselves through critique and resistance. By exaggerating expected elements of femininity, they were exposed as artificial constructions, thereby de-constructing and destroying the male fantasy.

Even within the mainstream consensus, this concept was powerful enough to occasionally emerge. One way in which this construction of femininity was revealed as knowing was in 1937, when *Vogue* described 'one of the maddest evening bags of the moment – a strap-handled box of clear, transparent Cellophane, through which could be seen, like an X-ray, all the owner's make-up implements'.[120] This continued ideas of voyeurism through transparency explored earlier in the period in fashion editorials. However, photographing models wearing transparent garments, as took place in the early 1930s, is ultimately a passive act. Actively using a transparent accessory within everyday life, such as during an evening out, as with the transparent bag described by *Vogue*, suggests more active agency, a deliberate choice. Furthermore, its usage within a handbag has further revealing implications. As the magazine described, it put on clear display all of the contents within, which primarily comprise 'make-up implements'.[121] This exposes the tools used to construct the feminine appearance of the woman carrying the bag. In this way, it is not flesh that is exposed, but the superficial trappings and underpinnings of sexualized femininity, showing it to be artificially constructed. The relation of looking through such a bag as being like an x-ray built on similar observations earlier in the decade, and added medical connotations, of a brutal, all-revealing act. Yet it also put on clear display the artificiality of the new, sexualized femininity, which depended on tools and props in order to entice, and exposed the desirous male gaze as being based on a falsehood.

Previously, feminine appeal had been defined as more sensual, and based on touch. Before the Second World War, the male fetishization of femininity and the emphasis of its sex appeal within so many examples of mainstream media, had been built up to such an extent that it was spectacularized. The Surrealist and female couturières' critique of this phenomenon highlighted that it was artificial and image-based, which distanced it from reality, and lessened its threat. This had built up from the sexual violation that occurred in literature early in the period, to the fears that were played out and fetishized on screen, and exposition that occurred within fashion illustration and photography, until they were adopted within fashion design itself, which enabled women to control their sexuality, and purposefully entice and rebuff the gaze. The potential for voyeurism, and therefore violation, that had dominated the previous years so strongly could now be used by women themselves at will.

4 Absence

Fashion and mourning

A grey figure floats ominously in the air [Figure 4.1]. It raises its wide arms above its head, its costume draping downwards and ending in feather-like fringing, evoking wings. One of its hands clutches an hourglass, with sand racing through its chamber to signify the passing of time. The other hand bears a scythe, as tall as the figure itself, with a large, sharply pointed blade. It forms a clear representation of the Grim Reaper, the very personification of death. All of the traditional elements of the character are included, which had appeared as early as the fifteenth century in English mythology, as a spectre who visits a victim before his or her death, in some versions causing the death, and in others to guide them to the afterlife.

This character made frequent appearances during the 1920s in a range of sources. It was used as a means through which to refer to death within literature, including novels and magazines, and was also referred to in official documents, such as governmental papers.[1] It frequently appeared in films, such as *The Ancient Mariner*, 1925, and it was even a popular costume choice in dressing up. *The Rotarian,* for instance, described in May 1922, 'the sombre robes and death-dealing scythe of the living personification of the Grim Reaper – otherwise Harry Hutchcroft' at an anniversary party.[2] Similarly, Figure 4.2 shows a couple dressed as the grim reaper and a maiden at a university costume party, *c*.1927.[3]

Whilst the personification was therefore not uncommon during the period, the context of Figure 4.1 was highly unusual. The illustration appeared in the *Gazette Du Bon Ton* in 1920, nestled amongst traditional fashion plates, and presented as though it was merely another style for consideration. The face appearing from within the costume, with its feminine features and rouged cheeks, is the only aspect that links it to what might be more typically expected within the prestigious fashion and cultural magazine. Death and fashion have shared a long-standing relationship over history, and dress traditionally played a crucial and well-defined

LE TEMPS

Figure 4.1 *Gazette Du Bon Ton, no. 2, March 1920.*

role within the mourning process. One of the most widespread and tangible traumatic consequences of the First World War was the catastrophic number of deaths, which had a significant impact upon women and culture. Bereavements were no longer suffered on a solely individual basis but experienced *en masse* instead. This chapter will examine the role fashion played within these changes, and how it affected attitudes towards women, their appearance and death.

Figure 4.2 *Photograph, People in Costumes of the Grim Reaper and a Maiden, c.1927, University of Iowa Libraries' Iowa City Town and Campus Scenes. F.W. Kent Collection University Archives The University of Iowa Libraries.*

The First World War brought about harrowing absence. Monumental losses of almost 3 million military personnel and civilians were suffered altogether in France, the UK and the United States. This marked the deadliest conflict that had ever been experienced by a vast margin. As has been discussed throughout this book, wartime devastation at large had a marked impact on civilization throughout the following interwar years. The war's impact on interwar attitudes towards death was also profound.[4] David Cannadine has stated, for example, that 'inter-war Britain was probably more obsessed with death than any other period in British history'.[5] The devastating losses, and their continued and significant impact on society, were openly acknowledged. For example, in 1920 Cope Morgan emphasized: 'we have just emerged from a devastating war – we haven't, we are just emerging.'[6] The war also had a 'devastating effect on [the] French household',[7] as Loleta I. Dawson and Marion Davis Huntting commented in 1921, and the 'devastation'[8] of the war was still widely discussed in America years later, for example in 1936 as having 'touched a new high in bringing disaster and misery'.[9]

Furthermore, the impact of the 1918 influenza pandemic should not be forgotten. The pandemic lasted from 1918 until December 1920 and resulted in considerably more deaths than the war itself: 50–100 million deaths across the world,[10] including approximately 280,507 in Britain,[11] 360,686 in France[12] and 675,000 in America.[13] This epidemic therefore gravely contributed to the widespread grief experienced during this period.

The extensive repercussions of this suffering, from both the war and the pandemic, were explicitly documented within the fashion press, within London, Paris and New York alike. In May 1920, *Vogue* stated the way in which 'War and the prevalence of death have made insistent the desire for immortality and for knowledge of the hereafter; and scientists and poets, philosophers and dramatists, seek to satisfy this great longing of humanity'.[14] The article went on to discuss the Belgian writer Maurice Maeterlinck, and his 'steadfast faith in the continuance of life after death, which he has voiced in plays and essays, came to us with "New Proofs of Immortality", and these proofs were well worth hearing'.[15] As in the *Gazette Du Bon Ton's* unorthodox representation of death, this was an uncustomary subject matter for *Vogue* to deal with. The poignant statements appeared seemingly in isolation within the edition, and with no further war-related context, as part of commentary on new literature. The writer's open curiosity towards these critical questions represented a growing tendency within society to explore the crucial matter of the possibility of life after death itself, which had recently become all too relevant.

One way in which to make sense of these questions was through the subconscious. Immediately after the war, forays into and explanations of the subject of death began to appear within academic circles, including psychoanalysis. Notably, Freud first published his thoughts on the possibility of a death drive in his *Beyond the Pleasure Principle*, 1920. Previously, Freud had asserted that the driving voice behind the id, the subconscious part of the human mind, was the 'pleasure principle', which is an instinct that seeks pleasure and avoids pain, at an innate level. This concept appeared within his early, fundamental works, including *Project for a Scientific Psychology*, 1895, and *The Interpretation of Dreams*, 1900. However, later observations, including the First World War itself, led Freud to revise these assertions. Indeed, Freud worked with traumatized returning soldiers, and noticed that they often re-enacted their experiences of conflict, despite being traumatic: 'dreams occurring in traumatic neuroses have the characteristic of repeatedly bringing the patient back into the situation of his accident.'[16] This developed his earlier association that the id seeks solely pleasure, and he concluded that 'even under the dominance of the pleasure principle, there are ways and means enough of making what is in itself unpleasurable into a subject to be recollected and worked over in the mind'.[17] These 'tendencies' were so strong that they were 'more primitive than [the pleasure principle] and independent of it'.[18] As a result, he proposed for the first time, in *Beyond the Pleasure Principle*, the possibility of 'a *death instinct*, the task of which is to lead organic life back into the inanimate state'.[19] This worked in 'opposition' to 'the sexual or life instincts',[20] which he deemed the 'pleasure principle'. The death drive entailed a constant 'pressure towards death … an urge in organic life to restore an earlier state of things',[21] 'whose function is to assure that the organism shall follow its own path to death'[22] and whose ultimate 'task … is to lead organic life back into the inanimate state'.[23] Not only was this development and addition to Freud's core principles a major development in psychoanalysis, and influenced directly by the war, but it also helped to underpin new attempts to understand death, both within academia and its frequent appearance and discussion within the wider media and fashion imagery.

The war also had a practical impact upon fashion's relationship with death. *Vogue* published two articles on mourning dress, in 1922 and 1927. Although each covered the subject in detail, the author did not mention the war directly in 1922, and instead merely described changes in style. By 1927, however, enough distance from the conflict had been gained that the vast impact that it had on the customs of mourning clothing could be articulated explicitly. The author explained the severity of its impact, on both sides of the Atlantic Ocean:

> the [First World] War had a great deal to do with this change. Mourning was abandoned by many people at that time, out of consideration for others, since a universal wearing of black as an expression of sorrow would have been

unthinkably depressing to the public. And women in America and England acquired a new view-point on this subject. They came to feel that they should not withdraw entirely from active life, except for a brief period, nor should they give themselves up to intimate and somber seclusion, wrapped up in deep habiliments of woe.[24]

Because of the total war nature of the conflict,[25] grief struck massive numbers of the population at once, rather than being a more individualistic experience, in which mourning dress could distinguish a bereaved individual, and allow others to treat them appropriately in public. As a result of the war, loss affected so many that it became a majority rather than minority, which required a shift in attitude, and, as *Vogue* described, a sense of society pulling together to move forward, as the only means through which to continue.

What did this mean practically, in terms of dress? In 1922, British *Vogue* explained:

> A generation ago there were absolutely strict rules for mourning, and in this respect no one who believed in the propriety of the conventions would have broken them. Today, every phase of life is being re-examined in the light of individual opinion, so that even mourning has become largely a question of personal feeling and the ultimate decision rests with the individual.[26]

However, certain conventions still existed regarding the proper etiquette, which had to be carefully followed. The author advised:

> It is generally conceded that whatever the degree of mourning, all black should be worn for the funeral and for the first few weeks. After that time, the black may correctly be relieved with a small distribution of white such as organdie collar and cuffs or a slight facing for the hat. All white is as strict mourning as the entirely black costume, but a more or less equal division of black and white, or grey and violet, is the accepted convention of second mourning.[27]

She did remark on 'marked changes in the etiquette of mourning', such as 'the decided abbreviation of the time that it is worn', which had previously been two years of full mourning, and half mourning for life or until a second marriage. By 1922, 'the widow rarely w[ore] the long crape veil for more than a year; some young widows, and even a few of the older matrons, now consider[ed] six months a sufficient period of deep mourning', which *Vogue* labelled 'a very modern interpretation'.[28] Discreet jewellery, such as 'fine pearls', was acceptable except for during the initial 'deepest mourning' period. The writer explained that the 'two reasons for wearing mourning' are 'to show respect for the person who has died' and 'for the protection of the person who is wearing it'.[29] Dress was used, therefore, to communicate a twofold message. Firstly, it made the status of the bereaved wearer known, and allowed them to receive an appropriate social reception, as discussed above. Secondly, wearing a colour that represented a deprivation of light was a clear link to the deprivation of the life of the deceased. This indicated that, despite their absence, they were still considered and commemorated in the present.

Several fashion historians have explored this intimate connection between clothing, memory and ghostliness through the dress of the departed. As Juliet Ash has written, 'real clothes … denote the absence of people … they have been discarded, but still bear the traces of their human wearers …. It is the sense and memory of the absent people which [is] … captured …'[30] She confirms that it is the delicate balance of 'previous presence and present absence' that makes clothing itself so ghostly.[31] Indeed, not only does 'worn clothing bear …. The individuating traces of its wearer', as Kitty Hauser has articulated, but, in accordance with Carlyle, it becomes part of an individual's 'unique identity', in much the same way as 'fingerprints, or in the DNA encoded in an eyelash'.[32] The remaining clothing of loved ones lost bear great pain and sentimentality, as Elizabeth Wilson has described: 'garments … [have] an intimate relationship with human beings … gone to their graves', and this phenomenon occurred at a mass level after the war.[33]

In addition to this primary purpose on an intimate, human level, style was also an important consideration in mourning-dress. *Vogue* cautioned in its above 1922 article, for instance:

> Mourning may be smart, but it should not be conspicuous, and it may and should be becoming, for there is never a time when a woman is not right in seeking to look her best. Above all, it is important that the apparel of mourning should be always in good taste.[34]

Indeed, the illustration accompanying the article featured two fashionably dressed women, praised in the caption for being 'extremely smart' and 'charmingly dignified'.[35] While each outfit is solely in black, the straight necklines, dropped waist, tubular shape and necklace accord with the demands of contemporary fashion. The black is broken up with various textures, layers and levels of sheerness. Therefore, while they conform to the (relaxing and loosening) requirements for mourning, they demonstrated an increasing link with fashion.

Alongside this growing relationship, there was also a noticeable rise in deathly language used within fashion magazines in the years following the war. This emphasized, and continued, a strong relationship between fashion and death that had already appeared within literature for many years. In 1911, for example, Georg Simmel had written that 'fashion always carries its own death within it',[36] as a result of its necessarily cyclical nature.[37] This connection was made apparent in fashion magazines throughout the 1920s through a tendency towards dramatic, deathly language. For example, in 1925, *Vogue* stated: 'Simplicity shows no signs of death; but severity – which is one form of it – will no longer be *de rigeur* for everybody.'[38] By the end of the decade, these lexical choices were still commonplace. In 1929, for instance, *Vogue* wrote that 'what is not wholly practical, or is for some reason inadequate, will fall and die like poisonous plants and mushrooms that, in their birth, are doomed to death'.[39] By this stage, then, the process of fashion itself was likened to being a deathly cycle by fashion magazines. Indeed, at its core is transience: clothing styles can, by definition, only be classed as fashionable for an ephemeral period of time, before they are replaced by a new season or style. In order to exist as a trend, each particular trend must eventually 'die'. This sense of temporality had particular resonance after the First World War, when the fragility and impermanence of life had been abruptly realized.

The unprecedented circumstances of the war built upon this longstanding relationship between fashion and death, and further developed it in an entirely new way. The widespread mourning that was undergone simultaneously at mass levels, due to the war's abundance of losses, also impacted the nature of mourning dress. Previously, when a woman wore a predominance of the colour black, it was strongly linked to death, and could be read as a clear sign of mourning. In 1916, for example, a black dress would not have been received as the height of fashion, as it would later be when Chanel popularized the 'little black dress' in 1926. While the black outfits produced in the years immediately following the war may now be looked back upon as being chic, this association would not have been made at the time, and smart black outfits were reserved for mourning.[40] However, with the war, thousands of mourners all wore black mourning outfits at the same time. Rather than being an individual event, it was carried out by necessity on a mass scale. This broke through the link between death and black. Because it was no longer solitary, black began to be re-conceptualized and be seen as more of a standard option for dress, that could have fashionable potential.

The increasing fashionability of mourning dress would only increase with passing years. In July 1927, British *Vogue* published an illustration of three elegantly dressed women stand together in a smart interior, turning to each other as if in deep conversation. They each wore fashionable cloche hats, knee length skirts with dropped, belted waists, and pointed high heels. Some wore fine necklaces and earrings, another gloves and a white organza ruffled trim. Like an illustration for a fashion spread, the caption announced the major designers behind the looks, including Chanel and Vionnet, and praised them for being 'chic', 'graceful' and 'skillfully cut'.[41] However, it was not a traditional fashion feature, but instead focused on mourning dress. On this first page, there was no indication towards death except for subtle qualifications in brackets after the description, that such attire was in fact suitable for mourning, for example '(a correct mourning fabric)'.[42] The writer also points out that the 'costume is correct for mourning or for general wear'.[43]

Similarly, on the following page of the article, an illustration of two women with bobbed, waved and lacquered hair was representative of typical, fashionable evening wear, with their sleeveless, straight lined, knee length gowns, decorated with long ruffles and pearls. The caption pointed out that even for mourning, 'the design must have simple dignity'.[44] The article stressed that 'the changes in fashion, in conduct, and in opinion have nowhere been so emphatically altered as in regard to mourning'.[45] Like the earlier 1922 version, the article explained that rules had been much stricter 'ten or twelve years ago', although even these 'were not so stringent as in the days of our grandmothers'.[46] However, by 1927, 'the wearing of mourning [had become] largely a matter of individual choice, and the rules [we]re far more flexible than ever before'.[47] This could entail 'refus[ing] to wear mourning altogether', which was admittedly 'difficult, if not impossible', although *Vogue* advised that 'it is the best taste to wear mourning that is not morbidly heavy, for a reasonable period, the exact length of time to be decided by the individual', and that 'the old fashioned degrees of mourning have been discarded', except for 'the black veil that one may wish to wear at first as a protection'.[48] This could simply entail 'all-black or all-white … with dull, lustreless surfaces … [which] may be lightened by such touches of white as a string of pearls'.[49]

By 1927, then, the increasingly lenient attitudes towards mourning of 1922 had loosened even further. The most important change by this stage was the fact that 'one need not wear clothes that are distinctly mourning clothes … the clothes that are in best taste for a woman in mourning are those that would be chic and correct for any woman',[50] and the writer went as far as announcing, in capital letters, that 'MOURNING MAY BE CHIC'.[51] This was helped by the 'present mode' which was 'so simple that a large number of smart dresses [we]re entirely suitable for mourning',[52] as the magazine advised that 'elaboration is not smart for any type'.[53] Rather, 'the tucks, pleats, and skillful cut sponsored by such designers as Vionnet and Chanel are ideal means of giving distinction to the mourning frock'.[54]

As a result, 'since mourning ha[d] become so much less spectacular, it [wa]s no longer necessary to go to a shop that sells nothing else', and appropriate outfits could be purchased from usual fashionable shops.[55]

However, while mourning wear was becoming more aligned with, and less distinguishable from, everyday fashionable clothes, it nevertheless had a significant and unique effect upon the body that subtly differentiated it. Whilst the remaining requirements for mourning dress could also pass as fashionable elements in their own right, their relationship with death and the process of mourning had further relevance. The most demanding requirement itself, for fabrics to be predominately black, involved a (non-)colour that, by its very nature, is composed entirely of absence, as it completely absorbs all light. Another requirement, for lustreless fabric, added to this effect, as it further prevented the wearer from reflecting light. By wearing absence on the skin, and strictly not emitting light, the wearer in a sense, then, became dead herself. This notion of carrying or wearing death on the body was further reinforced by heavy fabrics, both in weight and density, which hung from and enclosed the body. Indeed, *Vogue* itself personalized clothing with deathly characteristics, such as the above description of 'morbidly heavy' mourning wear, which was to be avoided, as mourning wear became less traditional and more aligned with fashion.[56] This sense of inherent deathliness within dress again drew on a long-standing precedent. For example, in Thomas Carlyle's 1831 *Sartor Resartus,* the protagonist visited the Old Monmouth Street Clothes Market. He dedicated an entire chapter to recording this experience, entitled 'Old Clothes', and explored their multifaceted meanings:

> With awe-struck heart I walk through that Monmouth Street, with its empty Suits, as through a Sanhedrim of stainless Ghosts. Silent are they, but expressive in their silence: the past witnesses and instruments of Woe and Joy, of Passions, Virtues, Crimes, and all the fathomless tumult of Good and Evil in 'the Prison men call Life.'[57]

For Carlyle, because the clothes at the old market had once been so connected with and surrounded by human life, when this life form is absent, they immediately become intricately associated with the opposite of life, death. Indeed, he describes clothes as 'Shells and outer Husks of the Body', as if they are part of the human body itself, so that when abandoned, they become dead themselves.[58] Furthermore, the absence of the human body, upon which they depend, becomes disturbing. Throughout the chapter, he refers to clothing as 'the Ghosts of Life', in affirmation of this stance. This has since become an important element of literature on fashion history, and Elizabeth Wilson has explored the 'eeriness' of 'old gowns', as 'a world of the dead', being 'congealed memories of the daily life of times past ... like souls in limbo'.[59] Clothes, when presented without people, are imbued with an inherent quality of deathliness. Dress is, in fact, the only design form that depends on the presence of a human body. Without it, clothes become a haunting reminder of absence.

Yet, during the 1920s, mourning no longer demanded the careful ritualization that it had previously. It became more closely aligned with everyday dress, as if by constant exposure, it could be habitualized and normalized into the quotidian, as if its ghostly effects and emotional powers could be diminished. This lessening of the sartorial display of grieving accorded with changes in attitude. By March 1929, *Vogue* proclaimed that women 'refuse to weep. Even when Death enters the household with ominous warning and the depressing draperies of destruction, they accept it – as accept it they must –, but they no longer bend and break beneath the burden.'[60] The magazine attributed this to their opinion that 'women are happier now than they used to be', because 'they are expressing themselves in terms of independence, gaiety, achievement'.[61] It suggested, then, that the new, modern form of independence that women had begun to enjoy after the war, 'as her horizon widens and her fields of activity become richer', had led to a more accepting attitude towards death.[62] Codes on mourning, which had previously been extremely strict, relaxed dramatically. However, the magazine's claim that women no longer wept over death conveyed a sense of disapproval, that they *shouldn't* weep when bereaved, and should instead focus on enjoying a modern, independent lifestyle. This suggested that it was no longer acceptable to dwell overtly on bereavement within society, and seen as selfish, for bereavement now affected so many simultaneously, rather than being on an individual scale, as a result of the mass deaths caused by the war. It implicitly advocated, then, a further example of repression.

The stark appearance of the grim reaper within the *Gazette Du Bon Ton* was a product of overwhelming trauma which was still extremely recent and raw. However, as the 1920s progressed, this began to be swept away and repressed. At the end of the decade, however, Elsa Schiaparelli produced a sweater in which a figure of death starkly emerged once more. Schiaparelli's couture career had begun in earnest when she produced a black-and-white jumper in 1927. It innovatively used a trompe-l'oeil technique, which featured a cravat bow indicated through white stitching upon the black jumper, as if it were a separate accessory rather than integral part of the garment. After wearing the piece to a society event, she received multiple orders and opened her first salon shortly afterwards. The style proved to be continually popular, and she went on to produce several variations, including a tie effect. In 1929, however, she produced another sweater which used the same technique to provoke an entirely different theme. As she described in her autobiography, 'white lines on the sweater followed the design of the ribs so that women wearing it gave the appearance of being seen through an X-ray'.[63] By her own admission, this was 'a skeleton sweater' which 'shocked the newspapers'.[64] She also mentioned that it 'hit the newspapers, which then took little notice of fashion'.[65] Indeed, on 6th January 1929, the *Chicago Tribune* featured a fashion illustration that includes one of the only surviving representations of the sweater.[66] The illustration, whilst simple, clearly denoted the white lines upon the black sweater, which evoked the bones of a female skeleton; however, the description only vaguely and minimally referred to it, as a 'black and white hand knitted sweater … knitted with an underweave of white and the odd scroll motif is white'.[67] Only once does the author, Bettina Bedwell, mention the fact that 'novelty in sports clothes [wa]s not absent', although by this she referred to the new Paris collections at large rather than Schiaparelli's piece in particular.[68] On one hand, the lack of reference to the sweater's unique theme could be attributed to the general nature of the publication, as a mainstream newspaper rather than a specialized fashion or women's magazine. However, Bedwell included considerably more details on other garments featured within the article, which is entitled 'The Last Word in Paris Fashions', suggesting in-depth coverage of the subject.[69] Deliberately or not, the rich subject matter of Schiaparelli's sweater goes unmentioned, as if exploring its implications would have been too difficult or disturbing, and were more comfortably repressed rather than acknowledged.

Certainly, the transformation that the sweater brought about, turning its wearer into a living skeleton, entailed a stark reminder of the losses faced by society at large. After the war, the topic of death had been very prevalent within many forms of culture. However, as the 1920s progressed, various attempts were made to move away from this unsettling subject. Women were instructed, both implicitly and explicitly, that it was no longer proper to dwell on grief, and instead they should focus on the new, faster-paced modern lifestyle. This shift in attitude and expectation was even reflected in mourning dress, which transformed so much that it became indistinguishable from current fashion. In her skeleton sweater, Schiaparelli drew upon this tension, which did not disappear and instead lurked under the surface, despite conventional media's attempts to repress it. Knowingly, she quite literally placed it upon wearers' chests, as walking reminders and embodiments of what was being repressed. The body was turned inside out, and matters that were banished to a subconscious level were displayed so that they could no longer be dismissed. This was characteristic of Schiaparelli's use of irony.

As death became more repressed and integrated into the everyday, Schiaparelli placed it as a striking feature upon an ubiquitous garment. The fact that the sweater was classed as sportswear increases this irony, for Schiaparelli used death as the major design feature within a category of clothing that traditionally celebrates the muscular, healthy, living body.

This oscillation between life and death was also being explored within psychoanalysis at this point at the end of the decade, when Freud had solidified his models of the death and pleasure drives. In *Civilisation and Its Discontents,* 1930, he admitted: 'to begin with it was only tentatively that I put forward the views I have developed [on the death drive in "Beyond the Pleasure Principle", 1920] … but in the course of time they have gained such a hold upon me that I can no longer think in any other way', and they had become an essential element of his psychoanalytic model, as they remain today.[70] An important aspect of the death drive model was its relationship with the repressed, which is essentially also what Schiaparelli drew upon with her skeleton sweater. Indeed, as a result of the death drive, 'patients repeat … unwanted situations and painful emotions', 'under pressure of a compulsion'.[71] This, he added, could very much be observed in the lives of both clinical patients and those he termed 'normal people … the impression they give is of being pursued by a malignant fate or possessed by some "daemonic power."'[72] The reason that such experiences are compulsorily repeated, even though they 'must cause the ego unpleasure' is because 'it brings to light activities of repressed instinctual impulses'.[73] In other words, traumatic experiences are often repressed and become subconscious, where they can be superficially pushed aside, but never healed. The death drive, then, 'has no other endeavour than to break through the pressure weighing down on it and force its way either to consciousness or to a discharge through some real action'.[74] Even though re-living such experiences is painful, it is necessary to do so in order to work through and resolve them. Immediately after the catastrophic suffering of the war, the figure of death emerged explicitly in an array of media forms, including fashion. However, just as the ego suppresses traumatic experiences in Freud's contemporaneous psychoanalytic model, throughout the decade various ways in which to repress this suffering emerged. Schiaparelli's sweater, then, with its overt and stark re-appearance of the deathly, performed a similar function to the death instinct: on one hand, by transforming the living wearer into a skeleton, which fulfilled the death drive's compulsion towards death, to return a living organism to its primary state. On the other hand, it similarly fulfilled the second function of the death drive, to usurp the repressed back into waking consciousness, to deal with a topic, that although harrowing, had to be addressed to find true relief.

Sinister shadows

In 1930, *Vogue* published an article on the new shapes of the season, titled 'Shadows of the Mode'. Its accompanying illustration depicted two panels, each containing a woman's outline, with only a dark silhouette apparent, as if illuminated before a window or light box, eradicating all sense of personal detail. The setting was composed entirely of black, flat darkness, upon a white background, evocative of comic strips, a genre that was particularly popular during the late 1920s and early 1930s.[75] The author preluded the article with an unusually poetic and descriptive passage:

> Now, let us turn out the lights and open the windows. The night is divine. Shall we walk up the middle path? The moon follows us with her pale, mocking smile. Look! Your shadow is taller than mine. How funny and narrow my shoulders, how slim your waist, how large my feet. What strange proportions. Is this the truth? Do I really look like that, move like that? Oh moon, you are making fun of us.[76]

The article 'wilfully ignor[ed] the personality and the details that go so far to complete the picture of the smart woman', and instead 'consider[ed] … only the first, but most important, essential – her silhouette'.[77] This allowed a higher degree of the reader's concentration to be placed upon her silhouette in isolation, considering the way in which the various garments that make up an outfit affect the overall figure, with style features and details such as tiered layers and hats creating a wide variety.[78] According to the magazine, this was an 'essential' element of a woman's appearance. However, the author also explained that there were deeper reasons behind focusing upon the 'shadows of fashion' in this way. Indeed, she declared that it offered a new perspective of 'reality'[79] which is 'exaggerated in a shadow'.[80] This 'instantaneous[ly]' offers a 'revelation of things as they are',[81] in a 'dramatic'[82] fashion. According to *Vogue's* logic, this was because 'the silhouette projected, for a moment' gives 'a detached and impartial view of yourself and your friends. Here, there is no escape from the truth about line and proportion.'[83] The implication was that while it offers an unbiased, objective view of superficial appearance, the shadow may also offer a glimpse into matters not usually apparent within everyday life.

In the Expressionist film genre, which had found widespread popularity during the preceding years (largely with films produced in Germany but popular with audiences internationally),[84] shadows played a similar and important character device. For example, *The Cabinet of Doctor Caligari,* 1920, frequently featured an enlarged projection of the protagonist's shadowy silhouette, which was much larger than the actor himself. Often, it would also appear twisted and distorted, which suggested that the sanity of the character was also to be questioned, and that reality itself was unstable. In *Nosferatu,* 1922, shadows were similarly used as a plot device to increase tension, and even the threat of imminent death. As Victor I. Stoichita has written, shadows in this genre of film reveal 'what is taking place inside the character' psychologically.[85]

This function has a precedent in psychoanalysis. Carl Jung referred to the 'shadow self' as 'the instinctive part of our psyche that we try to repress'.[86] His interest and belief in the significance of shadows were deep, and he explored the subject frequently throughout his oeuvre. The first mentions of the topic appeared in 1911 when he spoke of the shadow as being a 'dream motif', and by 1912 he wrote of the psyche having a 'shadow side'. It then began to appear regularly throughout his writings during the 1920s and 1930s, such as his prominent book on *Psychological Types,* 1922.[87] He strongly associated the shadow with the darker aspects of the human existence, and wrote that 'everyone carries a shadow … and the less it is embodied in the individual's conscious life, the blacker and denser it is'.[88] This can be read comparably to Freud's 'id' which revels in the human base instincts, as explored throughout the previous chapters. For Jung, the shadow self was an aspect of the unconscious, and the direct opposite of the persona that we create and usually present to the world. The shadow, then, across a range of media, both psychoanalytically and materially (when seen visually, whether in a film, magazine or real life), can be said to make present something that is usually absent.

This corresponded with explorations of the shadow and its effects in fashion photography throughout the 1930s, by photographers including Man Ray and Cecil Beaton. In publications such as *Vogue* in France, Britain and America alike, for example, it became common to shoot models before a plain white background, with dramatic lighting to deliberately cast an overt shadow, her own enlarged silhouette, or 'shadow self' looming above her. Occasionally, the projected shadow did not reflect the model herself, and in 1934, *Vogue* Paris published a photograph in which the model's shadow consisted of feathered shapes which did not correlate with her outfit, jutting out behind her as if shadowy wings. They presented an entirely different sight to that of her body itself, which was carefully styled and posed to present a highly controlled and polished manner.

Figure 4.3 *Cecil Beaton, photograph, Miss Sheldon Wearing a Maggy Rouff Shawl, 1935.*

This dualism between a restrained and unbridled self-corresponded to the binary being examined in contemporary psychoanalysis, between the Jung's authentic 'shadow self' and public persona. And in 1935, Cecil Beaton took this trend even further [Figure 4.3]. Miss Sheldon poses before a blank white backdrop, her arm outstretched to model a shawl by Maggy Rouff. Behind, the shadows of three men – who are not visible in the flesh – loom over her, two of them with arms and hands poised towards her. It is left ambiguous as to whether she is aware of their presence, and whether they are about to attack, or are being actively summoned by her. Her pose is deliberate, defiant, and confident, as if she retains control. Furthermore, the third shadow holds a cigarette, adding an element of social frivolity.

This increasing use of shadows within fashion photography has particular significance at the moment in history in which they appeared. The aforementioned *Vogue* article on shadows was published one year after the Wall Street Crash, and this trend grew in the midst of the Great Depression, which would last until 1939, with a devastating international impact that went far beyond the United States, including both France and the UK.[89] This directly correlated with the increasing appearance and exploration of the shadow in fashion photography in all three countries. Indeed, the interplay between presence and absence conjured by these images resonated on a macro as well as individual level. Whilst shooting high fashion represented glamour, and evoked occasions of fun and decadence where they may be worn, the appearance of shadows suggested the bleak reality that millions were living as a result of extreme economic difficulties, ever present and looming, even when it couldn't be explicitly seen. In Beaton's photograph, Miss Sheldon's floor-length gown and long gloves illustrate this sense of glamour in the face of adversity, and the Depression is an important contextual factor in this aesthetic development.

At the same time, there was also a peak in interest surrounding the association between women and evil or deathliness. While this had been made throughout history,[90] 1930 saw the publication of Mario Praz's *The Romantic Agony*, which was translated into English in 1933, and received considerable academic attention.[91] It was described by one contemporary reviewer as 'a study of the morbidly sexual elements in Romantic literature'.[92] She pointed out that such 'morbidly sexual elements' were not, however, solely limited to the Romantic period, and instead 'occur in all ages', including 'the present' time in which they were found 'everywhere'.[93] Certainly, morbidity and death were becoming particularly prevalent, and linked to women, through the trope of the femme fatale. She became a frequent protagonist in literature, such as within Lucie Delarue-Mardrus's, *Une Femme Mûre et l'Amour* 1935, which an American reviewer described as a 'delightful book' about a '"Femme Fatale" type'.[94] The trope also frequently appeared in women's and fashion magazines during the mid-late 1930s. For example, in 1937, the *Ladies' Home Journal* featured a short story by Josephine Bentham entitled 'Femme Fatale',[95] and women were even instructed to play the 'role' of the 'femme fatale' themselves, which *Women's Wear Daily*, for example, suggested could be achieved through dress, such as the application of a new perfume.[96] Dressed entirely in black, Miss Sheldon's outfit in Beaton's photograph also aligns with the trope of the femme fatale, and in this sense, the three shadowed men could be seen as unable to resist gravitating towards her.

This interpretation of women as being ghastly, or harbingers of violence or death, has a historical association with the interpretation of shadows. Between 1741 and 1801, the Swiss writer and thinker Johann Caspar Lavater produced his *Essays on Physiognomy,* which argued that 'physiognomy is a real science founded in nature',[97] and remained a reference during the 1930s.[98] Here, he argued that 'the soul of the person can be decoded in the interpretation of their profile',[99] and 'recognized man's soul in his shadow, and a shadow in his soul', interpreting the 'outlined profile' as a 'hieroglyph that has to be deciphered'.[100] The association between shadows and evil or deathliness remained strong during the 1930s, and was present in a range of sources from popular literature to figures of speech.[101]

This reading can be applied to shadows within mid-1930s fashion imagery. Their myriad presence within the representation suggests that shadows also offer a means of decoding in this context. For a fashion illustration, such as that in *Vogue*, it referenced traditional forms of recording dress, and offered a closer inspection for the reader, inviting them to focus on the most important details of an outfit's silhouette. In fashion photography, the frequent presence of shadows was a tool to significantly change the atmosphere of the image, and add another layer of expression. Frequently, this signified a darker meaning. Indeed, Stoichita has pointed out that 'the devil within was visualized in Lavater's science of physiognomy, projected in the shadow',[102] and a link between shadows within visual imagery and evil or violence can be traced all of the way back to Plato's cave.[103] Not only was the shadow itself dark, black and devoid of light but, as demonstrated above, the concept of the femme fatale was a popular contemporary reference during the mid-1930s, including within fashion, when the trend towards shadowy fashion photography manifested. This was contributed to by mourning dress itself, which effectively turned the wearer into a living shadow, with its heavy, dark, lustreless qualities, as discussed above. Therefore, women were being linked with dangerous deathliness across a range of media, and shadows upon the female figure and face within fashion photography denote a similar sinisterness.

As well as having a thorough historical tradition, these ideas were being examined in contemporary psychology concurrently to their appearance in fashion photography. In 1927, the Swiss psychologist Jean Piaget conducted a study of children's responses to shadows, which was widely read and reviewed within British, French and American literature, both academic and mainstream.[104] He discovered that children generally reach a relatively late age before they are able to understand the nature of shadows, and comprehend how and why they fall the way they do. He recognized that children first begin to realize that shadows are cast by an object at around the age of five years old. However, at this stage, they are only able to understand a shadow as either coming from an object or being part of an object: they perceive it as a substance in itself that is driven away by light. It is only by the age of around eight or nine years old that they begin to be able to identify their own shadow, which is a much more difficult process. Piaget concluded that it is 'at this age that the shadow finally becomes synonymous with the absence of light'.[105] Therefore, shadows in their very essence signify absence: it is their sole component. It is pertinent that these facts were being explored and noted at this point during the mid-interwar period, when shadows were so prevalent within fashion media. Furthermore, Stoichita has examined children's relationship with their shadow against Lacan's mirror stage. He wrote that while children do not fully understand their shadow until a later age, they still have a relationship and fascination with it beforehand. Whilst for Lacan, the mirror stage is a process of identification, the 'shadow stage' as Stoichita terms it, then, can be understood as an encounter with the strange, the alien, the other.

This concept of a menacing version of oneself continued to arise in relation to women and fashion. In 1938, Mainbocher produced a full-length couture gown, in plain black. Its flowing, elegant lines give way to a short slit towards the hem, revealing a small glimpse of the wearer's foot and lower leg. This elegant simplicity is contrasted by a dramatic, feather-adorned cape shape at the shoulders, which juts out behind the wearer's back, as if they were bird-like wings. This created a highly dramatic shape, which George Hoyningen-Huene displayed a nuanced understanding of when he captured the piece in a photograph of the same year. The model bowed her head forward and placed one foot in front of her to display all of the gown's detail. The lighting created a dark silhouette which was complemented by the monochromatic medium. What heightened the theatricality of the dress and photograph the most, however, was the enlarged shadow cast behind the model. It towered and loomed hauntingly above her, as if it were casting a spectre of herself. The shadow flattened and reduced the form of the dress even more, so that its silhouette became even more striking. With her face fallen forward, the model appeared unaware of this haunting background, poised menacingly. The careful setting of the photograph manipulates the interpretation and informs the meaning of the dress, showing how a thoroughly worked, elegant piece can also appear very sinister.

Horst P. Horst also explored similar ideas by creating shadows in his own fashion photography. During the same year again, 1938, he photographed Bunny Hartley for *Vogue* [Figure 4.4]. She sat upon the floor with her legs in a crossed position. Whilst her right hand was placed serenely upon her lap, her left-hand was held out before her, at a right angle to her body. Whilst the pose as a whole had calm, meditative associations, this was cancelled by her left hand, which formed a blocking gesture. However, what gave the photograph its menacing impact was once more the use of shadow. The light was deliberately directed so as to cast an oversized shadow directly behind Hartley, which loomed out above her. Furthermore, objects appeared in shadow that were not present physically within the frame, including organic, flower-like shapes. Their linear quality, in horizontal lines behind her served to add a sense of restriction, and they could be covered with thorns, or act like barbed wire. The fact that only their shadows were present created a ghostly atmosphere, the viewer was shown the spectre but not what it belonged to, heightening a sense of threatening absence. However, the most violent element of this absence appeared upon Bunny's own face. The dark, black shadow of a hand curved its way around the entirety of her face, blocking her eyes,

Figure 4.4 *Horst P. Horst, photograph, Bunny Hartley, 1938.*

nose and mouth, and therefore obliterating her senses and means of speaking, and even figuratively prevents her from breathing. Logically, we can see that the shadow belonged to her own outstretched hand, which tried to assertively block an outsider from touching her, as a means of protection. In the dark world of shadowy absence, however, the other had broken through, and appeared to smother her.

Actions such as smothering through shadow conveyed a sense of imminent death. However, there was also a concurrently growing trend within fashion photography to portray models as if they were already dead. In 1929, Man Ray had already anticipated this tendency. He shot a photograph entitled 'Woman with Long Hair'. Certainly, the model's long hair is a centrepiece of the image, and dominates a majority of the frame. It freely hangs, tumbling and flowing in uniform waves. Yet it did not fall from the model's head in a conventional manner: rather than framing her face, it hung below it. Instead of sitting or standing, her neck was draped backwards upon a vertical wooden block, and her head dangled. Her eyes and mouth are fixed shut, and there is nothing to prevent the viewer assuming that she is not alive. The shadowy background gives no impression of her surroundings, and her positioning looks too uncomfortable to be a believable chosen resting place. Her long hair and motionless face, among other visual similarities, recall John Everett Millais's painting of the drowning Shakespearean protagonist in his *Ophelia*, 1851–2, which may have informed an interpretation by Man Ray, and point towards a deathly reading.[106]

By 1935, this aesthetic became common within mainstream fashion photography. That year, Horst P. Horst shot his *Hair/Lace,* featuring actress Helen Bennett. Here, shadows were once more an important component of the work, and, due to Bennett's dress, were cast in intricate shapes upon the wall. She wore what appears to be a cape around her shoulders, made from abundant folds of lace. The lighting conditions again cast a shadow onto the model's face, which in this case transferred the details of the lace onto her skin. In this way, it was reminiscent of a veil, and the shadows worked in tandem as if shrouding her in lace, recalling traditional mourning wear. Lace and veils had long been an important feature of mourning dress, and remained major design elements into the early twentieth century; however, as discussed above, mourning wear became less and less segregated from typical dress, and more closely aligned with fashion during the 1920s. Therefore, women's expected role and behaviour when dealing with death had shifted considerably. Traditionally, it was only women who were able to express emotion and grief 'acceptably', and this was clearly displayed in the dress that they were expected to wear during the process. However, by the 1920s, the rules surrounding mourning wear loosened, and it became more aligned stylistically with everyday and fashionable dress. Alongside this decrease in the distinguishability of mourning dress, the message that women received from magazines such as *Vogue* encouraged them to lessen their expression of mourning, and instead become more stoic and 'modern', as discussed. Together, this suggested that mourning should become less overt, both sartorially and emotionally. Nevertheless, whilst changes in fashion and attitude happened in terms of expectations regarding the public persona, this by no means necessarily negated all grief; rather, it instead was buried beneath the surface. Therefore, it was incorporated into what Jung had appropriately deemed the 'shadow self'. The aesthetic of sinister shadows that appeared within fashion photography at this time was one way in which these repressed tendencies could momentarily slip out. Furthermore, wearing black, particularly in a veil, directly puts the wearer in shadow. Whilst developments in fashion and suggestions for behaviour encouraged a modern, controlled attitude to grief, by wearing black, which had become a common fashionable choice, a shadow could nonetheless be created, and offer some of the original sentiments behind mourning wear: respect for the deceased and protection of the wearer, allowing a socially acceptable means to subtly express the true 'shadow self'. Using black veiling within fashion photography allowed an outlet to further exaggerate and reveal this tendency.

In *Hair/Lace*, not only did the shadows have psychological associations in terms of grief, and the lace and dark colours link with mourning dress, but there are further deathly connotations within the image. Bennett's hair was stiffly lacquered and glossy in smooth curls. Whilst polished pin curls were fashionable at the time, the overt shine and slickness here suggested artificiality. Furthermore, due to makeup as well as harsh lighting, Bennett's skin was extremely smoothed and white, as if it were made of plastic. With her eyelids down, and fingers clenched to show off her lace, she appeared no different to an unliving mannequin. When the picture was published, *Vogue* even remarked on her 'remote, high-enamel look'.[107] In another photograph from the same shoot, the mourning associations were also apparent with her long transparent veil, which recalled traditional mourning veils, and her pose is awkward and uncomfortable, as if she has been manipulated like a mannequin or doll. Her eyes were not fully open in any of the shots. This uncanny oscillation between the living and the unliving, the artificial and organic, was an example of wider explorations of this boundary.

The frequent featuring of shadows within fashion photography from the late 1920s until the mid-1930s conflated the image of women with a range of connotations. The presence of a shadow was widely inferred as the revelation or uncovering of something that is usually absent, an interpretation that spanned a range of media and genres, from psychoanalysis, to the pages of *Vogue* itself. Furthermore, dating back to classical Philosophy, and made current and relevant by contemporary creative explorations, such as film and literature within all three countries, the absence that was uncovered through shadow was usually perceived to be sinister and as holding a threat. The pervading trend to photograph women amongst a variety of shadows within 1930s fashion photography both participated within, and commented upon, this tendency. It could be used as an aesthetic device to produce striking imagery, and it also offered a wealth of creative and cultural connotations, weaving together the Jungian 'shadow self' with changes in dress and attitudes related to death. By the mid-1930s, this evolved into photographing women to seem unliving, whereby any potential danger or morbid threat could be neutralized within imagery.

Death on the body

From the mid-1930s, the relationship between fashion and deathliness began to become more literal, visceral and thematic, and in addition to informing aspects of fashion images, began to play a main role within dress and fashion design. Schiaparelli had already begun to explore the aesthetic and expressive potential of the skeleton at the very beginning of her career with her 1927 skeleton sweaters, which had originally helped her to gain notoriety. In 1937, the theme appeared again as an important aspect of her oeuvre. That year, Paris hosted the World's Fair/Exposition, which included L'*Exposition Internationale des Arts et Techniques dans la Vie Moderne* as one of its six exhibits. This part of the exhibition showcased modern arts and techniques, and featured a 'Pavillon de l'Elégance', which exhibited the works of the most prominent Parisian couturiers, including Schiaparelli. The design of the pavilion was heavily influenced by concurrent developments in Surrealism, particularly biomorphism, which was reflected in the figures of the mannequins provided, with long, flowing, bulging and splayed limbs. Schiaparelli described the way in which she 'naturally protested' this enforced provision:

> Could I use Pascale, my wooden figure, and thus retain the atmosphere of the boutique Fantastique? Certainly not, cried the pundits. That would be conspicuous and revolutionary. So after much discussion I went and made my own show myself. I laid the dreary plaster mannequin, naked as the factory had delivered it, on some turf and piled flowers over it to cheer it up. I then stretched a rope across an open space and, as after washing day, hung up all the clothes of a smart woman, even to panties, stockings, and shoes. Nothing could be said. I had carried out most strictly the decrees of the Syndicat de la Couture, but in such a way that on the first day a *gendarme* had to be sent for to keep back the crowds![108]

Schiaparelli deliberately subverted the traditional, conservative elegance of the pavilion in its entirety, creating an alarming spectacle from the very conditions that were prescribed. Her set-up created such alarm and panic precisely because it enacted, to viewers, a funerary scene: Schiaparelli staged the mannequin as if it were a corpse. *Harper's Bazaar* reported on the viewers' reaction. While the description presented a respectable interpretation, it remarked that a traditional bereavement card was even placed at the scene:

> Schiaparelli stretches a nude figure on the ground, partially covered by a rug of flowers. On the opening day, someone threw a visiting card on the blanket with condolences, so now that lady has been jerked up to a sitting position, with her discarded dress and hat thrown on a garden chair.[109]

The controversy of the scene ensured that it was not included in the coverage of the Pavilion by any major French fashion magazine, such as *Femina, L'Art et la Mode,* and *Jardin de la Mode*. This repeated an earlier exclusion of Schiaparelli's thematic dalliance with death, as her skeleton sweater was also deliberately left out of major French fashion reporting. Schiaparelli's presentation of death was specifically constructed for a fashion magazine-reading audience, for the eyes of the fashionable women – or Parisiennes – that attended the Expo. Schiaparelli exposed abject inversions of the body with her skeleton sweater, placing impressions of a visceral, deathly body upon the living body of the wearer. At the Exposition, Schiaparelli used deathliness in a differing way: this time, she constructed a scene of death that explored the rituals that society surrounds it with. It was a dignified comment on the ceremony that society itself constructs around death, as a means through which to process it. Seeing an artificial imitation of this process within the context of the Exposition's Fashion Pavilion was an unexpected encounter, allowing the bourgeois audience to consider the pomp and formalities that death conventionally necessitated.

This focus on the artificial elements of funerary rituals was further exaggerated by the fact that Schiaparelli highlighted and played with the state of the mannequin itself. Christine Mehring has described the mannequin as being 'half-alive and half-dead'.[110] Its oscillation upon the boundary of life and death in this way contributed to its unsettling qualities. Manmade, inorganic materials are in their very nature unliving, yet when constructed as a mannequin, they are designed to resemble and even replace the living human body.

The International Exhibition was held from 25th May to 25th November, and towards the end of its display, in October 1937, *Vogue* published an article devoted to the mannequin itself: 'Wire, Wax, and Plaster of Paris: The Evolution of a Mannequin.'[111] The article gave a history of the development of the mannequin from 1885 dressmakers' dummies made of sawdust, to 'elegant figures of wax and wads of hair'[112] in 1893, to the 1918 mannequins which 'were waxen, buxom, and baby doll',[113] and a modernist 1924 version with 'a meta hook for a head, [and] spokes for arms',[114] for which the writer highlighted its lack of humanizing elements, instead 'a Brancusi elimination of matter'.[115] The writer's commentary frequently assesses how close to life each version was, emphasizing 'real hair'[116] and 'lashes an inch long',[117] sometimes anthropomorphizing them by using terms such as 'creatures'.[118]

Indeed, *Vogue* strongly emphasized 'the pulling fascination of mannequins' which 'has been constant ever since the first experimenter made a life-size figure with which to beguile the world'.[119] The reason given throughout the article for such allure was the lifelike qualities of the mannequin. Indeed, the article claimed that 'mannequins do approach art', and made a direct correlation between mannequins and real women.[120] Regarding the recent Exposition, it revealed that 'people copy the mannequins, pose like them, love them'.[121] The author went on to suppose that 'if life keeps on imitating art ... then we can expect women in the next few years to look divinely stretched out, with waists no wider than a wedding ring', just as the recent stylized mannequins were.[122] Furthermore, the magazine also noted that while the Exposition mannequins were abstract and stylized (which 'caused either a sigh of pleasure or ... a boo in Paris'),[123] the other branch of recent mannequin designs was much more lifelike, in the style of 'American photograph realism in plaster or Cellophane'.[124] The article demonstrated these differences with photographs, including a 1929 mannequin by the sculptor Archipenko for Saks Fifth Avenue, with a caption detailing that it had been 'the town's talk – beige ceramic, totally unreal'.[125] By 1937, when the 'seven-foot plaster abstractions of Paris' were displayed at the Exposition, mannequins had taken on a realistic aesthetic, and were carefully modelled to resemble the human form. This was illustrated with an example by Lester Gaba,[126] with its dainty arm leaning on a piano and smoking a cigarette, her hair and makeup perfectly and fashionably styled. The caption remarked that Gaba produced this mannequin as 'his own fireside companion', and it lived in his apartment 'with a wardrobe of her own'.[127]

Schiaparelli's mise-en-scène at the Exposition carefully considered and explored these recent developments in mannequins. She used elements of each of the two current polarized trends in mannequin design, of both realism and abstraction, in her critique of the mannequin's ambiguous state between semi-life and semi-death. Picking up on topical conversations and design developments regarding the mannequin's hovering between life and death, Schiaparelli subverted them by presenting the mannequin as a corpse, as being completely dead, rather than being an inorganic, unliving object presented to appear lifelike. Furthermore, the presence of a mannequin indicates the absence of a real, living body, and therefore serves as an uncanny reference to the death of the real body.

This strongly correlated with Walter Benjamin's observations on the links between fashion and death, which he was forming at approximately the same time when working on his *Arcades Project*.[128] An entire section was devoted to fashion, where Benjamin laid out his argument for death being at its very core: 'For fashion was never anything but the parody of the gaily decked-out corpse, the provocation of death through the woman, and (in between noisy, canned slogans) the bitter, whispered tête-à-tête with decay. That is fashion.'[129] Benjamin equated this with fashion's primary existence as being seasonal, temporal and fleeting, composed solely of trends which eventually 'die' and are replaced with new ones: 'for this reason she changes so rapidly, teasing death, already becoming something else again, something new, as death looks about for her in order to strike her down.'[130] He asserted that fashion 'lowers the barriers between the organic and inorganic world', as it is able to incite libidinal desire towards an inorganic product.[131] Schiaparelli, with her deathly Exposition set-up, directly performed and exaggerated his argument: any admirers of her couture on display would be, in actual fact, admiring a deathly funerary scene. For Benjamin, fashion 'prostitutes the living body to the inorganic world', and Schiaparelli highlighted this assertion and took it even further, by using the shock of a deathly body to reveal the interplay between unliving garments and the living body within the usual course of fashion. Benjamin argued that the modern woman could use fashion to resist the natural ageing and eventual death of the human body, which likens them to a mannequin, and turns them into 'gaily decked-out corpse'.[132] This 'gaily decked-out corpse' was precisely what Schiaparelli's display evoked, and can therefore be read as a comment on the nature of fashion, and its relationship to death.

The controversial statement that Schiaparelli made with her display was not just limited to Paris. The following year, Bonwit Teller, a traditionally conservative department shop in New York, unveiled a window display by Tom Lee. Lee made a clear reference to the recent Surrealist *Trompe l'Oeil* exhibition at the Julien Levy Gallery, also New York, with a subtle note in the bottom left-hand corner noting that he was inspired by it. While the influence of Surrealism was apparent in the work's overall mood, and indeed was produced at the height of the artistic movement's influence upon the commercial fashion industry, its content shared more with Schiaparelli's scene. Lee's version could be deemed a direct tribute, for it also presented a mannequin in a deathly manner. Its unliving status was emphasized with its cold, hard, pale skin, evoking a lifeless pallor. Her face was constructed with human features, including details such as eyebrows and eyelashes, yet her eyes were unnaturally blank. She knelt down before a grave marked by a tree (which was also barren, connoting deathliness), which, like Schiaparelli's set-up, was surrounded with flowers, as if they had been left to commemorate the deceased. The mannequin held a bunch of flowers herself, as if she had brought them to pay her own respects, yet her head had fallen to the side. It was left open to interpretation as to whether she was looking away in despair, or had just passed away herself. Her gown was constructed with lavish folds of black lace, and completed with a matching black veil, conjuring mourning dress. Yet in the window's scene, the dress was decorated with flowers, as if she were a corpse dressed for a funeral viewing herself. This unusually poetic and provocative scene approved by the conventional retailer demonstrates the great extent to which these themes and ideas brewed at this moment during the late 1930s, from a wide range of sources. Here, deathliness became part of the everyday, brazenly on display to New York's passing crowds.

Schiaparelli continued to explore deathliness in her fashion design, and the corpse in particular, as featured in her and Lee's displays, remained an important consideration. After examining the ritualization and uncanniness of death and absence during the Exposition, in her Circus collection of the following year, 1938, she returned to deathliness and decay within the body itself, with her Skeleton Dress. Silk crêpe, in jet black, clung to the skin, covering the entirety of the wearer's body in sheathed darkness. The shoulders, décolletage and each limb were fully enclosed. While the curved lines of the silhouette created adhered to fashionable evening wear of the season, as Valerie D. Mendes has written, 'the skeleton dress is so constricted that it became a second skin'.[133] Ghislaine Wood has also made a similar observation: 'Schiaparelli's realization of this corporeal imagery in "skin tight" black silk jersey provided the illusion of a second skin …'.[134]

In addition to the uncanny quality that this constriction provided, already conflating the states of living and unliving by giving an inorganic material uncomfortable and organic qualities, this effect was dramatically heightened by the addition of bones. Upon the surface of the matte silk, trapunto quilting was employed and exaggerated to create a skeletal anatomy on the exterior of the body. Six pairs of diagonal lines upon the chest (front and back) serve as the ribs, and further raised ridges indicate bones for the waist, legs, back and spine, on both sides of the dress, so that the skeleton was apparent to viewers whether they faced the wearer directly or not. As discussed, Schiaparelli had already conflated clothing with the skeleton in her 1927 skeleton sweater. For this later example, she collaborated with Salvador Dali, who produced an original sketch on the theme, which included skeletons wearing draped, transparent dress with prominent bones arranged in the same manner on those of Schiaparelli's final produced design. At the bottom of the drawing, he wrote: '*Cher Elsa j'aime enormement c'idee des os a l'exterieur*', suggesting that the pair had discussed their ideas on the theme previously.[135] Schiaparelli's design, with its matching bone structure, appears to have developed directly from this initial sketch.

Most items within the rest of the collection captured the fanciful, fun and frivolous aspect of the circus, and included design details such as decorated, dancing horse motifs, flying acrobats as buttons, jaunty circus leader-style top hats, clown hats, circus tent veils, glamorous tassels and hot pinks and purples. This was emphasized when the collection was shown, featuring performers alongside models. However, two ensembles stood out for emanating a sense of foreboding rather than frivolousness: the Tear Dress, which poignantly explored physical violence as discussed in Chapter 1, and the Skeleton Dress itself. Several writers, including Dilys Blum, Valerie Steele and Jennifer Park,[136] have reasonably interpreted that the design rationale behind the Skeleton dress was thematically connected to the overall subject of the collection, the circus, and that it represents the skeleton man in the traditional 'freak' sideshow included within the performance. This highlights a sense of fascination and horror to accompany the spectacle of the circus. Tod Browning's film, *Freaks,* for example, had emphasized the captivation of 1930s audiences with human 'freaks' as a source of entertainment, and promoted controversy for featuring real freakshow exhibitants, such as the conjoined sisters, Daisy and Violet Hilton. Using both the jovial and darker elements of a circus within the same collection allowed Schiaparelli to shed light on both the complete spectacle, and its seedy underbelly.

However, the Skeleton Dress conjures macabre, sinister and deathly connotations that seem to go even further in exploring death on the body. Certainly, the silk crepe material selected, in matte, is specifically a material that was suited to mourning wear. It was also designed with a hat that built on the outfit's aesthetic of mourning, which featured a black veil in the shape of a circus tent, topped with a cap. Furthermore, Caroline Evans has argued that images of the internal body are always associated with death:

> Before the advent of modern medicine, with its new technologies for imaging
> the body, the sight of the inside of the body was always an encounter with death.
> Today, despite medical advances, it still retains some of that charge, and a visual
> encounter with the inside of the body may be an encounter with disease and
> pathology.[137]

Schiaparelli produced her dress in between these two sides. Whilst x-ray technology was initially discovered at the end of the nineteenth century,[138] it wasn't until the mid-1920s that safety precautions began to be seriously recommended, and it would take over three further decades for them to approach universal adoption.[139] Its harmful effects remained highly prevalent during the 1930s when Schiaparelli was designing.[140] Therefore, Schiaparelli explored the technology at a point where it was still extremely harmful and relatively little understood, despite having existed for three decades. By turning the body inside out with her skeleton dress, she drew on both associations of glimpsing the internal body: both the pre-modern medicine link with death, the medically advanced link to disease and pathology. This was further fraught by the state of x-ray technology in the 1930s: it was widely used, and its dangers were well-reported, but ideal safety practices had not yet been implemented.

The skeleton dress enabled its wearer to embody death on multiple levels, from traditional mourning-wear, to associations with the dead or diseased body, and the added fear of a still dangerous medical technology employed in sickness. This allowed Schiaparelli to subvert traditional evening-wear. While the fabric clung to the body, which was common in contemporary fashion and allowed sensual display of the body's contours, Schiaparelli inverted this by revealing not just womanly curves, but the very bones beneath. In this way, she could toy with the male gaze, which expected to be rewarded with sexual pleasure by penetrating clothing to reveal the naked body beneath, but instead was taken deeper, and exposed to the visceral skeleton beneath: a theme that run through much of Schiaparelli's oeuvre. In this way, the skeleton dress transformed its wearer into the embodiment of a femme fatale, initially attracting men through her sexuality, but ensnaring them with her incarnation of death. As was typical with Schiaparelli, the shock that this design provoked was evident by its lack of media coverage: only *Harper's Bazaar* mentioned the dress, in relation to the Circus collection as a whole, and it suggested that the dress created the image of a malnourished figure, by proclaiming it to be 'designed especially for Coo Coo the Bird Girl'.[141]

This interpretation presented another significance of the exposition of bones upon a dress, which connected to the current context of the fashion industry, and expectations for women. From a distance, the skeleton dress appeared to conform precisely with the silhouette and style of current fashion for evening dresses, with its exaggerated shoulders and clinging contours. *Women's Wear Daily* gave a description of the dress of the season, which could be applicable to the skeleton dress: 'it is the sleeved evening gown that establishes the trend in formal dress fashions. The sleeves are larger; they grace the most formal dresses in the most formal fabrics, establishing a trend towards greater elegance.'[142] For

Figure 4.5 *Charles Frederick Worth, Black Satin Dinner Dress, c.1935.*

example, Charles Frederick Worth's 1935 black satin dinner dress had a very similar silhouette and overall effect as the skeleton dress itself, with its full length, high neckline, long sleeves and dark, single colour [Figure 4.5]. Furthermore, *Women's Wear Daily* even advised in August that for both day and evening dresses, 'surface decoration includ[ing] many appliques' was important.[143] Whilst such appliques were typically organic shapes such as flowers, much like jewellery as discussed above, Schiaparelli's bones do fit within the category. Furthermore, black had recently become fashionable, as elaborated above, and using it as the sole colour created an elegant ensemble. Only upon closer inspection would the raised bones, also constructed in black, become visible. Whilst this was clearly a bold and unique design tactic, it also necessitates a rethinking of standard contemporary evening dresses.

Indeed, in addition to the fashionable general style of the skeleton dress, it also raised a critical eyebrow at the demands placed on women's bodies by contemporary fashion. Bias cutting was one of the most prevalent trends in dress throughout the 1930s, as the following examples show. By necessity, due to the cutting of the fabric diagonally to the grain, it created slinky shapes that fit extremely closely to the body, darting over its contours and revealing its natural shape. Whilst the technique was largely pioneered by Madeleine Vionnet, and popular amongst many other Parisian couturiers, it was also prevalent within the New York and London fashion scene, and produced by couturiers including Norman Hartnell and Charles James circa 1933–4, with evening dresses that skimmed the body enough to reveal the real bones of the wearer, leaving no room for any slight physical imperfection, with clinging satin material and bias cut would have unforgivingly revealed every contour, including any boniness. By 1938, when Schiaparelli released her skeleton dress, this tendency had reached a new height. For example, *Women's Wear Daily* featured an illustration in 1938 of what they deemed 'a slim simple dress' by Norman Hartnell. Like many dresses released that year, the long silhouette was produced in a single dark colour. It drew attention to the tightness of the bias cut with a dramatic highlight surrounding the hips, where light hit the dark, shiny material, confirming the demanding and revelatory fit upon the body. When closely fitted in this popular way, a (suggestion of a) woman's 'bones' were literally revealed through her dress, and through exaggerating this process, Schiaparelli's Skeleton Dress served to comment on and expose these demands.[144]

This interplay of sex and death was also explored by writers at the end of the 1930s, including Georges Bataille, who was involved with the Surrealist group, and friends with Walter Benjamin. As Jonathan L. Owen has noted, 'Bataille's work … addresses "energy" … conceive[d] … in social and material, as well as psychic, terms.. concentrates more frequently on the excess of energy than on its scarcity.'[145] He argued that this 'energy' had to be disposed of 'correctly' when in surplus. This could be done through 'harmless expenditures', such as hedonistic feats of food and sex. However, if the energy was not spent in these ways, 'the irrepressible need or tendency to squander might express itself through the darker expenditures of, say, murder or war'.[146] He found that 'the most satisfying expenditures are the cruellest and most destructive ones', and as Owen has put it, 'Bataille's work revels in a fearsome iconography of human sacrifice, blood rituals, deviance and criminality, while his discussion of expenditure extends to modern warfare …'.[147]

In June 1939, Bataille published a text entitled 'La pratique de la joie devant la mort' in the journal *Acéphale*. Here, he outlined his theory on 'inner experience' and eroticism. According to Bataille, the violence of death cannot be escaped during life:' [man]cannot fulfill his life without surrendering to an inexorable movement, the violence of which he feels acting upon the most hidden aspects of his being with a rigour which frightens him.'[148] He asserted that one must find 'joy in the face of death', and 'laugh complacently at every human endeavour and to know every accessible delight.'[149, 150] Within this, Bataille emphasized ephemerality: 'it is an apotheosis of that which is perishable, apotheosis of flesh.'[151] This relates, then, to the spectre of death enacted by Schiaparelli's Skeleton dress. Rather than repressing death, the wearer of the dress embodies it, and, worn during the evening, where she is vulnerable to an objectifying gaze, it conflates sex and death in a Bataillean manner. This also lived out Benjamin's comment that fashion is 'the dialectical switching station between woman and commodity – desire and dead body'.[152]

Indeed, Bataille argued that 'Man's separation from an extravagant, exuberant, and excessive nature is signified by [the] establishment of two closely related taboos: murder and incest, the dead and the naked body, death and sexuality'.[153, 154] By repressing these taboos, 'man's self' is 'established by refusal, represses death and economizes sex'. With her Skeleton Dress, Schiaparelli exposed this repression, freeing women's sexuality from capitalist restraint, and forced society to be confronted by death. She did this not only by making the skeleton or corpse itself a fundamental design aspect, but also by candidly linking it to contemporary fashion, and the suffering that it demanded beneath the surface upon women's real, living bodies. Bataille noted that in traditional society, women are made passive, as taboos are artificially created by men, who then primally desire to transgress it through violence and death:

It is intentional like the act of the man who lays bare, desires and wants to penetrate his victim. The woman in the hands of her assailant is despoiled of her being … She is brusquely laid open to the violence of the sexual urges set loose in the organs of reproduction; she is laid open to the impersonal violence that overwhelms her from without.[155]

Schiaparelli's skeleton dress therefore transferred this power directly onto the female body. In this way, it could serve as both protection and empowerment. This sense of feminine empowerment mounted within Schiaparelli's oeuvre over the 1930s, and reached its peak at this point at the end of the decade, as the Second World War began to loom. Her protective, empowering dress could shield women from the dangers within society. This could provide comfort, figuratively, as the turbulent political scene unfolded, offering a sense of stability in the face of a world that was once again shifting, having scarcely recovered from the devastation of the First World War. In addition, its fundamentally deathly aesthetic could ward off the traditional fear and taboo of death, and instead acknowledge and liberate it, sparking Bataillean 'joy'.

Conclusion

Fashion is a sphere that has been typically perceived as being built on fantasy and escapism. On one hand, this can be interpreted as a criticism and dismissal of seemingly superficial frivolity. Yet it is the very fact that fashion works in the realm of fantasy and escapism that makes it possible to explore impulses of violence there. Here, trauma could be expressed upon an image-based level, and through doing so, it could be processed. This book has demonstrated fashion's unrelenting relationship with the context in which it occurs, and shows that, while it could reflect contemporary anxieties, fantasies and fears, it was also a place where, like in psychoanalysis, they could be explored and resolved. As Elizabeth Wilson has argued, fashion operates 'as a cultural phenomenon, as an aesthetic medium for the expression of ideas, desires and beliefs circulating in society'.[1] In this way, it 'may then be understood as ideological, its function to resolve formally, at the imaginary level, social contradictions that cannot be resolved'.[2] The interwar period was marked throughout its duration by a range of social contradictions and anxieties, many of which were based upon, or experienced and perceived with, violence. They manifested as representations of violence in fashion, placing them into a realm where they could be addressed, managed and processed. This in part involved the anxieties of mainstream conservatism, which were directed towards women, and absorbed by fashion. Yet high-end, female fashion, upon which this study has concentrated, had a direct relationship with femininity, and not only offered a 'safe' place for the resolution of trauma, but also offered women, in conjunction with Surrealists, the means, protection and empowerment to survive and thrive in the turbulence of post-war modernity.

Women and modernity

Another important factor behind violence in fashion is modernity. Particularly in the city, an aggressive form of modernity was experienced through sight, and visually bombarded the eye. A new, 'violent' use of colour became apparent within fashion, which could contend with the attack on sight that post-war modernity presented. In addition to visual violence, modernity in the city was also experienced fragmentarily, which created further anxieties within everyday life. This led to the isolation of the eye within contemporary makeup trends, which 'fragmented' it from the face, and the attention placed upon the eye within beauty marketing linked women with developments in modernity, and advocated a machine aesthetic, reflecting the progression of technology.

These developments in modernity were perceived as rapid, and could leave individuals feeling anxious and out of control as a result, as commentators described. Throughout this book, expressions of fear towards, and criticisms of, women are visited, and found to be a contributing factor to violence in fashion. For example, sex became more apparent within society from the early 1920s, leading to fears regarding the preservation of the status quo, and anxieties regarding the maintenance of traditional gender roles, even leading to women being presented as evil and as harbingers of death. In tandem with these moral condemnations of women, women were also placed under surveillance and control. For instance, at some points within the period, a traditionally feminine, and voluptuous figure was celebrated, yet at others, a tightly controlled and toned body shape was necessitated. These demands were not natural or effortless for the majority of women, and demonstrate a further attempt of controlling them. Even women's grief and mourning were regulated, and expected to be repressed.

However, women's role within this was by no means solely passive. Indeed, in each chapter of this book, the violence in fashion built up from early forays in text and image, to gradually gaining momentum and influencing dress itself, to eventually, by the mid-1930s, starting to appear as explicit interpretations of variations of violence. During the early interwar years, women's appearance was manipulated in beauty imagery, and violence was experienced visually as a result of everyday life. The female body was also a physical victim of fragmentation within fashion illustration. A more formal recognition of female sexuality, increased freedom in social conventions regarding sex, and the fact that it was being more freely explored within culture and as a leisure activity also continued the moral attack against women. Whilst the conservative, anxiety-driven backlash towards this took the form of sexual violence, at the same time, eroticism could also be enjoyed by women as escape, confounding such condemnation.

As the period progressed, the nature of violence in fashion began to shift, to allow women to develop a form of 'counter attack'. Colours described as 'violent' became fashionable, particularly when they 'violently' contrasted each other, which, as contemporary theorization detailed, physically strained the eye. Violence in fashion could therefore take part in a two-fold exchange: women received violence through sight, yet by adopting fashionable colours in their dress, or isolating the eye with makeup trends, they could draw on the violent potential of sight, and could reflect it back like a shield.

Towards the end of the period, this theme became more explicit, and was especially evident within fashion design, especially Schiaparelli's couture, from equipping her wearer for combat with literal weapons of assault, to turning women into the living embodiment of the femme fatale, offering them protection and empowerment. She and other designers such as Elizabeth Hawes toyed with the male gaze, and empowered women by offering them control and refusal of it. Rather than being a source of passive violence, manifestations of violence within high fashion design offered a resistance to negative mainstream attitudes towards the female body.

The framework of violence in fashion, in conjunction with psychoanalysis and Surrealism, was therefore able to counter the use of images of women within the mainstream, and present a new, subversive form of femininity that drew upon violence for its own gain.

Contexts

The First World War was a watershed event in creating trauma within society. This led to anxieties within wider, conservative society, which were directed towards the female body as an outlet. The assault of the conflict led to emotional war 'wounds' for women. Contemporary beauty advertising addressed these 'wounds', and in order to do so, drew upon the advances in medical knowledge and practice that had been necessitated during the war. However, rather than offering merely a safe, visual sphere upon which female trauma could be resolved, they in fact eventually placed women in dangerous, violent situations, with oversized, exaggerated medical implements that suggested potential visceral violence. In this way, violence towards women was a scapegoat for war-based trauma of wider society. The war also had a great impact on medicine and the body, including amputation, which was newly practised on a large scale as a result of the war. This literal fragmentation of the male body was transposed into imagery of fragmented women. Finally, an unprecedented number of deaths were suffered as a result of the war, which were also further compounded by the huge losses from the flu pandemic. This was directly addressed in the fashion industry, for example in fashion magazines, through direct discussions of death, the use of deathly language in relation to fashion, and even images of death itself, such as the grim reaper. Furthermore, the widespread, mass nature of grief at this time directly affected dress, by blurring the boundaries between mourning- and everyday-wear.

Whilst the aftermath of the war and the increasing demands of modernity were the main contextual factors considered by this book, at certain moments other events were also relevant. For example, the rise of fascism, and the fears it provoked internationally, presented an additional threat. This led to a move towards healing and reparation, as expressed in beauty advertisements, yet one that was ultimately marred with further violence, mimicking the surgical metaphors that were also presented by Mussolini. Likewise, a conflict emerged between the whole, classical body that was used within fascist and Nazi propaganda, and even national imagery used by the allied powers, and the image of the subverted and fragmented female body that Schiaparelli and the Surrealists used to counter this appropriation. Similarly, the Great Depression was another traumatic event that impacted the period, and values towards appearance and the body became more conservative as a result, in effort to reform traditional gender divides, and the emphasis of feminine characteristics such as wide hips, a nipped waist, and an emphasised bust became fashionable. Mae West and *Vogue* alike linked this with the current economic hardship. Yet this aesthetic of 'sex appeal', used for the first time by *Vogue* in 1937, was also a celebration of sexuality and its status as become more acceptably commonplace, and a rebellion against moral criticism towards women.

Therefore, the appearance of violence within fashion was irrevocably linked to its various contexts. Its manifestation and specific nature were closely linked to the traumatic aftermath of the First World War and flu pandemic, the changes it brought about within society, and the further pressures that developed over the course of the interwar period. These events implicated and were experienced by women, as the subsequent trauma experienced by wider society and men was re-directed towards them. Similarly, at certain points fashion itself represented and contributed to a sense of anxiety, such as through sight (in relation to both violent colour and the fragmentation of the eye), which was both a source of violence, but one that could ultimately be actively employed and used as a weapon of counter attack. The phenomenon of violence in fashion developed as the interwar period progressed: it was initially explored in fashion within text and image-based sources, appearing across a wide range of genres, and ultimately built up to such an extent that they appeared on the body through fashion design itself.

Psychoanalysis

It is no coincidence that psychoanalysis grew as a discipline in the years following the First World War, directly in tandem with the appearance of violence in fashion. Throughout this book, psychoanalysis has been drawn upon as both a historical source and methodological tool, helping to contextualize the deeper reasons behind violence's manifestations in fashion.

Freud's theory of wish fulfilment underpinned the need for healing women's war wounds, and medical attention, that was employed within beauty imagery. Furthermore, hysteria's link with women, notably by Lacan even amongst the myriad cases of male shellshock, further cement the notion of women having psychological war wounds, and advertising's deliberate tactics in taking advantage of them. Melanie Klein's theory of reparation also provides a crucial theoretical foundation of the many endeavours made towards reparation within society, including the ability of beauty advertisements to depict female trauma and offer apparent reparation of it.

Psychoanalysis also contributes towards the complexities of sight and vision during this period. Sigmund Freud's *Civilisation and Its Discontents* demonstrated modernity's dependence upon sight, and Jacques Lacan's theories regarding the gaze emphasized the precise nature of this modern emphasis of sight for women. This demonstrated the anxiety that came from being the object of many observers, but also revealed that they could in turn reflect back this visual attention and anxiety as a two-fold dialogue.

Psychoanalysis also informed the division between head and mind that was occurring within fragmented fashion illustration. Not only was psychoanalysis itself directly informed by physical fragmentation, such as Schilder's concept of body image based on amputee soldiers, but fragmentation was at the core of many psychoanalytic theories that were developed at the time, such as Freud's very notion of the psyche, as outlined in 'The Ego and the Id', 1923. In addition, according to Jacques Lacan, the fragmented body is a fundamental element of human experience. His concept of the mirror stage, from which this notion of the fragmented body arose, revealed the ways in which, towards the end of the period, Schiaparelli and Surrealists engaged with both this and the notion of Sadism and Masochism, which each 'protected' women from fragmentation.

Another form of violence was also intrinsic within the human psyche according to Freud, who argued that aggression always forms part of (particularly male) sexuality, which can be seen to frame the array of sexual violence women were subjected to. In contrast, Joan Riviere's concept of 'Womanliness as a Masquerade' worked in tandem with Duchamp to offer a foil to sexual violence for women, by demonstrating that the erotic gaze was based on spectacularized, superficial appearance rather than reality. This built upon the concurrent theorization of sight and constructed the complex map of seeing and being seen.

Deathliness in fashion can be understood through Freud's contemporary solidification of his model of the death drive. This offers one crucial factor behind the appearance of violence in fashion at large. Even though fashion has been traditionally interpreted as an area of fantasy and escape, which accords with Freud's pleasure principle, during the interwar period, Freud came to the conclusion that the death drive is stronger than this within human psychology, that an impulse to violence is stronger than that of pleasure. Psychoanalysis also offered a deeper insight of this phenomenon of shadows in fashion photography, and Carl Jung's concept of the 'shadow self', and Jean Piaget's studies on responses to shadows illustrate its significance, that they signify the 'true' self being unleashed despite contemporary demands for repression and control. Julia Kristeva's definitions of abjections are also essential in underpinning the empowerment that Schiaparelli was able to assert through deathliness, by making those who saw her clothing undergo a violently visceral reaction through confrontation with deathliness, as Kristeva surmised.

Intermediality

Throughout this book, the various manifestations of violence in other genres have been examined in relation to its expressions in fashion. For example, the return to classicism from abstraction in art can be linked to the desire for wholeness within society, which were evidenced in both Klein's psychoanalytical theory of reparation and national governmental agendas, which were then drawn upon by violence in beauty advertising. Increasing colour in photography and film contributed to the increased presence of colour in modern life, which was an underlying reason for perceptions of violence within colour, and fuelled fashion's use of this. Literature has been another important consideration: it helped to exemplify the way in which modern city life was experienced fragmentarily, and it could also offer both pleasure and threat for women, providing sexual violence or punishment, yet also the possibility of private fantasy, a safe way to indulge in sex and its newly visible popularity, whilst avoiding moral condemnation.

Art and Surrealism

This book has demonstrated the ways in which violence in fashion relates to art, in particular the Surrealist group of artists and writers, and how can this help to re-interpret their own aims and representations of women. Certain Surrealists depicted violence towards vision, which expressed the anxiety that could come from modernity's violent visual experience. Sonia Delauna's bold use of colour directly reflected the age of modernity it was produced in, and placed the violence of colour upon women's bodies through her fashion design, as well as contributing to colour's overt presence within her art. Strong links are also found between Schiaparelli's Tear Dress and the contemporaneous paintings of Salvador Dali and Leonor Fini, through which the explorations of vulnerability, violation and attack within each were strengthened. A newfound focus upon the eye in Surrealist artwork also paralleled a similar attention drawn to the eye by 1920s makeup trends.

As the interwar years progressed, the Surrealists' engagement with Schiaparelli, which even included direct collaborations, continued to be essential, as together they offered a new subverted form of femininity. Marcel Duchamp's deconstruction of femininity exposed its superficial aspects, which similarly offered ways in which women could be shielded from the mainstream's erotic exploitation of them. Meanwhile, the Surrealist writer Bataille's theory of eroticism worked in tandem with Freud's death drive, as he argued that joy should be found in the face of death, that life could not be lived without facing this. This offered another factor, then, behind the appearance of violence in fashion.

Violence in fashion

Women were faced with a range of types of violence throughout the interwar period, both through experience and representation. This was both reflected, and contributed to, by fashion. This manifestation of violence in fashion played a critical role in expressing, navigating and processing the many demands of the interwar period. Not only were women's roles changing, but sustained turbulence within wider society created widespread unease and even affected perceptions of femininity itself. The female body became the site upon which this trauma was expressed and addressed, through violence in fashion. Whilst fashion could be a source of violence in this way, it also offered women means to counter it and 'attack' back, appropriating their own forms of violence through the range of violent trends that emerged in fashionable dress. This gained momentum over the course of the interwar period, moving from the printed page to the body itself.

The strong and complex relationship between fashion and violence is irrefutable, and they each play an important role in helping us to understand the other, as well as shedding light into the crevices of what drives society. This book has established the crucial role that violence in fashion played during the interwar period, and this occurrence has not melted away. Far from it: fashion's intricate relationship with its many contexts continually pushes forward in tandem with unfolding events, incidents and episodes. Building upon this groundwork, there is much potential to pursue the nuances of violence in fashion in relation to other periods, and with focus on voices from other countries, classes and genders. For as *Vogue* magazine put it, in a statement that remains as true today as when it was casually uttered in a 1928 review, 'violence is and will continue to be the vogue'.[3]

Notes

Introduction

1 See Chapter 4.

2 See Chapter 1.

3 See Chapter 3.

4 Joanne B. Eicher and Mary Ellen Roach-Higgins, 'Definition and Classification of Dress', in Ruth Barnes and Joanne B. Eicher (eds.), *Dress and Gender: Making and Meaning in Cultural Contexts* (Oxford: Berg, 1993), p. 15.

5 *Vogue* in London, Paris and New York; *Harper's Bazaar* in London and New York.

6 *Life*, 6th September 1937, pp. 32–9.

7 Ibid.

8 As *Life* put it: 'Their influence is inestimable. Key people in every branch of the $300,000,000 women's apparel industry read them religiously.' Ibid.

9 Howard Cox and Simon Mowatt, 'Vogue in Britain: Authenticity and the Creation of Competitive Advantage in the UK Magazine Industry', *Business History*, vol. 54, 2012, pp. 140–53.

10 Mary E. Davis, *Classic Chic: Music, Fashion, and Modernism* (Berkeley, Los Angeles and London: University of California Press, 2006), p. 48.

11 For example, the publication was distributed by Condé Nast in the United States under the title *Gazette du Bon Genre* and included American advertisements.

12 André Breton, 'Manifesto of Surrealism', [1924] in Patrick Waldberg (ed.), *Surrealism* (New York: Oxford University Press, 1965), p. 66.

13 In Breton's words: 'Credit for this must go to Freud. On the evidence of his discoveries a current of opinion is at last developing which will enable the explorer of the human mind to extend his investigations, since he will be empowered to deal with more than merely summary realities. Perhaps the imagination is on the verge of recovering its rights.' Ibid.

14 Benjamin Crémieux, *Inquiétude et reconstruction: Essai sur la littérature d'après*-guerre (Paris: Editions R.-A. Corrêa, 1931), p. 18. 'L'éclairage de 1914 faisait apparaître un monde fixe, stable, immobile, ou se déplaçant Presque imperceptiblement selon une lente évolution. L'éclairage de 1918 enseignait soudain à tous l'instabilité de ce monde, l'instabilité de la civilisation occidentale, comme de toutes les autres, l'instabilité des régimes collectifs, le pouvoir de la violence, le mépris de la vie humaine, les mutilations apportées aux fondements mêmes de la vie spirituelle.'

15 Ibid.

16 Henry Seidel Canby, *Education by Violence: Essays on the War and the Future* (New York: The Macmillan Company, 1919), p. 2.

17 *Vogue*, New York, 1st October 1919, p. 186.

18 Ibid., p. 232.

19 Trudi Tate, *Modernism, History and the First World War* (Manchester and New York: Manchester University Press, 1998), p. 85.

20 Margaret R. Higgonet, *Nurses at the Front: Writing the Wounds of the Great War* (Boston, MA: Northeastern University Press, 2001), p. viii.

21 Pearl James, 'Images of Femininity in American World War I Posters', in Pearl James (ed.), *Picture This: World War I Posters and Visual Culture* (Nebraska: University of Nebraska Press, 2009), p. 283.

22 The giant ape, prevalent in folklore and explorers' tales since at least the eighteenth century, saw a resurgence of interest during the interwar period. For example, in 1924 Albert Otsman claimed to have been captured by a Sasquatch (Bigfoot) for six days, and J.W. Burns published Bigfoot legends in magazines and newspapers during the 1920s. It was later further popularized by Merian C. Cooper and Ernest B. Schoedsack's 1933 film, *King Kong*. See Joshua Blu Bluhs, *Bigfoot: The Life and Times of a Legend* (London: University of Chicago Press, 2009).

23 Richard Overy, *The Morbid Age: Britain and the Crisis of Civilisation, 1919–1939* (London: Penguin, 2010), p. 2.

24 Martin Pugh, *We Danced All Night: A Social History of Britain between the Wars* (London and New York: Vintage, 2009), p. 4. Other writers who have emphasized the ongoing impact of the war include Samuel Hynes in his *A War Imagined: The First World War and English Culture*, in which he wrote that the war was a 'great disruption' and 'transforming force' within society and culture. Paul Fussell in his *The Great War and Modern Memory* (1975) also presented a thorough and convincing argument for the war's prolonged impact, and Modris Eksteins, in his *Rites of Spring: The Great War and the Birth of the Modern Age* (1989), similarly classed it as a transformative event, with long-lasting effects.

25 Including Susan R. Grayzel, *Women and the First World War* (Abingdon: Routledge, 2002); Katie Adie, *Fighting on the Home Front: The Legacy of Women in World War One* (London: Hodder & Stoughton: 2013); and Maurine Weiner Greenwald, *Women, War, and Work: The Impact of World War I on Women Workers in the United States*, (Westport, CT: Greenwood Press, 1980).

26 It was dealt with briefly by Grayzel and Adie, in a final chapter each (ibid.). The former looks at tangible consequences, such as political rights, employment, social welfare policy, whilst the latter focuses on commemoration and memory.

27 'Women and War Strain', *Our Empire* (19th August 1919), p. 2.

28 Some publications, such as Mary Louise Roberts, *Civilization without Sexes: Reconstructing Gender in Postwar France, 1917–1927* (Chicago: University of

Chicago Press, 1994), and Susan Kingsley Kent, *Making Peace: The Reconstruction of Gender in Interwar Britain* (Princeton: Princeton University Press, 1993), have illustrated that society and gender were in fact deeply inflected by the war, which accords with the stance taken by this book.

29 Ibid., p. 77.

30 Ibid., p. 79.

31 Ibid., p. 77.

32 Such as Maggie Andrews and Mary Talbot (eds.), *All the World and Her Husband: Women in Twentieth-century Consumer Culture* (London: Bloomsbury, 2000).

33 Similarly, imagery of the First World War itself is currently surprisingly limited. An exception is Pearl James (ed.), *Picture This: World War I Posters and Visual Culture* (Nebraska: University of Nebraska Press, 2009), which focuses on visual culture in a number of countries during the war, including Britain, France and America, including a chapter which contextualizes the use of the female form in posters. This book extends James's approach by focusing on women and incorporating fashion.

34 Hynes, *A War Imagined*, p. xi.

35 See, for example, Atsuko Ichijo, *Nationalism and Multiple Modernities* (Basingstoke and New York: Palgrave Macmillan, 2013).

36 Martin Dauton and Bernhard Rieger, 'Introduction', in Daunton and Rieger (eds.), *Meanings of Modernity: Britain from the Late-Victorian Era to World War I* (Oxford: Berg, 2001), pp. 1–24, p. 1.

37 Pugh, *We Danced All Night*, p. 2.

38 The trope of the 'new woman' began to appear within popular culture from the late-nineteenth century, and signified a more liberal, progressive form of femininity. The term was still being used to describe women after the war, and became represented by the image of the 'flapper', which predominantly referred to young, fashionable and single women. Deidre Berdoe has summarized, for example, that 'the image of the flapper is partly an elaboration of the New Woman theme, but she is the New Woman stripped of her serious side and hell-bent on having a good time'. [*Back Home to Duty: Women Between the Wars, 1918–1939* (London: Pandora, 1989), p. 10.] This trope appeared throughout discussions in Britain, France and America alike. For contemporary examples, see Roberts, *Civilization without Sexes*, pp. 19, 52, 100, 227; and Estelle B. Freedman, 'The New Woman: Changing Views of Women in the 1920s', *The Journal of American History*, vol. 61, no. 2 (September 1974), pp. 372–93.

39 *Vogue*, [U.S.] 1st October 1920, p. 85, among many other examples, as discussed in Chapter 1, Section 1.

40 Andreas Huyssen, *After the Great Divide: Modernism, Mass Culture and Postmodernism* (Indiana: Indiana University Press, 1987). Here, Huyssen commented that the dawning of mass modernism in the late-nineteenth

century induced 'fears, and anxieties (both personal and political), which were brought about by modernization' (p. 52). Furthermore, this publication included his essay on 'Mass Culture as Woman: Modernism's Other.'

41 Elizabeth Wilson, *Adorned in Dreams: Fashion and Modernity* (London: I.B. Tauris, 1985), p. 10.

42 Wilson, *Sphinx in the City: Urban Life, the Control of Disorder, and Women* (Oakland, CA: The University of California Press, 1992), p. 7.

43 Dilys Blum, *Shocking! The Art and Fashion of Elsa Schiaparelli* (New Haven: Yale University Press, 2003), p. 121.

44 Here she described, for example, that while Paris gave her great 'inspiration', it was not always 'hospitable and friendly … [or] made it possible for [her] to obtain a unique place in the world' [p. 112] and recounted, in the third person: 'Schiap was an ugly child as standards go', a feeling which prevailed throughout her life [p. 15]. Elsa Schiaparelli, *Shocking Life: The Autobiography of Elsa Schiaparelli* (London: V&A Museum, 2007).

45 For example, by Mary Ann Caws, Rudolf Kuenzli and Gwen Raaberg (eds.), *Surrealism and Women* (Cambridge, MA: MIT Press, 1993) and Whitney Chadwick, *Women Artists and the Surrealist Movement* (London: Thames & Hudson, 1985).

46 Katharine Conley, *Automatic Woman: The Representation of Woman in Surrealism* (Nebraska: University of Nebraska Press, 1996), p. 4.

47 Rebecca Arnold, *Fashion, Desire and Anxiety: Image and Morality in the Twentieth Century* (London: I.B. Tauris, 2001), p. 34.

48 Caroline Evans, 'Masks, Mirrors and Mannequins: Elsa Schiaparelli and the Decentered Subject', *Fashion Theory*, vol. 3, no. 1, pp. 3–31.

49 Wilson, *Adorned in Dreams*, p. 11.

50 *Vogue*, New York, 1st September 1927, p. 77.

Chapter 1

1 Florence Warden, *The Beauty Doctor* (London: Robert Hayes Ltd., 1920), p. 19.

2 Marinello advertisement, *Vogue*, [U.S.] 15th September 1922.

3 Ibid.

4 Ibid.

5 Sigmund Freud, *The Interpretation of Dreams* (New York: Macmillan, 1913), p. 107.

6 Stephen Gundle has described the way in which, during the early twentieth century, printed articles and photographs, particularly in *Vogue*, 'became a key component of the dreamscape of the period'. [*Glamour: A History* (Oxford and New York: Oxford University Press, 2008), p. 36.] Rebecca Arnold has situated magazines as 'part of the culture that spawns them', which allows them to act as a temporary refuge. For example, she related Russian *Vogue* during the late 1990s, and the 'couture luxury and excess' it published as 'a dreamscape from which to forget economic crisis'. [*Fashion: A Very Short Introduction* (Oxford and New York: Oxford University Press), pp. 61–2.]

7   Gary Cross, *An All-Consuming Century: Why Commercialism Won in Modern America* (New York: Columbia University Press, 2000), p. 38.

8   Walter S. Mass, 'Subconscient et Publicité', Arts et Métiers Graphiques, no. 1 (15th September 1927), pp. 56–7. Translation by Amy Lyford, *Surrealist Masculinities: Gender Anxiety and the Aesthetics of post-World War I Reconstruction in France* (California: University of California Press, 2007), p. 40.

9   Freud, 'Introduction', in Drs. S. Ferenczi, Karl Abraham, Ernst Simmel and Ernest Jones (eds.), *Psychoanalysis & War Neuroses* (London, Vienna and New York: The International Psycho-Analytical Press), p. 1.

10 Élisabeth Roudinesco, *Jacques Lacan: An Outline of a Life and a History of a System of Thought* (Cambridge, Oxford and Boston: Polity Press, 1999), p. 10.

11 Ibid., p. 15.

12 Ibid.

13 Ernest Jones, letter to Sigmund Freud, 21st December 1918. Published in R. Andrew Paskauskas (ed.), *The Complete Correspondence of Sigmund Freud and Ernest Jones* (Cambridge, MA: Harvard University Press, 1993), p. 327.

14 Jacques Lacan, 'Abasia in a War-traumatized Female Patient', described to the Société neurologique on 2nd November 1928. Printed within his doctoral book, *De la psychose paranoïaque dans ses rapports avec la personnalité* (Paris: Le François, 1975 [1932]).

15 For example, R. Satow has written "hysteria' has been a label used for a pot pourri of female ailments and non-ailments alike since antiquity … the Greeks and Romans called almost all female complaints hysteria and believed the cause of all these female maladies to be a wandering uterus', ['Where Has All the Hysteria Gone?', *Psychoanalytic Review,* vol. 66 (1979/80), pp. 463–77, pp. 463–4], and similarly, several writers, including Helen King, have reinforced this association through the term hysteria's etymology, pointing out that 'the Greek adjective *hysterikos* means "from the womb."' ['Once Upon a Text' in Sander L Gilman, *Hysteria beyond Freud* (Berkeley, Los Angeles and London: University of California Press, 1993), pp. 13–91]. Jean-Martin Charcot [*Iconographie Photographique de la Salpêtrière* (1879–80)] and later Freud re-theorized it as an illness of the mind rather than the womb, associating it with the psychic rather than biological state of femininity.

16 Viabella advertisement, British *Vogue*, early December 1924.

17 Marinello advertisement, *Vogue*, [U.S.] 15th December 1925.

18 l'Université de Beauté 'CÉDIB' advertisement, *Vogue* Paris, July 1927.

19 Romy Golan, *Modernity and Nostalgia: Art and Politics in France between the Wars* (Yale University Press: New Haven and London, 1995), p. ix.

20 Ibid.

21 Whilst this plan was eventually sacrificed in light of the economy's staggering inflation and debts, it nevertheless shows a drive towards reparation.

22 Daniel T. Rodgers, *Atlantic Crossings: Social Politics in a Progressive Age* (Cambridge, MA: Harvard University Press, 1998), p. 4.

23 Beth Linker, *War's Waste: Rehabilitation in World War I* (Chicago: University of Chicago Press, 2011), p. 4.

24 Ibid., p. 91.

25 Hannah Segal, *Introduction to the Work of Melanie Klein* (London: The Hogarth Press, 2008), pp. 91–2.

26 Ibid., p. 92.

27 Ibid.

28 Ibid.

29 Jay Winter, *Sites of Memory, Sites of Mourning* (Cambridge: Cambridge University Press, 1998), p. 223.

30 Ibid.

31 Christopher Reed, *A Roger Fry Reader* (Chicago and London: The University of Chicago Press), p. 307; Sir Roy C. Strong, *The Spirit of Britain: A Narrative History of the Arts* (New York: Fromm International Publishing Corporation, 2000), p. 625.

32 Michael Auping (ed.), *Modern Art Museum of Fort Worth: 110* (London: Third Millennium Information Ltd), p. 233.

33 Viabella advertisement, British *Vogue*, early December, 1924.

34 Marinello advertisement, *Vogue*, [U.S.] 15th September 1922.

35 This correlates with Michel de Certeau's later theorization that 'the Expert is growing more common in … society, to the point of becoming its generalized figure', *The Practice of Everyday Life*, trans. Steven Rendall (Berkeley, Los Angeles, London: University of California Press, 2011), p. 7.

36 Lt.-General T.H.J.C. Goodwin, C.B., C.M.G., etc., Director-General of Army Medical Service, 'Foreword', in Colonel H.M.W. Gray (ed.), *The Early Treatment of War Wounds* (Oxford: Oxford University Press, 1919), p. vii.

37 Marinello advertisement, *Vogue*, [U.S.] (15th September, 1922).

38 Warden, *The Beauty Doctor*, p. 16.

39 Ibid.

40 Ibid., p. 19.

41 Ibid.

42 Ibid., p. 15.

43 Ibid.

44 Ibid., p. 25.

45 Michel Foucault, *The Birth of the Clinic* (London: Routledge, 2003), p. 38.

46 Ibid., p. 39.

47 *Vogue* [U.S.] (1st March, 1928), p. 108.

48 Gilbert Guilleminault, *Less Années folles* (Paris: editions Denöel, 1958), p. 5. Translated by Mary Louise Roberts, *Civilization without Sexes: Reconstructing Gender in Postwar France, 1917–1927* (Chicago, University of Chicago Press, 1994), p. 19.

49 *Vogue* [U.S.] (1st October, 1920), p. 85.

50 Sally Alexander, *Becoming a Woman: And Other Essays in 19th and 20th Century Feminist History* (New York: New York University Press, 1995), p. 218.

51 Jacques Boulenger, 'La Femme moderne: Devant le feu', *Illustration*, 6th December 1924.

52 Adrian Rifkin, *Street Noises: Parisian Pleasure, 1900–40* (Manchester: Manchester University Press, 1993), p. 9.

53 As pointed out, for example, by Alexander, *Becoming a Woman*, p. 219.

54 Viabella advertisement, British *Vogue*, early December 1924

55 Helena Rubinstein advertisement, *Vogue* [U.S.], December 1920

56 Elizabeth Arden advertisement, British *Vogue*, late November 1924. Also reproduced in the Paris edition.

57 See, for one of a vast number of examples of appeals to natural beauty, Yardley's perfume advertising *c*. 1910–19.

58 Madame Theux advertisement, *Vogue* Paris, June 1926.

59 As Rebecca Arnold has commented in *The American Look: Fashion, Sportswear and the Image of Women in 1930s and 1940s America* (London: I.B. Tauris, 2009), p. 46.

60 De Certeau, *The Practice of Everyday Life*, p. 6.

61 Ibid.

62 Ibid.

63 Viabella advertisement, British *Vogue*, early December 1924.

64 The 'New Woman' is a phrase first used at the end of the nineteenth century in relation to women's growing independence and consumerism, and evolved with each generation, into the interwar period.

65 Roberts, *Civilization without Sexes*, p. 20.

66 Norman Douglas, *South Wind* (South Dakota: NuVision Publications, 1925), p. 20.

67 Zane Grey, *The Call of the Canyon* (Maryland: Phoenix Rider, Arc Manor, 2008 [1923]), p. 107.

68 Amy Lyford, 'André Kertész in Paris', in Raymond Spiteri and Donald LaCosse (eds.), *Surrealism, Politics and Culture* (Aldershot and Burlingon, VT: Ashgate Publishing, 2003), pp. 74–5.

69 Boulenger, trans. Roberts, *Civilization without Sexes*, p. 19.

70 Roberts, *Civilization without Sexes*, p. 9.

71 This advertisement appeared in several editions of *Vogue* Paris, 1927–8. Versions also appeared in the British and U.S. editions. More generally, the bandaged face itself was a widespread trope in Arden's advertising around this time.

72 This advertisement for Contouré Laboratories, Inc. appeared, for example, in *Vogue* [U.S.], 8th December 1928.

73 Lyford, 'André Kertész in Paris', p. 84.

74 Philip Morgan, *Fascism in Europe, 1919–1945* (Oxford and New York: Routledge, 2007), p. 29.

75 For anti-fascism in Britain, France and America during the interwar period, see, for example: Nigel Cospey and Andrzej Olechnowicz (eds.), *Varieties of Anti-Fascism: Britain in the Inter-War Period* (Basingstoke: Palgrave Macmillan, 2010); Nigel Copsey, 'Communists and the Inter-War Anti-Fascist Struggle in the United States and Britain', *Labour History Review*, vol. 76, no. 3 (December 2011), p. 184; and Emmanuelle Carle, 'Women, Anti-Fascism and Peace in Interwar France: Gabrielle Duchêne's Itinerary', *French History*, vol. 18, no. 3 (2004), pp. 291–314.

76 Duncan Aikman, 'American Fascism', *Harpers Magazine*, New York, April 1925, pp. 513–9.

77 Ibid.

78 Margherita Sarfatti, *Dux*, p. 250, cited by David Forgacs, 'Fascism, Violence and Modernity', in Jana Howlett and Rod Mengham (eds.), *The Violent Muse: Violence and the Artistic Imagination in Europe, 1910–1939* (Manchester and New York: Manchester University Press), p. 6.

79 Mussolini, cited ibid.

80 For example, Benito Mussolini came to power in 1922 in Italy, and seized total power as dictator in 1926. Adolf Hitler had joined the German Workers' Party in 1919, from whence it developed over the 1920s party into the Nazi party it is known as. Hitler took governmental control when he was appointed chancellor in 1933.

81 *La Gazette Du Bon Ton*, no. 5 (1923), p. 185.

82 *Vogue* [U.S.] (1st March 1925), p. 65.

83 Aileen Ribeiro, *Dress and Morality* (London, Oxford and New York: Berg, 2003), p. 14.

84 *Ladies' Home Journal* (May 1922), p. 159; *Vogue* [U.S.] (1st April 1922), p. 131, and reprinted monthly in this publication until 1st October 1922.

85 Ibid.

86 Kathy Peiss, *Hope in a Jar: The Making of America's Beauty Culture* (Pennsylvania: University of Pennsylvania Press, 2011), p. 19.

87 Frances Maule, 'The Woman Appeal', *J. Walter Thompson News Bulletin*, no. 105 (January 1924), pp. 1–2.

88 Cited in Peiss, *Hope in a Jar*, p. 40.

89 Jean Baudrillard, *The System of Objects* (London and New York: Verso, 2005), p. 30.

90 Ibid.

91 *Vogue* [U.S.] (1st March 1925), p. 65.

92 Advertisement, *Dorin of Paris*, American *Vogue* (15th August 1922), back cover.

93 Martin Jay, *Downcast Eyes: The Denigration of Vision in Twentieth-Century French Thought*, (Berkeley, CA: University of California Press, 1993) p. 153.

94 Jay, *Downcast Eyes*, p. 151.

95 Ibid., p. 154.

96 Ibid.

97 *Vogue* [U.S.] (15th October 1934), p. 41.

98 Ibid. (1st February 1927), p. 58; (20th July 1929), p. 66.

99 Ibid. (15th March 1927), p. 174,

100 Sir John Herbert Parsons, *Introduction to the Study of Colour Vision* (Cambridge: Cambridge University Press, 1924), p. 138.

101 Ibid.

102 *Vogue* [U.S.] (1st March 1925), p. 65.

103 *Vogue* [U.S.] (1st April 1925), p. 60.

104 *Vogue* [U.S.] (1st March 1925), p. 65.

105 *Vogue* [U.S.] (10th November 1928), p. 102.

106 Adrian Stokes, *Colour and Form* (London: Thompson, 1937), p. 24.

107 Sigmund Freud, *Civilization and Its Discontents*, ed. and trans. James Strachey (New York: W. W. Norton & Company, 2010), Ibid. p. 88.

108 Ibid.

109 Ibid.

110 Jay, *Downcast Eyes*, p. 213.

111 Georges Bataille, *Histoire de l'oeil* (Paris: Fernand Lefèvre, 1928).

112 Jay, *Downcast Eyes*, p. 212.

113 *Vogue* [U.S.] (1st March 1925), p. 65.

114 Ibid.

115 Maurice Merleau-Ponty, *Phenemology of Perception* (Oxford: Taylor & Francis, Psychology Press, 2002), p. 79.

116 *Vogue* [U.S.] (15th May 1931), p. 104.

117 Ibid.

118 *Vogue* [U.S.] (15th April 1931), p. 112.

119 Nancy Koehn, 'Estée Lauder: Self-Definition and the Modern Cosmetics Market', in *Beauty and Business: Commerce, Gender, and Culture in Modern America* (New York: Routledge: 2001), p. 247.

120 Sarah Hill, Christopher Rodeheffer, Vladas Griskevicius, Kristina Durante, Andrew White, 'Boosting Beauty in an Economic Decline: Mating, Spending, and the Lipstick Effect', *Journal of Personality and Social Psychology*, vol. 103, no. 2 (2012), pp. 275–91.

121 Charles Tepperman, 'Color Unlimited: Amateur Color Cinema in the 1930s', in Simon Brown, Sarah Street, Liz Watkins (eds.), *Color and the Moving Image: History, Theory, Aesthetics, Archive* (New York and London: Routledge, 2013), pp. 138–49, p. 138.

122 Bryony Dixon, 'Surveying the Screen: Fashion and Film 1896 to 1929', lecture, The Courtauld Institute, The Courtauld Spring 2014 Friends Lecture Series, 28th January 2014. See also Michelle Tolini Finamore, *Hollywood before Glamour: Fashion in American Silent Film* (London: Palgrave Macmillan, 2013), p. 22.

123 Cited in Arthur Allen Cohen, *Sonia Delaunay* (New York: H. N. Abrams, 1975), p. 15.

124 Matilda McQuaid, Susan Brown (eds.), *Color Moves: Art & Fashion by Sonia Delaunay* (New York: Cooper Hewitt, Smithsonian Design Museum, 2011), p. 16.

125 Jacques Lacan, *The Four Fundamental Concepts of Psychoanalysis*, trans. Alan Sheridan (Harmondsworth: Penguin, 1986), p. 72.

Notes

126 Ibid., p. 74.

127 *Vogue* [U.S.] (15th January 1935), p. 40.

128 Ibid.

129 Ibid.

130 Advertisement, *Savage*, 'New Kind of Dry Rouge', 1935.

131 Advertisement, *Savage*, 'Maddening Hues for Lips and Cheeks', 1935.

132 Martin Jay, 'The Disenchantment of the Eye', in Lucien Taylor (ed.), *Visualizing Theory: Selected Essays from V.A.R* (New York and Oxford: Routledge, 2009), pp. 173–204, p. 186.

133 *Vogue* [U.S.] (1st March 1928), pp. 81, 108.

134 *Vogue* [U.S.] (1st November 1936), p. 71.

135 *The Manchester Guardian* (26th October 1914). In 1959 the publication acquired its present name, *The Guardian*.

136 *International Press Correspondence*, vol. 13, 1933, p. 631.

137 Ibid.

138 *Life* (10th April 1939), vol. 6, no. 15, p. 20.

139 Benjamin Munn Ziegler, *The International Law of John Marshall* (New Jersey: The Lawbook Exchange, Ltd., 2006), p. 11.

140 Anonymous, 'The Sword and the War', *The Saturday Review of Politics, Literature, Science and Art* (9th April 1921), p. 301.

141 As discussed in the first section of this chapter.

142 Evans, 'Masks, Mirrors and Mannequins', pp. 3–31, p. 11.

143 Palmer White, *Elsa Schiaparelli: Empress of Paris Fashion* (New York: Rizzoli, 1986), p. 26.

144 For more details on political tension during the 1930s and the factors leading to the Second World War, see Richard Overy, *The Origins of the Second World War* (London and New York: Routledge, 2009).

145 Richard Martin, *Fashion and Surrealism* (New York: Rizzoli, 1987), p. 136.

146 Ibid.

Chapter 2

1 *Gazette du Bon Ton,* no. 10 (1921), p. 111.

2 Jim Wolveridge, *Ain't It Grand (Or This Was Stepney)* (London: The Journeyman Press, 1981), p. 19.

3   Caroline E. Playne, *Britain Holds on 1917, 1918* (London: Allen and Unwin, 1933), pp. 76–7.

4   Joanna Bourke, *Dismembering the Male: Men's Bodies, Britain, and the Great War* (Chicago: University of Chicago Press, 1996), p. 56. Citing Edward Marshall, 'Introduction' in H.H. Thomas, *Help for Wounded Heroes* (London: Essential Limb Co., 1920), p. i.

5   Ibid., p. 74.

6   *The Times* (5th April 1916), p. 5.

7   Although set in the post-Civil War years, it was written in 1925, and drew on many shared concerns between the two periods, past and contemporary. Henry Adams, *Democracy: An American Novel* (Los Angeles, CA: Library of Alexandria, 1925), p. 193.

8   Joanna Bourke has stated: 'The First World War led to amputations on a scale never seen before, or since the nineteenth century', *Dismembering the Male: Men's Bodies, Britain, and the Great War* (Chicago: University of Chicago Press, 1996) p. 33.

9   *Vogue* [U.S.] (1st July 1924), pp. 104, 106.

10 Ibid.

11 Ibid., p. 104.

12 Paul Schilder, *The Image and Appearance of the Human Body* (London: Routledge, 1999), p. 13.

13 Ibid., p. 11.

14 Ibid.

15 Schilder was not the first to relate physicality with mental activity. Wilhelm Reich, in 1924, for example, strongly connected emotions with the muscles, through a process that he labelled 'orgastic potency'. Nevertheless, it was Schilder's study of First World War amputees that paved the way for a more thorough, comprehensive and complete understanding of the fundamentality of the dependency between body and mind, which drew together, developed and expanded existing theories. Reich, *The Function of the Orgasm: Sex-Economic Problems of Biological Energy: The Discovery of the Orgone*, Volume I, trans. Vincent R. Carfagno (London: Souvenir Press, 1999 [1924]).

16 Jacques Lacan, conference paper, 'Le stade du miroir', Merienbad, August 1936. It was published and translated into English in 1937: 'The Looking-Glass Phase', *The International Journal of Psychoanalysis*, vol. 18, part 1 (January 1937).

17 Henri Wallon, 'Comment se développe chez l'enfant la notion de corps proper', *Journal de Psychologie* (November-December 1931), pp. 705–48.

18 Lacan, 'The Mirror Stage as Formative of the Function of the I as Revealed in Psychoanalytic Experience', in *Écrits: A Selection*, trans. Alan Sheridan (London: Routledge, 1977), p. 506.

19 Ibid., p. 503.

20 Ibid., p. 506.

21 Lacan, 'Aggressivity in Psychoanalysis', in *Écrits: A Selection*, trans. Alan Sheridan (London: Routledge, 1977), p. 11.

22 Ibid.

23 Lacan, 'Mirror Stage', p. 508.

24 Lacan, 'Aggressivity … ', p. 11.

25 Ibid.

26 Ibid.

27 'The Well-Gowned Woman as a Poster', *Vogue* [U.S.] (15th March 1913), p. 51.

28 Golan, *Modernity and Nostalgia*, p. 18.

29 According to the Gospel of Matthew 14:6–11:' … on Herod's birthday, the daughter of Herodias [Salome] danced before them: and pleased Herod. Whereupon he promised with an oath, to give her whatsoever she would ask of him. But she being instructed before by her mother, said: Give me here in a dish the head of John the Baptist. And the king was struck sad: yet because of his oath, and for them that sat with him at table, he commanded it to be given. And he sent, and beheaded John in the prison. And his head was brought in a dish: and it was given to the damsel, and she brought it to her mother'.

  As a result, Salome became an icon for female seductiveness and superficiality, and the dangers of this. This motif has a widespread presence within the History of Art and literature. It became particularly popular at the end of the nineteenth century, and Salome appeared, for example, as a femme fatale in Oscar Wilde's Salome, 1891 (French language) and 1984 (English language), and in a depiction by Gustave Moreau, L'Apparition, *c.*1876. Joris-Karl Huysmans described the latter depiction as 'reveal[ing Salome] in a sense as the symbolic incarnation of world-old Vice, the goddess of immortal Hysteria, the Curse of Beauty … indifferent, irresponsible, insensible, poisoning.' *Against the Grain: À rebours* (Berlin: Hofenberg, 2015), p. 44.

30 William Fox, *Salome,* 1918. Charles Bryant, *Salome*, 1923.

31 Sigmund Freud, 'New Introductory Lectures on Psychoanalysis,' 1933, in *The Standard Edition of the Complete Psychological Works of Sigmund Freud,* vol. 22, trans. James Strachey (London: Random House, 2001), p. 72.

32 Ibid.

33 Ibid., p. 78.

34 It was initially published in the American journal, *The Little Review,* from March 1918 to December 1920.

35 James Joyce, *The Little Review: Ullyses* (New Haven and London: Yale University Press, 2015), p. 134.

36 T. S. Eliot, *The Wasteland* (New York: Liveright, 1922), p. 60.

37 Georg Simmel, 'The Metropolis and Mental Life' (1903), in Gary Bridge and Sophie Watson (eds.), *The Blackwell City Reader* (Oxford and Malden, MA: Wiley-Blackwell, 2002), pp. 11–19, p. 11.

38 Ibid., pp. 11–12.

39 Barbara Low, *Psycho-Analysis: A Brief Account of the Freudian Theory* (New York: Harcourt, Brace and Company, 1920), p. 36.

40 Virginia Woolf, *Mrs Dalloway* (Ontario and London: Broadview Press, 2012), p. 118.

41 'World Urbanisation Trends as Measured in Agglomerations, 1920–1960' and 'Alternative Estimates and Trends Derived from 'Metropolitan Area … 1920–1960', *UN Dept. of Economic and Social Affairs, Population Studies*, no. 44 (New York: United Nations, 1969), pp. 19–38, 44–9.

42 For figures, see: Kathleen Morgan Drowne and Patrick Huber, *The 1920's* (Westport, CT: Greenwood Publishing Group, 2004), p. 189 [America]; Laura King, *Family Men: Fatherhood and Masculinity in Britain, 1914–1960* (Oxford: Oxford University Press, 2015), p. 9 [Britain]; W. Scott Haine, *Culture and Customs of France* (Westport, CT: Greenwood, 2006), p. 157 [France].

43 Theodore Peterson, *Magazines in the Twentieth Century* (Illinois: University of Illinois Press, 1964), p. 268.

44 John Dos Passos, *Manhattan Transfer* (Boston: Houghton Mifflin, 1925), p. 15.

45 Karen Lucic, *Charles Sheeler and the Cult of the Machine* (Cambridge, MA: Harvard University Press, 1991), p. 34.

46 Le Corbusier, *The Decorative Art of Today*, trans. James Dunnett (Cambridge, MA: MIT Press, 1987 [1925]), p. 112.

47 Susan Stanford Freidman, *Psyche Reborn: The Emergence of H. D. Bloomington* (Indiana: Indiana University Press, 1981), p. 97.

48 Ibid.

49 Ibid.

50 Andreas Huyssen, *After the Great Divide: Modernism, Mass Culture, Postmodernism* (Bloomington: Indiana University Press, 1986), p. 62.

51 F. Scott Fitzgerald, *The Great Gatsby* (Cambridge: Cambridge University Press, 1999), p. 63.

52 Elizabeth Burris-Meyer, *Color and Design in the Decorative Arts* (New Jersey: Prentice Hall, 1935), p. 159.

53 Emily Post and Elizabeth L. Post, *The New Emily Post's Etiquette* (New York: Funk & Wagnalls, 1975), p. 824.

54 Advertisement, *Maybell Laboratories,* various versions published in *Red Book Magazine* (January 1920), p. 154; (April 1920), p. 156.

Notes

55 Advertisement, *Maybelline,* various versions published 1920–3: *Red Book Magazine* (July 1920), p. 167 and (March 1923), p. 138.

56 Ibid.

57 Advertisement, *Winx Waterproof Mascara,* 1925.

58 Ibid.

59 Elza Adamowicz, 'Hats or Jellyfish? André Breton's Collages', in Ramona Fotiade (ed.), *Andre Breton – The Power of Language* (Exeter: Elm Bank Publications, 2000), pp. 83–96, p. 90.

60 See, for example, Werner Spies, *Max Ernst Collages: The Invention of the Surrealist Universe* (New York: Harry N. Abrams, 1991), for a selection and discussion of Ernst's collages.

61 Max Ernst, 'Au-delà de la peinture' (1936), in Ecritures (Paris: Gallimard, 1970), pp. 258–9.

62 Ibid., p. 262.

63 Elza Adamowicz, *Surrealist Collage in Text and Image: Dissecting the Exquisite Corpse* (Cambridge: Cambridge University Press, 2005), p. 7. See also J. H. Matthews, *The Imagery of Surrealism* (Syracuse, New York: Syracuse University Press, 1977).

64 Ibid.

65 Printed in Jennifer Mundy (ed.), *Man Ray: Writing on Art* (Los Angeles, CA: Getty Research Institute, 2015), p. 105.

66 *Harper's Bazaar*, UK (October 1934), pp. 52–3.

67 Caroline Evans and Minna Thornton, *Women & Fashion: A New Look* (London: Quartet Books, 1989), p. 118.

68 See, for example, the contemporaneous work of William Reid Dick, which also employed a smooth, classical style, including *Bust,* 1935 and *Torso,* 1937 (Royal Academy of Arts, London).

69 Adolph Hitler, speech at Nuremberg, 11th September 1935, quoted in Kenneth E. Silver, 'A More Durable Self', in Silver, *Chaos and Classicism: Art in France, Italy, and Germany, 1918—1936*, exh. cat. (New York: Solomon R. Guggenheim Foundation, 2010), p. 46.

70 For a detailed description of the exhibition, see Valentina Follo, *The Power of Images in the Age of Mussolini,* PhD thesis, University of Pennsylvania, 2013, pp. 20–35.

71 Salvador Dali, *The Secret Life of Salvador Dali*, trans. Haakon M. Chevalier (New York and London: Dial Press, 1961).

72 *Vogue* [U.S.] (15th September 1936), p. 70.

73 *Vogue* [U.S.] (15th September 1936), p. 153.

74 White, *Elsa Schiaparelli*, p. 97.

75 See, for example: Tirza True Latimer, 'Equivocal Gender: Dada/Surrealism and Sexual Politics between the Wars', in David Hopkins (ed.), *A Companion to Dada and Surrealism* (Malden, MA, and Oxford: Wiley, 2016), pp. 352–65, p. 354; Roxana Marcoci and Geoffrey Batchen, *The Original Copy: Photography of Sculpture, 1839 to Today* (New York: Museum of Modern Art, 2010), p. 186; Jean Clair and Pierre Théberge, *The 1930s: The Making of 'the New Man'* (Ottawa: National Gallery of Canada, 2008), p. 73.

76 Constantin Jelenski, *Les Dessins de Hans Bellmer* (Paris: Denoel, 1966), p. 21.

77 See, for example, Therese Lichtenstein, *Behind Closed Doors: The Art of Hans Bellmer* (California: University of California Press, 2001), p. 102; and Sue Taylor, *Hans Bellmer: The Anatomy of Anxiety* (Cambridge, MA: MIT Press, 2002), pp. 11–12.

78 Hal Foster, *Prosthetic Gods* (Cambridge, MA: The MIT Press, 2004), p. 233.

79 Ruth Ronen, *Aesthetics of Anxiety* (New York: State University of New York Press, 2010), p. 51.

80 Jacques Lacan, *The Seminars of Jacques Lacan*, ed. Jacques-Alain Miller, trans. Dennis Porter, book VII (New York and London: Routledge, 1992), p. 243.

81 Rosalind Krauss, 'Uncanny', in Yve-Alain Bois and Rosalind Krauss (eds.), *Formless: A User's Guide* (New York: Zone Books, 1997), pp. 192–7.

82 Wilson, *Adorned in Dreams*, p. 246.

83 See, for example: Sandra Zalman, *Consuming Surrealism in American Culture* (Surrey: Ashgate, 2015); Robin Walz, *Pulp Surrealism: Insolent Popular Culture in Early Twentieth-Century Paris* (California: University of California Press, 2000); and Ghislaine Wood (ed.), *Surreal Things: Surrealism and Design* (London: V&A Publishing, 2007).

84 British *Vogue* (August 1938), p. 26.

85 Ibid.

86 See the above discussion on Bellmer.

87 Mainstream cinema also began to incorporate violent fragmentation. Tod Browning's *Freaks*, 1932, included many tropes in particular which resonated with this theme. For example, the 'freak' characters include a pair of 'living torsos', each with no legs, and one with no arms. At one point, the group of 'freaks' take revenge on the Cleopatra character, by violently dismembering her until she is reduced to a squawking chicken. The act of castration also appears frequently.

Chapter 3

1 William Bolitho, 'The New Skirt Length', *Harper's Bazaar* (February 1930), p. 293.

2 Walter G. Muirheid, 'Fashion Follies Follow War', *Mentor* (1st September 1921), p. 32.

3 F. Scott Fitzgerald, 'Echoes of the Jazz Age', *Scribner's Monthly*, vol. 90 (November 1931), pp. 459–60.

4 'Is the Younger Generation in Peril?' *Literary Digest,* vol. 69 (14th May 1921), p. 1.

5 Hugh A. Studdert Kennedy, 'Short Skirts', *The Forum* (June 1926), pp. 829–35, p. 835.

6 Ibid.

7 Cited in 'The Catholic Crusade for Modesty', *Literary Digest,* vol. 82, no. 9 (1924), pp. 25–6.

8 Angela J. Latham, *Posing a Threat: Flappers, Chorus Girls, and Other Brazen Performers of the American 1920s* (Connecticut: Wesleyan University Press, 2000) p. 48.

9 Bruce Bliven, *Literary Digest* 92 (29th January 1927), pp. 27–8.

10 Ibid., pp. 27–8.

11 Latham, *Posing a Threat*, p. 54.

12 Susan R. Bordo, 'The Body and the Reproduction of Femininity: A Feminist Appropriation of Foucault', in Alison M. Jaggar and Susan R. Bordo (eds.), *Gender/Body/Knowledge: Feminist Reconstructions of Being and Knowing* (New Jersey: Rutgers University Press, 1989), pp. 13–33, p. 13.

13 Mary Alden Hopkins, 'Do Women Dress for Men?', *Delineator*, no. 98 (July 1921), p. 3.

14 Cited by Hopkins, ibid.

15 Ibid.

16 Sigmund Freud, in James Strachey, Anna Freud and Angela Richards, *The Standard Edition of the Complete Psychological Works of Sigmund Freud* (London: Hogarth Press, 1966), vol. 23, 1940a, p. 186. For a detailed and contemporaneous account of Freud's theory, see Dr. Eduard Hitschmann, *Freud's Theories of the Neuroses* (New York: New York Psychiatrical Society, 1913).

17 Maria LaPlace, 'Mothering, Feminism and Representation: The Maternal in Melodrama and the Woman's Film, 1910–40', in Christine Gledhill, ed., *Home Is Where the Heart Is: Studies in Melodrama and the Woman's Film* (London: BFI Publishing, 1987), pp. 138–66, p. 153.

18 Jay A. Gertzman, *Bookleggers and Smuthounds: The Trade in Erotica: 1920–1940* (Pennsylvania: University of Pennsylvania Press, 2001), p. 10.

19 Margaret Anderson and Howard Taylor, *Sociology: Understanding a Diverse Society* (Belmont, CA: Thomson Wadsworth, 2006), p. 338.

20 Ibid.

21 Freud, *Three Contributions to the Sexual Theory*, trans. A. A. Brill (New York: The Journal of Nervous and Mental Disease Publishing Company, 1910), p. 21.

22 Laura Claridge, *Emily Post: Daughter of the Gilded Age, Mistress of American Manners* (New York and London: Random House, 2008), p. 292.

23 Madeleine Pelletier, *L'Émancipation sexuelle de la femme* (Paris: Brochure Mensuelle, 1926); Angus McLaren, *Twentieth Century Sexuality: A History* (Oxford: Blackwell, 1999), p. 43; Anna Clark, *Desire: A History of European Sexuality* (New York and London: Routledge, 2008), pp. 167–8.

24 Elizabeth Roberts, *A Woman's Place: An Oral History of Working Class Women 1890–1940* (Oxford: Wiley-Blackwell, 1995), pp. 72–80.

25 Judy Giles, *Women, Identity and Private Life in Britain, 1900–50* (London: Palgrave Macmillan, 1995), p. 211.

26 Georgette Heyer, 'The Historical Romance and the Consumption of the Erotic', in Maggie Andrews and Mary M. Talbot (eds.), *All the World and Her Husband* (London and New York: Cassel, 2000), p. 83.

27 Charles Eckert, 'The Carole Lombard in Macy's Window', in Christine Gledhill (ed.), *Stardom: Industry of Desire* (London: Routledge, 1991), p. 109.

28 Alison Light, *Forever England: Femininity, Literature and Conservatism between the Wars* (London and New York: Routledge, 1991), p. 256.

29 Nicola Beauman, *A Very Great Profession: The Women's Novel, 1914–39* (London: Virago, 1989), p. 9.

30 Andrews and Talbot, p. 86.

31 Elinor Glyn, *The Man and the Maid* (New York: A. L. Burt Company, 1922), p. 5.

32 Ibid., p. 33.

33 Ibid.

34 The woman's marital status as a divorcée was not a concern in the novel, and indeed, was not necessarily a scandal in reality: 'the reputation of Paris divorcées [did] not [suffer] one jot' in high New York society, for example. Dorothy Dunbar Bromley, 'The Market Value of a Paris Divorce', *Harper's Magazine*, May 1927, pp. 669–681, p. 679.

35 Ibid., p. 168.

36 Ibid., p. 11.

37 Ibid., p. 168.

38 *The Bookman* (May 1922), p. 106.

39 Elinor Glyn, 'Elinor Glyn Tells How to Keep Men in Their Place', *Nash's and Pall Mall Magazine* (October 1922), pp. 97–103, p. 97.

40 Ibid., p. 98.

41 *Saturday Review of Politics, Literature, Science and Art* (13th May 1922), p. 499.

42 Mary Ann Caws, *The Surrealist Look: An Erotics of Encounter* (Cambridge, MA, and London: The MIT Press, 1999), p. 143.

43 Ibid., p. 306.

44 This observation, along with many others, was recorded and reprinted as an anthology in 1931: Lamar Beman, *Selected Articles on Censorship of the Theatre and of Moving Pictures* (New York: Wilson, 1931), p. 312.

45 Billy Sunday, printed in 'Theater, Cards and Dance', in John R. Rice (ed.), *The Best of Billy Sunday: 17 Burning Sermons from the Most Spectacular Evangelist the World Has Ever Known* (Murfreesboro, TN: Sword of the Lord Publishers, 1965). The author suggests that Sunday preached this sermon multiple times, starting from approximately 1915.

46 Gabrielle Chanel, 'Fait Expres – by Chanel', *Ladies' Home Journal* (June 1929), p. 46.

47 *Women's Wear Daily* (3rd March 1933), p. 116.

48 *Women's Wear Daily* (17th May 1934), p. 1.

49 André Breton, *Nadja* trans. Richard Howard (New York: Grove Press, 1960), p. 160.

50 John Roberts, *The Art of Interruption: Realism, Photography, and the Everyday* (Manchester: Manchester University Press, 1998), p. 102.

51 Jill Berk Jiminez (ed.), *Dictionary of Artists' Models* (London and Chicago: Fitzroy Dearborn Publishers, 2001), p. 415.

52 See Anne O. Nomis, *The History and Arts of the Dominatrix* (London and Melbourne: Anna Nomis Ltd., 2013), p. 52.

53 Ibid., p. 200.

54 Ibid., p. 201.

55 André Breton, 'Manifesto of Surrealism', 1924 in André Breton, *Manifestoes of Surrealism* trans. Richard Seaver and Helen R. Lane (Michigan: The University of Michigan Press, 1969), p. 9.

56 Johanna Malt, *Obscure Objects of Desire: Surrealism, Fetishism, and Politics* (Chicago: The University of Chicago Press, 2005), p. 5.

57 Ibid.

58 *Minotaure*, no. 3/4, Paris (1933), p. 81.

59 Mary Ann Doane, 'The Woman's Film: Possession and Address', in Gledhill, Christine (ed.), *Home Is Where the Heart Is: Studies in Melodrama and the Woman's Film* (London: BFI Publishing, 1987), pp. 283–298, p. 289.

60 Samuel Weber, 'The Sideshow, or Remarks on a Canny Moment', *MLN*, vol. 88, no. 26 (December 1973), p. 1131.

61 James Laver, *Modesty in Dress* (London: Heinemann, 1969), p. 121.

62 Tim Dant, 'Fetishism and the Social Value of Objects', *Sociological Review*, vol. 44, no. 3 (1996), pp. 495–516.

63 Rosalind Krauss, 'Photography in the Service of Surrealism', in Rosalind Krauss and Jane Livingston (eds.), *L'Amour Fou, Photography and Surrealism* (Washington D.C.: Corcoran Gallery of Art, 1985), pp. 15–56, p. 40.

64 Jane Livingston, 'Man Ray and Surrealist Photography', in *L'Amour Fou, Photography and Surrealism*, pp. 115–54, p. 147.

65 Walter Benjamin, *The Arcades Project*, trans. Howard Eiland and Kevin McLaughlin (Cambridge, MA, and London: Harvard University Press, 1999), p. 69.

66 Ibid., p. 79.

67 *Women's Wear Daily* (26th January 1937), p. 23.

68 *Vogue* (U.S.) (September 1937), p. 163.

69 Rebecca Arnold, *The American Look: Sportswear, Fashion, and the Image of Women in 1930s and 1940s New York* (London: I.B. Tauris, 2009), p. 81.

70 *Vogue* (U.S.) (15th May 1939), p. 46.

71 Ibid.

72 Cited in Jill Watts, *Mae West: An Icon in Black and White* (Oxford: Oxford University Press, 2001), p. 164.

73 Ibid., p. 165.

74 Ibid., p. 164.

75 Ibid.

76 Ibid., p. 165.

77 Ibid.

78 Ibid.

79 Ibid.

80 *Vogue*, New York, (15th May 1939), p. 46.

81 Ibid.

82 Elizabeth Hawes, *Fashion Is Spinach* (New York: Random House, 1938), pp. 288–9.

83 Ibid.

84 *Vogue* [U.S.] (1st September 1933), p. 67.

85 Indeed, West generated much scandal within her personal life, and was even imprisoned for ten days due to the perceived indecency of the play she authored and starred in, *Sex*, 1926. Certainly, her actions and vocal beliefs demonstrate that while her image was sexualized, she was in control rather than objectified. While she used elements of Victorian fashion within her appearance, she exposed the hypocrisy of the era as she was not demure.

86 See, for example, Oswell Blakeston's yearly review, 'The Cinema in 1933', *The Bookman* 85, 507 (December 1933), pp. 163–5.

87 *Photoplay* (July 1933), p. 20.

88 *The Bend Bulletin* (16th July 1954), p. 7.

89 *Picture Play Magazine* (January 1933), p. 26.

90 Particularly Salvador Dali, who featured her explicitly in several works, including his *Mae West's Face,* 1934, and *Mae West Lips* sofa, 1937.

91 Cited by Meryle Secrest, *Elsa Schiaparelli: A Biography* (New York: Random House, 2014), p. 80.

92 *Women's Wear Daily* (December 1937), p. 17.

93 Ibid.

94 *Women's Wear Daily* (9th December, 1937), p. 14.

95 Ibid.

96 See, for example: *Ladies' Home Journal* (November 1935), p. 92; Women's *Wear Daily* (9th March 1939), p. 17.

97 Secrest, *Elsa Schiaparelli.*

98 *Vogue* [U.S.] (September 1937), p. 79.

99 Ellis Havelock, *Studies in the Psychology of Sex: Vol. 5, Erotic Symbolism* (Philadelphia: F. A. Davis, 1927), p. iv.

100 *Vogue* [U.S.] (September, 1937), p. 77.

101 Jan Giler Reeder, *High Style: Masterworks from the Brooklyn Museum Costume Collection at the Metropolitan Museum of Art* (New York: Metropolitan Museum of Art, 2010), p. 122.

102 *Women's Wear Daily* (21st September 1937), p. 1.

103 *Women's Wear Daily* (16th September 1937), p. 3.

104 Ibid.

105 Ibid.

106 Ibid.

107 *Vogue* [U.S.] (1st September 1937), p. 75.

108 Ibid.

109 Ibid.

110 Ibid.

111 Ibid.

112 *Vogue* [U.S.] (15th February 1939), p. 44.

113 Ibid.

114 *Vogue* [U.S.] (15th December 1935), p. 27.

115 Ibid.

116 Watts, *Mae West*, p. 166.

117 *Vogue* [U.S.] (15th May 1939), p. 46.

118 *Vogue* [U.S.] (1st September 1933), p. 67.

119 Ibid.

120 *Vogue* [U.S.] (15th September 1937), p. 99.

121 Ibid.

Chapter 4

1 From novels, such as L.B. Yates' 1922 *Picking Winners with Major Miles,* which include the grim reaper as a constant threat throughout the narrative: 'The grim reaper is hidin' behind every woodpile in the country … ' [(Bobbs-Merrill Company, 1922), p. 266]; to magazines: 'The grim reaper has again visited the family … ', *Typographical Journal,* vol. 64 (1924), p. 403; 'A workman … narrowly escaped the Grim Reaper in the course of his daily tasks … ' *Everybody's Magazine,* vol. 55 (1926), p. 108; and official proceedings: *New York State Safety Congress* (New York, 1920), p. 27, and *California Board of Medical Examiners Annual Report* (1920), p. 5.

2 *The Rotarian* (May 1922), p. 238.

3 University of Iowa Libraries' Iowa City Town and Campus Scenes Digital Collection.

4 Peter C. Jupp and Tony Walter, 'The Healthy Society: 1918–98', in Peter C. Jupp and Clare Gittings (eds.), *Death in England: An Illustrated History* (Manchester: Manchester University Press, 1999), pp. 256–82, p. 256.

5 Cited ibid.

6 Cope Morgan, *The Cambridge Review,* vol. 42 (1920), p. 315.

7 Loleta I. Dawson and Marion Davis Huntting, *War Fiction and Personal Narratives* (Massachusetts: F. W. Faxon, 1921), p. 18.

8 *United States Investor,* vol. 34, no. 2 (1923), p. 2415.

9 Leo Huberman, *Man's Worldly Goods* (New York: New York University Press, 1936), p. 100.

10 K. D. Patterson, G.F. Pyle, 'The Geography and Mortality of the 1918 Influenza Pandemic', *Bull Hist Med,* vol. 65, no. 1 (Spring 1991), pp. 4–21.

11 Séverine Ansart, Camille Pelat, Pierre-Yves Boelle, Fabrice Carrat, Antoine Flahault and Alain-Jacques Valleron, 'Mortality Burden of the 1918–1919 Influenza

Pandemic in Europe', *Influenza and Other Respiratory Viruses*, no. 2 (May 2009), pp. 99–106.

12 Ibid.

13 Alfred W. Crosby, *America's Forgotten Pandemic: The Influenza of 1918* (Cambridge: Cambridge University Press, 2003), p. 206.

14 *Vogue* [U.S.] (1st May 1920), p. 146.

15 Ibid.

16 Freud, *On Metapsychology: The Theory of Psychoanalysis: 'Beyond the Pleasure Principle', 'The Ego and the Id' and Other Works*, ed. Angela Richards (London: Penguin, 1987), p. 282.

17 Ibid., p. 433.

18 Ibid.

19 Ibid., p. 380.

20 Ibid., p. 316.

21 Ibid., p. 308.

22 Ibid., p. 311.

23 Ibid., p. 380.

24 *Vogue* [U.S.] (15th July 1927), p. 76.

25 See Roger Chickering and Stig Förster, *Great War, Total War, Combat and Mobilization on the Western Front, 1914–1918* (Cambridge: Cambridge University Press, 2006).

26 British *Vogue* (June 1922), p. 32.

27 Ibid.

28 Ibid.

29 Ibid.

30 Juliet Ash, 'The Aesthetics of Absence: Clothes without People in Paintings', in Amy De La Haye and Elizabeth Wilson (eds.), *Defining Dress: Dress as Object, Meaning and Identity* (Manchester and New York: Manchester University Press, 1999), pp. 128–42, p. 135.

31 Ibid.

32 Kitty Hauser, 'The Fingerprint of the Second Skin', in Christopher Breward and Caroline Evans (eds.), *Fashion and Modernity* (Oxford and New York: Berg), pp. 153–70, p. 156.

33 Wilson, *Adorned in Dreams*, p. 1.

34 British *Vogue* (June 1922), p. 32.

35 Ibid.

36   Georg Simmel, 'Die Mode', in *Gesamtausgabe*, xiv (Suhrkamp: Frankfurt am Main, 1989), pp. 196.

37   James Laver went on to produce a text, *Taste and Fashion*, that presented a formula for the cyclical nature or deathliness of fashion, 1938.

38   *Vogue* [U.S.] (15th January 1925), p. 35.

39   *Vogue* [U.S.] (21st January 1929), p. 35.

40   For example, Valerie Cumming and C. W. Cunnington, *The Dictionary of Fashion History* (London: Bloomsbury, 2010), p. 122.

41   British *Vogue* (July 1927), p. 76.

42   Ibid.

43   Ibid.

44   Ibid., p. 77.

45   Ibid.

46   Ibid.

47   Ibid.

48   Ibid.

49   Ibid.

50   Ibid., p. 92.

51   Ibid.

52   Ibid.

53   Ibid.

54   Ibid.

55   Ibid.

56   Ibid.

57   Thomas Carlyle, *Sartor Resartus: The Life and Opinions of Herr Teufelsdröckh in Three Books* (London: Chapman and Hall, Limited, 1831), p. 192.

58   Ibid, p. 191.

59   Wilson, *Adorned in Dreams*, p. 1.

60   *Vogue* (2nd March 1929), p. 80.

61   Ibid.

62   Ibid.

63   Schiaparelli, *Shocking Life*, pp. 46–7.

64   Ibid.

65   Ibid.

66   Victoria Rose Pass, 'Strange Glamour: Fashion and Surrealism between the World Wars', PhD book, University of Rochester, New York, 2011, p. 130.

67 *Chicago Daily Tribune* (6th January 1929), p. E2.

68 Ibid.

69 Ibid.

70 Freud, 'Civilization and Its Discontents', p. 311.

71 Ibid.

72 Ibid.

73 Freud, *On Metapsychology*, p. 435.

74 Ibid., p. 434.

75 See, for example, Joel E. Vessels, *Drawing France: French Comics and the Republic* (Oxford and Mississippi: University Press of Mississippi, 2012) and Christina M. Knopf, *The Comic Art of War: A Critical Study of Military Cartoons, 1805–2014* (North Carolina: McFarland, 2015).

76 *Vogue* [U.S.] (26th April 1930), p. 56.

77 Ibid.

78 This evoked the eighteenth-century custom of producing silhouettes, which was an accessible and popular for portraiture and recording dress styles. For a general overview of this custom, see Georges Vigarello, *La silhouette du XVIIIe siècle à nos jours: naissance d'un défi* (Paris: Éditions de Seuil, 2012).

79 Ibid.

80 Ibid.

81 Ibid.

82 Ibid.

83 Ibid.

84 Kristin Thompson and David Bordwell have noted that the genre had become popular with international audiences by 1922, partly as a result of the post-First World War attitudes against the country having begun to diminish. Kristin Thompson and David Bordwell, *Film History: An Introduction*, 3rd edn. (Columbus, OH: McGraw Hill, 2010), p. 87.

85 Victor I. Stoichita, *A Short History of the Shadow* (Chicago: Reaktion Books, 1997), p. 150.

86 Carl Jung, *Memories, Dreams, Reflections*, trans. Richard and Clara Winston (London: Flamingo, 1983), p. 262.

87 For an overview of the shadow in Jung's oeuvre, see Ann Casement, 'The Shadow', in Renos K. Papadopoulos, *The Handbook of Jungian Psychology* (Sussex and New York: Routledge, 2006), pp. 94–112.

88 Jung, 'Psychology and Religion', 1938, in *The Complete Works of C.G. Jung*, vol. 11 (New Jersey: Princeton, 1969), pp. 131.

89 See, for example, Dietmar Rothermund, *The Global Impact of the Great Depression 1929–1939* (Routledge: London and New York, 1996).

90 Praz summarizes the myriad appearances of this trope throughout history, from sirens in ancient Greek mythology, to the biblical figure Eve, to the vampiresses of Romantic poetry, and the popular revival of these figures in fin-de-siècle culture. Mario Praz, *The Romantic Agony*, trans. Angus Davidson, 2nd edn. (London and New York: Oxford University Press, 1951[1930]).

91 For example, it was frequently reviewed in international literary journals, such as Pinto's review above, and also by Howard Mumford Jones in *Modern Language Notes*, vol. 51, no. 6 (June 1936), pp. 295–397.

92 Vivian de Sola Pinto, *The Review of English Studies*, vol. 11, no. 41 (January 1935), pp. 109–11, p. 109.

93 Ibid., p. 111.

94 Florence White Thomas, *Books Abroad* (Fall 1935), p. 414.

95 *Ladies' Home Journal* (April 1937), pp. 14–15, 106, 108, 110–11.

96 *Women's Wear Daily* (22nd November 1928), p. 6.

97 Johann Caspar Lavater, *Essays on Physiognomy*, vol. 2 (London: C. Whittingham, 1804), p. 34.

98 This text was still read and discussed frequently during the 1930s. See, for example: *Vocational Guidance Magazine*, vol. 11 (Bureau of Vocational Guidance, Harvard University, 1932), p. 7; *Life and Letters Today*, vols. 13–14 (London: Brendin Publishing Company, 1935), p. 188; Reginald Howard Wilenski, *Masters of English Painting* (Hale: Cushman and Flint, 1934), p. 234; Johann Wolfgang von Goethe, *Conversations with Goethe* (London: J. M. Dent & Sons, Limited, 1935), p. 295; Studies in History, Economics, and Public Law, Issues 396–8 (1934), Columbia University Press, p. 71; Charles T. Gilden, *The Human Face: A Symposium* (Philadelphia: Philadelphia County Medical Society, 1935), pp. 63, 64, 82; John Clemans Flanagan, *Factor Analysis in the Study of Personality* (Stanford: Stanford University Press, 1935); John Spon, *Faces. What They Mean and How to Read Them: The Physiognomist's Pocket Book* (London: E. & F.N. Spon, 1934).

99 Lavater, *Essays on Physiognomy*, p. 34.

100 Ibid.

101 For example, one popular crime novel was entitled *The Sinister Shadow*, by Henry Holt, 1934 (New York: Caxton House). The phrases 'sinister shadow' and 'shadow of death' were frequently used as figures of speech to evoke sinistrous and deathly concepts in general, and to introduce a sense of violence and tension. This was present in sources from encyclopaedias [e.g. *The Cambridge History of the British Empire* (Cambridge: Cambridge University Press, 1936), which

described death as casting 'the darkest and most sinister shadow … ', p. 239]; to plays [such as *Good Night, Caroline*, by Conrad Seiler (New York: Dramatists Play Service, 1938), which featured 'the sinister shadow of a man', p. 5]. One book on the disease, syphilis, by Thomas Parran, was even entitled 'Shadow on the Land: Syphilis' (New York: Reynal & Hitchcock, 1937). It was also used as a language device within poetry, such as *Race with Death: A Collection of Poems* by Caroline Parker-Smith (New York: Hastings House, 1939), within which the shadow was a frequent means by which to refer to death, for example: 'was that black shadow so close at hand?', p. 108.

102 Lavater, Essays on Physiognomy, p. 34.

103 Inside Plato's cave were prisoners, who were turned away from the light opening, which signified the illumination of knowledge. Instead, they were bound and able only to look at the shadows that were cast upon the cave wall, rather than the direct objects in reality. Therefore, they were prevented from viewing reality, and were only privy to its shadow. The underlying rationale was, therefore, that truth, knowledge and goodness were signified by the light, indicating, then, that darkness and shadows were sinister and evil. Furthermore, Stoichita has commented on the inherent violence within this origin myth, that it was, in essence, a 'sadistic' scene and 'unnecessarily cruel to imagine, as he did, the people in the cave as bound, their legs and necks fastened,' and he described the philosopher as 'being blatantly sadistic' [Stoichita, *A Short History of the Shadow*, p. 21].

104 See, for example: Bird Thomas Baldwin, *Child Psychology: A Review of the Literature*, 1 January 1923 to 31 March 1928 (London: n.p, 1928), p. 661; *The Journal of Educational Research*, vol. 26 (1933), p. 540; *Studies in Psychology*, Issues 1–4, The College (1930), p. 4; *Studies in Psychology from the William Allan Neilson Research Laboratory*, Issue 1 (1930), p. 4; *The Illinois Teacher*, vol. 22, *Illinois Education Association.*, 1933, pp. 107–8; *Saturday Review*, vol. 5, Saturday Review Associates (1928), p. 208.

105 Jean Piaget, *La Causalité physique chez l'enfant* (Paris: Alcan, 1927), pp. 203–18.

106 This canonical painting remained a current reference during the 1930s. See, for example: Violet Hunt, *Saturday Review of Politics, Literature, Science and Art* (29th August 1931), pp. 261–1; Gervase Smith, 'Taste for Nature', *The English Review* (November 1936), pp. 414–21, p. 420; E. H. W. Meyerstein, 'Landscape in English Art and Poetry', *Saturday Review of Politics, Literature, Science and Art* (23rd May 1931), p. 764; *Country Life* (11th July 1936), p. 35.

107 British *Vogue* (6th February 1935), p. 85.

108 Schiaparelli, *Shocking Life*, pp. 73–4.

109 *Harper's Bazaar* (15th September 1937), p. 78.

110 Christine Mehring, *Wols Photographs* (Cambridge: Busch-Reisinger Museum, 1999), p. 20.

111 *Vogue* [U.S.] (15th October 1937), pp. 100–1.

112 Ibid., p.100.

113 Ibid.

114 Ibid.

115 Ibid.

116 Ibid.

117 Ibid.

118 Ibid.

119 Ibid.

120 Ibid.

121 Ibid.

122 Ibid.

123 Ibid.

124 Ibid., p. 101.

125 Ibid.

126 Ibid., p.100

127 Ibid., p. 101.

128 Benjamin worked on the manuscript from 1927 to 1940. The notes were not discovered until after the Second World War, during which they had been hidden by Georges Bataille, a friend of Benjamin. Within the text, several writers and publications are referred to, the latest being in 1935, which indicates that Benjamin was considering the issue at or shortly after this time. We can therefore assess his argument as being within approximately the same context as Schiaparelli's work.

129 Walter Benjamin, cited in Susan Buck-Morss, *Dialectics of Seeing* (Cambridge, MA: MIT Press, 1991), p. 101.

130 Ibid.

131 Benjamin, cited in Buck-Morss, *Dialectics of Seeing*, p. 101.

132 Ibid.

133 Valerie D. Mendes, *Black in Fashion* (London: V&A Publications, 1999).

134 Ghislaine Wood, *The Surreal Body: Fetish and Fashion* (New York: Harry N. Abrams, 2007), p. 65.

135 'Dear Elsa, I like this idea of bones on the outside enormously.' The sketch is reproduced in Dilys Blum, 'Fashion and Surrealism', cited in Ghislaine Wood, *Surreal Things: Surrealism and Design* (London: V&A Publishing, 2014), pp. 139–59, p. 147.

136 See Blum, ibid.; and Valerie Steele and Jennifer Park, *Gothic: Dark Glamour* (New Haven and London: Yale University Press, 2008), p. 65.

137 Evans, *Fashion at the Edge …*, p. 224.

138 Whilst there are no affirmative records of who made the first x-ray discovery, it was first studied by Wilhelm Röntgen in 1895. The technology was first used under clinical conditions in Birmingham, England, in January 1896 by John Hall-Edwards, and he used the x-ray in a surgical operation for the first time in February that year. At this early developmental stage, however, the technology was inherently dangerous, and in early 1896, Ivan Romanovich Tarkhanov discovered that x-rays 'not only photograph, but also affect the living function' ['THE X-RAYS', *Science,* vol. 3, no. 67 (10th April 1896), pp. 562–3]. One paper published by Dr E. A. Codman in 1902 revealed that, of the 88 injuries that had been published as a result of x-rays since its discovery in 1895, that '55 had occurred in 1896, 12 in 1897, 6 in 1898, 9 in 1899, 3 in 1900 and 1 in 1901' [E. A. Codman, *Philadelphia Medical Journal,* vol. 9 (1902), pp. 438–42].

139 In 1929 the U.S. Advisory committee on X-Ray and Radiation Protection was first formed, and permitted recommended doses of radium were regularly published; however, this number was still fine-tuned until 1950.

140 For example, Dr Cannon, an early x-ray pioneer from its discovery, who had begun to use x-rays in 1896, developed recurring lesions all over his body in 1931, and he continued to study the process, and make suggestions on how it could be better understood, such as through biopsies. K. Sansare, V. Khanna and F. Karjodkar, 'Early Victims of X-rays: A Tribute and Current Perception', *Dentomaxillofac Radiol*, vol. 40, no. 2 (February 2011), pp. 123–5.

141 *Harper's Bazaar* (15th March 1938), p. 71.

142 *Women's Wear Daily* (8th September 1938), p. 32 (section 2).

143 *Women's Wear Daily* (25th August 1938), p. 4.

144 The fashion press itself highlighted this connection between fashionable, clinging dresses and a skeletal frame. In 1935, *Women's Wear Daily* reported: 'When the Haute Couture decrees that the waistline shall be high and the hipline long, it is the foundation garment that makes it possible for the vast majority of women, not naturally high-waisted or long of hip, to wear the new fashions. When Paris says the Princess Silhouette is in, and dresses must be skin-tight through the diaphragm, it is the foundation that molds the figure into such a silhouette that women of all sizes and proportions may have the fashionable silhouette' [*Women's Wear Daily* (5th September 1935), p. 17]. In 1937, The *London Bureau of Women's Wear Daily* described Victor Stiebel's new collection as featuring 'slim' and 'slender' gowns. When reporting on a collection by British designer Norman Hartnell in 1939, *Women's Wear Daily* categorized them as 'Slim dresses' in the headline, and emphasized within the text that these 'slim dresses' and 'slim evening gowns' were for 'ultra slender types', 'characteristic of Norman Hartnell' for both day and evening respectively[*Women's Wear Daily* (31st March 1939), p. 1]. Towards the end of the decade, this developed into a tendency to re-introduce internal corsetry into dresses to create the desired figure. *Women's Wear Daily* reported on this phenomenon in 1939: 'the current silhouette trend towards an ever narrowing waistline and the importance generally of period fashions makes a recall of the corset types worn a generation or more ago logical' [*Women's Wear Daily* (25th May 1939), p. 18]. By 1939, American *Vogue* confirmed, within its report on the Paris openings: 'you'll have to count on a corset this year. You'll have to learn how to lace yourself in – a lesson that even your mother has forgotten ... ' [American *Vogue* (15th September 1939), p. 59].

145 Jonathan L. Owen, *Avant-garde to New Wave: Czechoslovak Cinema, Surrealism and the Sixties* (New York and Oxford: Berghahn, 2011), p. 94.

146 Bataille published a developed version of these theories in his 1949 book, *The Accursed Share: An Essay on General Economy*, vol. 1 (New York: Zone Books, 1988 [1949]).

147 Owen, *Avant-garde to New Wave*, p. 94.

148 Bataille, 'The Practice of Joy Before Death', in *Visions of Excess: Selected Writings, 1927–1939*, ed. and trans. Allan Stoekl (Minneapolis: University of Minnesota Press, 1985), pp. 235–239, p. 235.

149 Ibid., p. 238.

150 Ibid., p. 236.

151 Ibid., p. 237.

152 Benjamin, cited in Buck-Morss, *Dialectics of Seeing*, p. 101.

153 As summarized by Karla L. Schultz, 'Bataille's "L'Erotisme" in Light of Recent Love Poetry', *Pacific Coast Philology*, vol. 22, no. 1/2 (November 1987), pp. 78–87, p. 81.

154 Benjamin, who was friend with Bataille, also proposed a similar concept of the social constructs around death: 'Birth is a "natural" condition, death is a "social" one. Fashion is the "transcendence" of the former as a new source of newness; it "transcends" the latter by making the inorganic commodity itself the object of human desire.' Cited in Buck-Morss, *Dialectics of Seeing*, p. 101.

155 Georges Bataille, *Eroticism: Death & Sensuality*, trans. Mary Dalwood (City Light Books: San Francisco, 1986 [1957]), p. 90.

Conclusion

1 Wilson, *Adorned in Dreams*, p. 9.

2 Ibid.

3 *Vogue*, New York, 8th December 1928, p. 98.

Bibliography

Primary Materials

Magazines

Editions published c.1919–1939
Art, Gout, Beauté
Arts et Métiers Graphiques
Black Mask
British Vogue
Daily Telegraph, London
Femina
Harper's Bazaar UK
Harper's Bazaar (U.S.)
Jardin de la Mode
L'Art et la Mode
La Gazette du Bon Ton
La Révolution Surréaliste
Ladies' Home Journal
Life
Minotaure
Motion Picture Magazine
Photoplay
Pinpoints
Red Book Magazine
Vogue (U.S.)
Vogue Paris

Journals, Articles, and Book Chapters

All issues c.1919–1939, unless otherwise indicated.
'Is the Younger Generation in Peril?' *Literary Digest*, vol. 69 (14th May 1921).
'The Well-Gowned Woman as a Poster', *American Vogue* (15th March 1913).
'Within the Pavillon d'Elegance', *Harper's Bazaar* (15th September 1937).
Anonymous, 'The Sword and the War', *The Saturday Review of Politics, Literature, Science and Art* (9th April 1921), p. 301.
Benjamin, Walter, 'Critique of Violence', 1921 in *Selected Writings, vol. 1* (Harvard University Press, 1999), pp. 277–300.

Benjamin, Walter, 'Surrealism: Last Snapshot of the European Intelligentsia' [1929], trans. Jephcott, Edmond, *New Left Review*, no. 108 (March/April 1978), pp. 47–56.

Bolitho, William, 'The New Skirt Length', *Harper's*, vol. 160 (February 1930).

Boulenger, Jacques, 'La Femme moderne: Devant le feu', *Illustration* (6th December 1924).

Books Abroad Vol. 9, No. 4, (Autumn, 1935).

Breton, André, 'La beauté sera convulsive', *Minotaure*, no. 5 (June 1934), pp. 9–16.

Breton, André, 'Prestige d'André Masson', *Minotaure*, nos. 11–12 (May 1939), p. 13.

Breton, André and Louis Aragon, 'La Cinquantenaire de l'hysterie', *La Revolution surréaliste*, no. 11 (15th March 1928).

British *Harper's Bazaar* (October 1934), pp. 52–3.

Bliven, Bruce, *Literary Digest*, vol. 92 (29th January 1927), pp. 27–8.

California Board of Medical Examiners Annual Report (1920).

Chanel, Gabrielle, 'Fait Expres – by Chanel', *Ladies' Home Journal* (June 1929).

Cope, Morgan, *The Cambridge Review*, vol. 42 (1920).

Ernst, Max, 'Au-delà de la peinture' (1936), in *Ecritures* (Paris: Gallimard, 1970), pp. 258–9.

Everybody's Magazine (vol. 55, 1926).

Fitzgerald, F. Scott, 'Echoes of the Jazz Age', *Scribner's Monthly*, vol. 90 (November 1931).

Gazette du Bon Ton, no. 10 (1921).

Glyn, Elinor, 'Elinor Glyn Tells How to Keep Men in Their Place', *Nash's and Pall Mall Magazine* (October 1922), pp. 97–103.

Goodwin, Lt.-General T.H.J.C., Director-General of Army Medical Service, 'Foreword', in Colonel H.M.W. Gray, *The Early Treatment of War Wounds* (Oxford: Oxford University Press, 1919).

'Howard Mumford Jones', *Modern Language Notes*, vol. 51, no. 6 (June 1936), pp. 295–397.

Hurlock, Elizabeth B., 'Motivation in Fashion', *Archives of Psychology*, no. III (1929).

Huysmans, Joris-Karl, *Against the Grain: À rebours* (Berlin: Hofenberg, 2015).

International Press Correspondence, vol. 13, 1933.

Kennedy, Hugh A. Studdert, 'Short Skirts', *The Forum* (June 1926), pp. 829–35.

Leonard, Hall, *Photoplay* (January 1930).

Life and Letters Today, vols. 13–14 (London: Brendin Publishing Company, 1935).

Life (6th September 1937).

Life, vol. 6, no. 15 (10th April 1939).

Mass, Walter S., 'Subconscient et Publicité', *Arts et Métiers Graphiques*, no. 1 (15th September 1927).

Maule, Frances, 'The Woman Appeal', *J. Walter Thompson News Bulletin*, no. 105 (January 1924), pp. 1–2.

Minotaure, no. 3/4, Paris (1933).

Muirhead, Walter G., 'Fashion Follies Follow War', *Mentor*, vol. 9 (1st September 1921).

New York State Safety Congress (New York, 1920).

Orwell, George, 'Raffles and Miss Blandish' (1944).

Oswell Blakeston's yearly review, 'The Cinema in 1933', *The Bookman*, vol. 85, no. 507 (December 1933), pp. 163–5.

Photoplay (July 1933).

Picture Play Magazine (January 1933).

'"Queen of Sheba," William Fox's Greatest Screen Production', *Women's Wear* (11th April 1921).

Rosenberg, Harold, 'Life and Death of the Amorous Umbrella', 1942 in Mary Ann Caws (ed.), *Surrealist Painters and Poets: An Anthology* (Cambridge, Massachusetts: MIT Press, 2002), pp. 363–6.

Saturday Review, vol. 5, Saturday Review Associates (1928).

Saturday Review of Politics, Literature, Science and Art (13th May 1922).

Saturday Review of Politics, Literature, Science and Art (29th August 1931).

Simmel, Georg, 'Die Mode', in *Gesamtausgabe, xiv* (Frankfurt am Main, 1989).

Studies in History, Economics, and Public Law, Issues 3. 396–8 (1934), Columbia University Press.

Studies in Psychology, Issues 1–4, The College (1930).

Studies in Psychology from the William Allan Neilson Research Laboratory, Issue 1 (1930).

The Bend Bulletin (16th July 1954).

The Bookman (May 1922).

'The Catholic Crusade for Modesty', *Literary Digest*, vol. 82, no. 9 (1924).

The Illinois Teacher, vol. 22, Illinois Education Association, 1933.

The Journal of Educational Research, vol. 26 (1933).

The Manchester Guardian (26th October 1914).

The Review of English Studies, vol. 11, no. 41 (January 1935).

The Rotarian (May 1922).

The Times (5th April 1916).

Typographical Journal, vol. 64 (1924).

United States Investor, vol. 34, no. 2 (1923).

Vocational Guidance Magazine, vol. 11 (Bureau of Vocational Guidance, Harvard University, 1932).

Wallon, Henri, 'Comment se développe chez l'enfant la notion de corps proper', *Journal de Psychologie* (November–December 1931), pp. 705–48.

Woolf, Virginia, 'Modern Fiction' (1919).

Young, Estelle de, 'A Psychological Analysis of Fashion Motivation', *Archives of Psychology*, no. 171 (1934).

Books

Abbott, Berenice, *New York in the Thirties: As Photographed by Berenice Abbott* (New York: Dover Press, 1973 [1939]).

Adams, Henry, *Democracy: An American Novel* (Los Angeles, CA: Library of Alexandria, 1925).

Alexandrian, Sarane, and Gordon Clough, *Surrealist Art* (London: Thames & Hudson, 1970).

Allen, Frederick Lewis, *Only Yesterday: An Informal History of the 1920s* (New York and London: Harper and Brothers, 1931).

Aragon, Louis, *Paris Peasant [Le Paysan de Paris]*, trans. Simon Watson Taylor (London: Cape, 1971).

Artaud, Antonin, *Selected Writings* (Berkeley, CA: University of California Press, 1988).

Ballard, Bettina, *In My Fashion* (London: Seeker and Warburg, 1960).

Barling, Seymour, and John T. Morrison, *Manual of War Surgery* (London: Henry Frowde; Hodder & Stoughton, 1919).

Georges Bataille, *Eroticism: Death & Sensuality*, trans. Mary Dalwood (City Light Books: San Francisco, 1986 [1957]).

Bataille, Georges, *Histoire de l'œil* [1928] (Paris: Gallimard, 1998).

Bataille, Georges, *La pratique de la joie devant la mort* (Paris: Mercure de France, 1967).

Bataille, Georges, *Visions of Excess: Selected Writings, 1927–1939* (Minneapolis: University of Minnesota Press, 1985).

Beaton, Cecil, *Fashion: An Anthology*, ed. Madeleine Ginsburg, 2nd edn. (London: Victoria and Albert Museum, 1971).

Beaton, Cecil, *The Glass of Fashion* (London: Cassell, 1989 [1954]).

Benjamin, Walter, *The Arcades Project* [1927–1940], ed. Rolf Tiedemann (Cambridge, MA: Harvard University Press, 1999).

Bergler, Edmund, *Fashion & the Unconscious* (New York: Robert Brunner, 1953).

Bourneville, D.M., and P. Regnard, *Iconographie photographique de la Salpêtrière*: service de M. Charcot (Paris: Aux bureaux du Progrès medical, 1876–80).

Bradley, Dennis H., *The Eternal Masquerade* (London: T. Werner Laurie Ltd., 1922).

Breton, André, *Communicating Vessels*, trans. Mary Ann Caws and Geoffrey T. Harris (Lincoln: University of Nebraska Press, 1990).

Breton, André, *Mad Love [L'amour fou, 1937]*, trans. Mary Ann Caws (Lincoln: University of Nebraska Press, 1987).

Breton, André, *Manifestoes of Surrealism* (Ann Arbor, MI: University of Michigan Press, 1969).

Breton, André, *Manifestoes of Surrealism*, trans. Richard Seaver and Helen R. Lane (Michigan: The University of Michigan Press, 1969).

Breton, André, *Nadja* (London: Penguin, 1999).

Breton, André, *Nadja*, trans. Richard Howard (New York: Grove Press, 1960).

Breton, André, *What Is Surrealism?* trans. David Gascoyne (London: Faber and Faber, 1936).

British Medical Journal (eds.), *War Wounds and Air Raid Casualties* [articles republished from the British Medical Journal] (London: Lewis, 1939).

Brophy, John, *The Soldier's War: A Prose Anthology* (London and Toronto: J.M. Dent & Sons Ltd., 1929).

Burbank, Emily, *Woman as Decoration* (New York: Dodd, Mead and Co., 1920).

Byers, Margaretta, *Designing Women: The Art, Technique and Cost of Being Beautiful* (New York: Simon and Schuster, 1938).

Cahun, Claude, *Disavowals or Cancelled Confessions [Aveux non avenus],* trans. S. De Muth (London, 2007).

Canby, Henry Seidel Ph.D., *Education by Violence: Essays on the War and the Future* (New York: The Macmillan Company, 1919).

Centers, Richard, *The Psychology of Social Classes: A Study of Class-Consciousness* (Princeton, NJ: Princeton University Press, 1949).

Charcot, Jean-Martin, *Iconographie Photographique de la Salpêtrière* (1879–80).

Chevreul, M.E., De la loi du contraste simultanée des coleurs (Paris: Pitois-Levrault, 1839).

Coles, Bertha Lippincott, *Wound-Stripes: Stories of after the War* (Philadelphia and London: J.B. Lippincott, 1921).

Daw, S.W., *Orthopedic Effects of Gunshot Wounds*, with a Foreword by Major-General Sir Robert Jones and an Appendix on Functional Disabilities by Dr. W. Cuthbert Morton (London: Henry Frowde, 1919).

De Ligt, Bart., *The Conquest of Violence: An Essay on War and Revolution*, with an Introduction by Aldous Huxley, trans. Honor Tracy from the French, text revised and enlarged by the author (London: George Routledge & Sons, Ltd., 1937).

De Monzie, A. (ed.), *Encyclopédie française*, vol. 8 (Paris: Sté de l'Encyclopédie française, 1938).

Ellis, Albert, *The American Sexual Tragedy* (New York: Twayne, 1954).

Ferenczi, S., Karl Abraham, Ernst Simmel, and Ernest Jones, *Psychoanalysis & War Neuroses* (London, Vienna and New York: The International Psycho-Analytical Press, 1921).

Finkelstein, Haim N. (ed.), *The Collected Writings of Salvador Dali* (Cambridge: Cambridge University Press, 1998).

Flügel, J. C., *The Psychology of Clothes* (London: Hogarth Press, 1930).

Friedan, Betty, *The Feminine Mystique* (London: Penguin, 1993 [1963]).

Glyn, Elinor, *The Man and the Maid* (New York: A. L. Burt Company, 1922).

Gray, Colonel H.M.W., *The Early Treatment of War Wounds* (London: Oxford University Press, 1919).

Guillaume, P., *L'imitation chez l'enfant* [Imitation in children] (Paris: Alcan, 1925).

Halsted, William, *Surgical Papers*, vol. 2 (Baltimore: John Hopkins Press, 1924).

Hawes, Elizabeth, *Anything but Love: A Complete Digest of the Rules for Feminine Behavior from Birth to Death, Given Out in Print, on Film and over the Air [...]* (New York and Toronto: Rinehartand Co, 1948).

Hawes, Elizabeth, *Fashion Is Spinach* (New York: Random House, 1938).

Hawes, Elizabeth, *Men Can Take It* (New York: Ramndom House, 1939).

Hawes, Elizabeth, *Why Is a Dress?* (New York: Viking Press, 1942).

Hawes, Elizabeth, *Why Women Cry, or, Wenches with Wrenches* (New York: Reynal and Hitchcock, 1943).

Henri, Wallon, *Comment se développe chez l'enfant la notion de corps propre* (in *Journal de Psychologie*, November–December 1931, pp. 705–748).

Huelfer, Evan Andrew, *The 'Casualty' Issue in American Military Practice: The Impact of World War I* (Westport, CT: Praeger Publishers, Greenwood Publishing Group, 2003).

Hull, Alfred J., F.R.C.S., Major, 'Royal Army Medical Corps: Surgeon, British Expeditionary Force, France: Late Lecturer on Surgical Pathology', in *Surgery in War, with a Preface by Sir Alfred Keogh, K.C.B., M.D.* (London: J. & A. Churchill, 1916).

Hurlock, Elizabeth B., *The Psychology of Dress: An Analysis of Fashion and Its Motives* (New York: The Ronald Press Company, 1929).

Jean, Marcel, *The History of Surrealist Painting*, with the collaboration of Arpad Mezei, trans. Simon Watson Taylor (London: Weidenfeld & Nicolson, 1960).

Keen, William Williams, *The Treatment of War Wounds* (Philadelphia: W.B. Saunders, 1918).

Kempton, Murray, *Part of Our Time: Some Ruins and Monuments of the Thirties* (New York: New York Review Books, 1998 [1955]).

Kinsey, Alfred, et al., *Sexual Behavior in the Human Female* (Philadelphia and London: W.B. Saunders and Co., 1953).

Lautréamont, Comte de [Isidore Ducasse], *Les Chants de Maldoror* (New York: New Directions Books, 1965).

Lavater, Johann Caspar, *Essays on Physiognomy*, vol. 2 (London: C. Whittingham, 1804).

Laver, James, *Modesty in Dress* (London: Heinemann, 1969).

Le Corbusier, *The Decorative Art of Today*, trans. James Dunnett (Cambridge, MA: MIT Press, 1987 [1925]).

Ludovici, Anthony, *Violence, Sacrifice and War* (London: Holders Press Limited, 1933).

Lundberg, Ferdinand and Marynia F. Farnham, *Modern Woman; The Lost Sex* (New York: Harper and Brothers, 1947).

MacKintosh, J.M., *War and the Doctor: Essays on the Immediate Treatment of War Wounds* (Edinburgh: Oliver and Boyd, 1940).

Makins, Sir George Henry, *On Gunshot Injuries to the Bloodvessels: Founded on Experience Gained in France during the Great War, 1914–1918* (Bristol: J. Wright, 1919).

Man, Ray, *Les Mannequins* (Paris, 1966).

Mitchell, T.J., and Miss G.M. Smith, *History of the Great War Based on Official Documents, Medical Services: Casualties and Medical Statistics of the Great War* (London: published by his majesty's stationery office, 1931).

Muller, Cecilie, *Fresh Hope and Health for Hospital Patients and Invalids* (London: G. Bell and Sons, 1919).

National American Women's Suffrage Association, *Victory: How Women Won It*, A Centennial Symposium, 1840–1940 (New York: The H. W. Wilson Co., 1940).

Neather, Carl Albert, *Advertising to Women* (New York: Prentice-Hall, 1928).

Parran, Thomas, *Shadow on the Land: Syphilis* (New York: Reynal & Hitchcock, 1937).

Parsons, Frank Alvah, *The Art of Dress* (Garden City, New York: Doubleday, 1928).

Parsons, Frank Alvah, *The Psychology of Dress* (Garden City, New York: Doubleday, 1923).

Piaget, Jean, *La Causalité physique chez l'enfant* (Paris: Alcan, 1927).

Pickerill, H. P., *Facial Surgery* (Edinburgh: E. & S. Livingstone, 1924).

Rauschenpush, Winifred, *How to Dress in Wartime* (Los Angeles: Coward McCann Ltd., 1942).

Reich, *The Function of the Orgasm: Sex-Economic Problems of Biological Energy*, The Discovery of the Orgone, Vol. I, trans. Vincent R. Carfagno (London: Souvenir Press, 1999 [1924]).

Rudofsky, Bernard, *Are Clothes Modern?* (Chicago: Paul Theobold, 1947).

Ruth, O'Brien, Ruby Kathryn Worner, and Esther Peterson Daniel, *Bibliography on the Relation of Clothing to Health* (Washington: [U.S. Govt. Print. Off.], 1929).

Rutherford, Nathaniel John Crawford, *Memories of an Army Surgeon* (London: Paul, 1939).

Sarfatti, Margherita G., *The Life of Benito Mussolini*, trans. Frederic Whyte (London: T. Butterworth, 1925).

Schiaparelli, Elsa, *Shocking Life* (London: J. M. Dent, 1954).

Sorel, Georges, *Réflexions sur la violence: huitième edition avec plaidoyer pour Lénine* (Paris: Rivière, 1936).

Stokes, Adrian, *Colour and Form* (London: Thompson, 1937).

Storey, Thomas Andrew, *Principles of Hygiene* (Stanford University Press, 1930).

Virginia Woolf, *Mrs Dalloway* (Ontario and London: Broadview Press, 2012).

Warden, Florence, *The Beauty Doctor* (London: Robert Hayes Ltd., 1920).

Wilenski, Reginald Howard, *Masters of English Painting* (Boston: Hale, Cushman and Flint, 1934).

Yates, L.B., Picking Winners with Major Miles (Indianapolis: Bobbs-Merrill Company, 1922).

Yezierska, Anzia, *Bread Givers* (New York: Persea Books, 1975 [1925]).

Theoretical Texts

Barthes, Roland, *Mythologies*, trans. Annette Lavers (London: Vintage, 1993).

Bataille, Georges, *Visions of Excess: Selected Writings*, ed. and trans. Allan Stoekl (Minneapolis: University of Minnesota Press, 1985).

Baudelaire, Charles, *Complete Poems*, trans. Walter Martin (Manchester: Carcanet, 1997).

Baudelaire, Charles, *Selected Writings on Art and Literature* (London: Penguin, 1992).

Baudelaire, Charles, *The Painter of Modern Life and Other Essays,* 2nd ed., trans. Jonathan Mayne (London: Phaidon, 1995).

Baudrillard, Jean, *Fatal Strategies* (New York: Semiotext(e), 1990).

Baudrillard, Jean, *Seduction*, trans. Brian Singer (London: Macmillan, 1990 [1979]).

Baudrillard, Jean, *Simulcra and Simulation*, trans. Sheila Faria (University of Michigan, 1994).

Baudrillard, Jean, *Symbolic Exchange and Death* (London: Sage, 1995).

Baudrillard, Jean, *The Ecstasy of Communication*, trans. Bernard and Caroline Schutze (Brooklyn, NY: Semiotext(e) Autonomia, 1998).

Baudrillard, Jean, *The Illusion of the End*, trans. Chris Turner (Cambridge: Polity Press, 1994).

Baudrillard, Jean, *The System of Objects*, trans. James Benedict (London and New York: Verso, 2005).

Beauvoir, Simone de, *The Second Sex* (London: Vintage, 1997 [1949]).

Benjamin, Walter, *Illuminations*, trans. Harry Zohn (London: Fontana/ Collins, 1973 [1955]).

Benjamin, Walter, *Reflections: Essays, Aphorisms and Autobiographical Writing*, edited by Peter Demetz (New York: Harcourt Brace Jovanovich Inc., 1978).

Benjamin, Walter, *The Origin of German Tragic Drama*, trans. John Osborne with an intro. by George Steiner (London: New Left Books, 1977).

Bourdieu, Pierre, *Distinction: A Social Critique of the Judgement of Taste* (London: Routledge, 1996).

Bourdieu, Pierre, *The Rules of Art: Genesis and Structure of the Literary Field*, trans. Susan Emanuel (California: Stanford University Press, 1995).

De Certeau, Michel, *The Practice of Everyday Life* (Berkeley, Los Angeles, London: University of California Press, 1998).

Debord, Guy, *Society of the Spectacle*, trans. Donald Nicholson-Smith (London: Zone Books, 1994 [1967]).

Derrida, Jacques, *Specters of Marx: The State of Debt, the Work of Mourning, and the New International*, trans. Peggy Kamuf (New York and London: Routledge, 1994).

Foucault, Michel, *Discipline and Punish: The Birth of the Prison*, trans. Alan Sheridan (New York: Vintage Books,1995).

Foucault, Michel, *The Birth of the Clinic* (London: Routledge, 2003).

Foucault, Michel, *The History of Sexuality* [all vols.], trans. Robert Hurley (New York: Pantheon, 1985 [1984]).

Freud, Sigmund, A Case of Hysteria, Three Essays on Sexuality, and Other Works, in trans. James Strachey and Anna Freud, ed. James Strachey, *The Standard Edition of the Complete Psychological Works of Sigmund Freud*, Vol. 7 (London: Hogarth Press, 1953).

Freud, Sigmund, An Infantile Neurosis, and Other Works, in trans. James Strachey and Anna Freud, ed. James Strachey, *The Standard Edition of the Complete Psychological Works of Sigmund Freud*, Vol. 17 (London: Hogarth Press, 1955).

Freud, Sigmund, Beyond the Pleasure Principle, Group Psychology, and Other Works, in trans. James Strachey and Anna Freud, ed. James Strachey, *The Standard Edition of the Complete Psychological Works of Sigmund Freud*, Vol. 17 (London: Hogarth Press, 1955).

Freud, Sigmund, *Civilization and Its Discontents*, ed. and trans. James Strachey (New York: W. W. Norton & Company, 2010).

Freud, Sigmund, 'Fetishism' [1927], in James Strachey (ed.), *Miscellaneous Papers, 1888–1938*, vol. 5 (London: Hogarth and Institute of Psycho-Analysis, 1950), pp. 198–204.

Freud, Sigmund, Five Lectures on Psycho Analysis, Leonardo Da Vinci, and Other Works, in trans. James Strachey and Anna Freud, ed. James Strachey, *The Standard Edition of the Complete Psychological Works of Sigmund Freud*, Vol. 11 (London: Hogarth Press, 1957).

Freud, Sigmund, Hysteria [1893–1895], in trans. James Strachey, ed. James Strachey, *The Standard Edition of the Complete Psychological Works of Sigmund Freud*, vol. 2 (London: Hogarth Press and the Institute of Psychoanalysis, 1995).

Freud, Sigmund, 'Inhibitions, Symptoms and Anxiety', *The Standard Edition of the Complete Psychological Works of Sigmund Freud*, vol. 20 (1926), pp. 75–175.

Freud, Sigmund, 'Introductory Lectures on Psycho Analysis', in trans. James Strachey and Anna Freud, ed. James Strachey, *The Standard Edition of the Complete Psychological Works of Sigmund Freud*, vols. 15 and 16 (London: Hogarth Press, 1963).

Freud, Sigmund, *La science des rêves*, trans. Ignace Meyerson (Paris: Félix Alcan, Bibliothèque de philosophie contemporaine, 1926).

Freud, Sigmund, 'New Introductory Lectures on Psychoanalysis' 1933, in trans. James Strachey *The Standard Edition of the Complete Psychological Works of Sigmund Freud*, vol. 22 (London, 2001).

Freud, Sigmund, *On Metapsychology: The Theory of Psychoanalysis: 'Beyond the Pleasure Principle', 'The Ego and the Id' and Other Works*, ed. Angela Richards (London: Penguin, 1987).

Freud, Sigmund, On the History of the Psycho Analytic Movement, Papers on Metapsychology, and Other Works, in trans. James Strachey and Anna Freud, ed. James Strachey, *The Standard Edition of the Complete Psychological Works of Sigmund Freud*, vol. 14 (London: Hogarth Press, 1957).

Freud, Sigmund, 'The Dissolution of the Oedipus Complex' [1924], in *The Standard Edition of the Complete Psychological Works of Sigmund Freud*, vol. 19 (London: Hogarth Press, 1955), pp. 173–82.

Freud, Sigmund, The Ego and the Id, and Other Works, trans. James Strachey and Anna.

Freud, Sigmund, *The Interpretation of Dreams* (New York: Macmillan, 1913).

Freud, Sigmund, The Interpretation of Dreams and on Dreams, in trans. James Strachey and Anna Freud, ed. James Strachey, *The Standard Edition of the Complete Psychological Works of Sigmund Freud*, vol. 4 (London: Hogarth Press, 1953).

Freud, Sigmund, The Psychopathology of Everyday Life, in trans. James Strachey and Anna Freud, ed. James Strachey, *The Standard Edition of the Complete Psychological Works of Sigmund Freud*, vol. 6 (London: Hogarth Press, 1960).

Freud, Sigmund, *The Uncanny [1919]*, trans. David McLintock (London: Penguin, 2003).

Freud, Sigmund, *The Standard Edition of the Complete Psychological Works of Sigmund Freud*, ed. James Strachey, vol. 19 (London: Hogarth Press, 1961).

Freud, Sigmund, *Three Contributions to the Sexual* Theory, trans. A. A. Brill (New York: The Journal of Nervous and Mental Disease Publishing Company, 1910).

Freud, Sigmund, *Three Contributions to the Theory of Sex*, trans. A. A. Brill (New York and Washington: Nervous and Mental Disease Publishing Co., 1920).

Freud, Sigmund, Totem and Taboo, and Other Works, in trans. James Strachey and Anna Freud, ed. James Strachey, *The Standard Edition of the Complete Psychological Works of Sigmund Freud*, vol. 13 (London: Hogarth Press, 1955).

Freud, Sigmund, Two Case Histories: Utile Hans' and the 'Rat Man'', in trans. James Strachey and Anna Freud, ed. James Strachey, *The Standard Edition of the Complete Psychological Works of Sigmund Freud*, vol. 10 (London: Hogarth Press, 1955).

Freud, Sigmund, James Strachey, Anna Freud, and Angela Richards, *The Standard Edition of the Complete Psychological Works of Sigmund Freud* (London: Hogarth Press, 1966), vol. 23, 1940a.

Jung, Carl, *Memories, Dreams, Reflections* (London: Harper Collins/Fontana Press, 1993).

Jung, Carl, 'Psychology and Religion', 1938, in *The Complete Works of C.G. Jung*, vol. 11 (New Jersey: Princeton, 1969).

Klein, Melanie, *The Selected Melanie Klein*, ed. Juliet Mitchell (Harmondsworth: Penguin, 1986).

Kristeva, Julia, *New Maladies of the Soul*, trans. Ross Guberman (New York: Columbia University Press, 1995).

Kristeva, Julia, *Powers of Horror: An Essay on Abjection* (New York: Columbia University Press, 1982).

Lacan, Jacques, 'Abasia in a War-traumatized Female Patient', described to the Société neurologique on 2nd November 1928. Printed within his doctoral book, *De la psychose paranoïaque dans ses rapports avec la personnalité* (Paris: Le François, 1975 [1932]).

Lacan, Jacques, *Feminine Sexuality: Jacques Lacan and the Ecole Freudienne*, trans. Jacqueline Rose, ed. Juliet Mitchell and Jacqueline Rose (New York: WW Norton, 1983).

Lacan, Jacques, 'Le stade du mirroir', Merienbad, August 1936. Translated as 'The Looking-Glass Phase', *The International Journal of Psychoanalysis*', vol. 18, part 1 (January 1937).

Lacan, Jacques, *On Feminine Sexuality: The Limits of Love and Knowledge* (the Seminar of Jacques Lacan: Book XX), trans. Bruce Fink (New York and London: Norton, 1998).

Lacan, Jacques, *The Ecrits*, trans. Bruce Fink (New York: W.W. Norton and Co., 2006).

Lacan, Jacques, *The Four Fundamental Concepts of Psychoanalysis*, trans. Alan Sheridan, ed. Jacques-Alain Miller (London: Karnak, 2004).

Lacan, Jacques, 'The Mirror Stage as Formative of the Function of the I as Revealed in Psychoanalytic Experience', in trans. Alan Sheridan, *Écrits: A Selection* (London: Routledge, 1977).

Lacan, Jacques, *The Seminars of Jacques Lacan*, ed. Jacques-Alain Miller, trans. Dennis Porter, book VII (New York and London: Routledge, 1992).

Lacan, Jacques, *The Seminars of Jacques Lacan Book II: The Ego in Freud's Theory and in the Technique of Psychoanalysis*, trans. Sylvana Tomaselli, ed. Jacques Alain Miller (Cambridge: Cambridge University Press, 1988).

Laplanche, Jean, *The Unconscious and the Id* (London: Rebus, 1999).

Lefebvre, Henri, 'The Everyday and Everydayness', *Yale French Studies*, no. 73, Everyday Life (1987).

Levine, D.N. (ed.), *Georg Simmel, On Individuality and Social Forms* (Chicago: University of Chicago Press, 1971).

Mestrovic, Stjepan Gabriel (ed.), *Thorstein Veblen: On Culture and Society* (London: Sage, 2003).

Nietzche, F., *On the Genealogy of Morals* (Oxford: Oxford University Press, 1996).

Riviere, Joan, 'Womanliness as a Masquerade' [1929], repr. in V. Burgin, J. Donald and C. Kaplan (eds.), *Formations of Fantasy* (Routledge: London, 1986), pp. 35–44.

Schilder, Paul, *The Image and Appearance of the Human Body: Studies in Constructive Energies of the Psyche* (New York: International Universities Press Inc., 1970).

Simmel, Georg, 'Fashion' [1904], and 'The Metropolis and Mental Life' [1903], in ed. and with an intro. by Donald N. Levine *On Individuality and Social Forms*, (Chicago, ILL: University of Chicago Press, 1971) pp. 294–323 and pp. 324–39.

Secondary Materials

Journal Articles and Book Chapters

Adamowicz, Elza, 'Hats or Jellyfish? André Breton's Collages', in Ramona Fotiade (ed.), *Andre Breton – The Power of Language* (Exeter: Elm Bank Publications, 2000), pp. 83–96.

Adams, Parveen, 'Representation and Sexuality', m/ f,1: 1(1978), pp. 65–82.

Arnold, Rebecca, 'Heroin Chic', *Fashion Theory*, vol. 3, no. 3, (September 1999), pp. 279–95.

Arnold, Rebecca, 'The Brutalized Body', *Fashion Theory*, vol. 3, no. 4 (December 1999), pp. 487–501.

Bailey, Peter, 'Pansexuality and Glamour: The Victorian Barmaid as Cultural Prototype', *Gender and History*, vol. 2, no. 2 (1990), pp. 148–72.

Barthes, Roland, 'Where the Garment Gapes', in Malcolm Banard (ed.), *Fashion Theory: A Reader* (Routledge: Abingdon, 2007).

Bernd, Herzogenrath, 'Tod Browning's Freaks and the Fraternity of the Fragmented', in Heinz Tschachler, Maureen Devine, and Michael Draxlbauer (eds.), *The EmBodyment of American Culture* (Münster: LIT Verlag, 2003), pp. 203–15.

Bill, Katina, 'Attitudes towards Women's Trousers: Britain in the 1930s', *Journal of Design History*, vol. 6, no. 1 (1993), pp. 45–54.

Bourke, Joanna, 'Effeminacy, Ethnicity and the End of Trauma: The Sufferings of 'Shell-Shocked' Men in Great Britain and Ireland, 1914–39', *Journal of Contemporary History*, vol. 35 (2000), pp. 57–70.

Breward, Christopher, 'Femininity and Consumption: The Problem of the Late Nineteenth-Century Fashion Journal', *Journal of Design History*, vol. 7, no. 2 (1994), pp. 71–89, p. 75.

Buckley, Reka C. V., 'Flash Trash: Gianni Versace and the Theory and Practice of Glamour', in Stella Bruzzi and Pamela Church Gibson (eds.), *Fashion Cultures: Theories, Explanations and Analysis* (London and New York: Routledge, 2000), pp. 331–48.

Carle, Emmanuelle, 'Women, Anti-Fascism and Peace in Interwar France: Gabrielle Duchêne's Itinerary', *French History*, vol. 18, no. 3 (2004), pp. 291–314.

Carter, Michael, 'J.C. Flügel and the Nude Future', *Fashion Theory*, vol. 7, no. 1 (2003).

Cocks, H. G., 'Saucy Stories: Pornography, Sexology and the Marketing of Sexual Knowledge in Britain, c.1918–70', *Social History*, vol. 29, no. 4 (November 2004), pp. 465–84.

Copsey, Nigel, 'Communists and the Inter-War Anti-Fascist Struggle in the United States and Britain', *Labour History Review*, vol. 76, no. 3 (December 2011).

Cox, Howard and Simon Mowatt, '*Vogue* in Britain: Authenticity and the Creation of Competitive Advantage in the UK Magazine Industry', *Business History*, vol. 54 (2012), pp. 140–53.

Crawforth, Hannah, 'Surrealism and the Fashion Magazine', *American Periodicals*, vol. 14, no. 2 (2004), pp. 212–46.

Dant, Tim, 'Fetishism and the Social Value of Objects', *Sociological Review*, vol. 44, no. 3 (1996), pp. 495–516.

Doane, Mary Ann, 'Film and Masquerade: Theorising the Female Spectator', *Screen*, vol. 23, no. 3–4 (1982).

Duncan, Carol, 'Virility and Domination in Early Twentieth Century Vanguard Painting', in Norma Broude and Mary D Garrard (eds.), *Feminism and Art History* (New York, 1982), pp. 293–314.

Eicher, Joanne B. and Mary Ellen Roach-Higgins, 'Definition and Classification of Dress', in Ruth Barnes and Joanne B. Eicher (eds.), *Dress and Gender: Making and Meaning in Cultural Contexts* (Oxford: Berg, 1993).

Evans, Caroline, 'Living Dolls: Mannequins, Models and Modernity', in Julian Stair (ed.), *The Body Politic*, Crafts Council (London, 2000), pp. 103–16.

Evans, Caroline, 'Masks, Mirrors and Mannequins: Elsa Schiaparelli and the Decentred Subject', *Fashion Theory*, vol. 3, no. 1 (1999), pp. 3–31.

Evans, Caroline, 'Yesterday's Emblems and Tomorrow's Commodities: The Return of the Repressed in Fashion Imagery Today', in Stella Bruzzi and Pamela Church

Gibson (eds.), *Fashion Cultures: Theories, Explorations, and Analysis* (London; New York: Routledge, 2000), pp. 93–113.

Foster, Hal, 'The Art of Fetishism', *The Princeton Architectural Journal*, vol. 4, 'Fetish' (1992), pp. 6–19.

Foster, Hal, 'Trauma Studies and the Interdisciplinary: An Interview', in Alex Colesand and Alexia Defert (eds.), *The Anxiety of Interdisciplinary* (London: BACKless Books and Black Dog, 1998).

Freedmen, Estelle B., 'The New Woman: Changing Views of Women in the 1920s', *The Journal of American History*, vol. 61, no. 2 (September 1974), pp. 372–93.

Friedman, Jonathan, 'Narcissism, Roots and Postmodernity: The Constitution of Selfhood in the Global Crisis', in Scott Lash and Jonathan Friedman (eds.), *Modernity and Identity* (Oxford: Basil Blackwell, 1992), pp. 331–6.

Fuss, Diana, 'Fashion and the Homospectatorial Look', *Critical Enquiry*, vol. 18, no. 4 (1992), pp. 713–37.

Gibson, Robyn, *Surrealism into Fashion: The Creative Collaborations between Elsa Schiaparelli and Salvador Dali* (RMIT University, 2001).

Greenwood, Jeremy and Nezih Guner, 'Social Change: The Sexual Revolution', *PSC Working Paper Series* (April 2009), accessed at University of Pennsylvania Scholarly Commons, http://repository.upenn.edu/psc_working_papers/12, September 2016.

Haiken, Beth, 'Plastic Surgery and American Beauty at 1921', *Bulletin of the History of Medicine*, vol. 68, no. 3 (Fall 1994), pp. 429–53.

Hume, Marion, 'McQueen's Theatre of Cruelty', *Independent*, 21 October 1993.

Hume, Marion, 'Scissorhands', *Harper's and Queen*, August 1996.

Hutchison, Sharla, 'Convulsive Beauty: Images of Hysteria and Transgressive Sexuality: Claude Cahun and Djuna Barnes', *Symploke*, vol. 11, nos. 1–2 (2003), pp. 212–26.

Jay, Martin, 'The Disenchantment of the Eye', in Lucien Taylor (ed.), *Visualizing Theory: Selected Essays from V.A.R* (New York and Oxford: Routledge, 2009), pp. 173–204.

Johnston, Claire, 'Femininity and the Masquerade: *Anne of the Indies*', in E. Ann Kaplin (ed.), *Psychoanalysis and Cinema* (London and New York: Routledge, 1990), pp. 64–72.

Jupp, P. C. and Walter, 'The Healthy Society: 1918–98', in Jupp, P. C., and C. Gittings (eds.), *Death in England: An Illustrated History* (Manchester: Manchester University Press, 1999).

Kenneth, E. Silver, 'A More Durable Self', in *Silver, Chaos and Classicism: Art in France, Italy, and Germany*, 1918–1936, exh. cat. (New York: Solomon R. Guggenheim Foundation, 2010).

Koehn, Nancy, 'Estée Lauder: Self-Definition and the Modern Cosmetics Market', in Philip Scranton (ed.), *Beauty and Business: Commerce, Gender, and Culture in Modern America* (Routledge, 2001), p. 247.

Latimer, Tirza True, 'Equivocal Gender: Dada/Surrealism and Sexual Politics between the Wars', in David Hopkins (ed.), *A Companion to Dada and Surrealism* (Malden, MA and Oxford: Wiley, 2016).

Leslie, Esther, 'Souvenirs and Forgetting: Walter Benjamin's Memory-work', in Marius
    Kwint Christopher Breward, and Jeremy Aynsley (eds.), *Material Memories: Design
    and Evocation* (Oxford and New York: Berg, 1999), pp. 107–22.
Loschek, Ingrid, 'The Deconstructionists', in Gerda Buxbaum (ed.), *Icons of Fashion: The
    Twentieth Century* (Munich, London and New York: Prestel, 1999), p. 146.
Luijten, Ger, 'Frills and Furbelows: Satires on Fashion and Pride around 1600', *Simiolus:
    Netherlands Quarterly for the History of Art*, vol. 24, no. 2/3.
Mansén, Elisabeth, 'Fingertip Knowledge: Meret Oppenheim on the Sense of Touch',
    The Senses & Society, vol. 9, no. 1 (2014), pp. 5–15.
Martin, Richard, 'Destitution and Deconstruction: The Riches of Poverty in the
    Fashions of the 1990s', *Textile and Text*, vol. 15, no. 2 (1992).
Monahan, Laurie J., 'Radical Transformations: Claude Cahun and the Masquerade
    of Womanliness', in Catherine de Zegher (ed.), *Inside the Visible* (Institute of
    Contemporary Art, Boston: MIT Press, 1996).
Peiss, Kathy, 'Making Faces: The Cosmetics Industry and the Cultural Construction of
    Gender, 1890–1930', *Genders*, no. 7 (Spring 1990), pp. 143–69.
Pumphrey, Martin, 'The Flapper, the Housewife and the Making of Modernity', *Cultural
    Studies*, vol. 1, no. 2 (1987), pp. 79–194.
Radford, Robert, 'Dangerous Liaisons: Art, Fashion and Individualism', *Fashion Theory*,
    vol. 2, no. 2 (June 1998), pp. 151–63.
Ragland, Ellie, *The Logic of Sexuation: From Aristotle to Lacan* (New York, 2004).
Rajchman, John, 'Lacan and the Ethics of Modernity', *Representations*, vol. 15 (summer
    1986), pp. 42–56.
Richard Butsch, 'American Movie Audiences of the 1930s' *International Labor and
    Working Class History*, no. 59, 'Workers and Film: As Subject and Audience' (Spring
    2001), pp. 106–20.
Rose, Jacqueline, 'Fleshly Memories', *Times Literary Supplement* (17 June 1993).
Rothenberg, Molly Ann, and Joseph Valente, 'Fashionable Theory and Fashion-Able
    Women: Returning Fuss's Homospectatorial Look', *Critical Enquiry*, vol. 22, no. 2 (1996).
Roudinesco, Élisabeth, 'The Mirror Stage: An Obliterated Archive', in J.-M. Rabaté (ed.),
    The Cambridge Companion to Lacan (Cambridge: Cambridge University Press,
    2003).
Roudinesco, Élisabeth, and Peter Schöttler, 'Lucien Febvre à la rencontre de Jacques
    Lacan, Paris 1937', *Genèses*, vol. 13, no. 13 (1993), pp. 139–50.
Sansare, K., Vikram Khanna, and Freny Karjodkar, 'Early Victims of X-rays: A Tribute and
    Current Perception', *Dentomaxillofac Radiol*, vol. 40, no. 2 (February 2011), pp. 123–5.
Savage, Gail, 'Erotic Stories and Public Decency', *The Historical Journal*, vol. 41, no. 2
    (1998), pp. 511–28.
Schultz, Karla L., 'Bataille's "L'Erotisme" in Light of Recent Love Poetry', *Pacific Coast
    Philology*, vol. 22, no. 1/2 (November, 1987).
Seltzer, Mark, 'Wound Culture: Trauma in the Pathological Public Sphere', *October*, vol.
    80 (spring 1997), pp. 3–26.

Shottenkirk, Dena, 'Fashion Fictions: Absence and the Fast Heartbeat', *ZG*, 'Breakdown Issue', 9, (1983), n.p.

Silverman, Kaja, 'Dis-Embodying the Female Voice', in Mary Ann Doane, Patricia Mellencamp and Linda Williams (eds.), *Re-Vision: Essays in Feminist Film Criticism* (Los Angeles: AFI, 1984), pp. 131–49.

Silverman, Kaja, 'Fragments of a Fashionable Discourse', in Tania Modleski (ed.), *Studies in Entertainment: Critical Approaches to Mass Culture* (1986), pp. 139–54.

Silverman, Kaja, 'Histoire d'O: The Story of a Disciplined and Punished Body', *Enclitic*, vol. 7, no. 2 (1983), pp. 63–81; also published in *Pleasure and Danger: Exploring Female Sexuality*, ed. Carol S. Vance (London: Routledge & Kegan Paul, I984), pp. 320–49.

Silverman, Kaja, 'Male Subjectivity and Masochism', *Camera Obscura*, no. 17 (1988), pp. 31–68.

Silverman, Kaja, 'Masochism and Subjectivity', *Framework*, no. 12 (1980), pp. 2–9.

Specter, Michael, 'Le freak, c'est chic', *Observer*, 30 November 2003.

Stewart, Mary Lynn, and Nancy Janovicek, 'Slimming the Female Body?: Re-evaluating Dress, Corsets, and Physical Culture in France, 1890s–1930s', *Fashion Theory*, vol. 5, no. 2 (2001), pp. 173–94.

Troy, Nancy, 'The Theatre of Fashion: Staging Haute Couture in Early 20th Century France', *The Theatre Journal*, vol. 53 (2001), pp. 1–32.

Books

Adamowicz, Elza, *Surrealist Collage in Text and Image: Dissecting the Exquisite Corpse* (Cambridge: Cambridge University Press, 2005).

Adams, Parveen, *The Emptiness of the Image: Psychoanalysis and Sexual Differences* (London: Routledge, 1996).

Adie, Kate, *Corsets to Camouflage: Women and War* (London: Hodder and Stoughton, 2003).

Aikman, Duncan, 'American Fascism', *Harpers Magazine*, New York, April 1925.

Alexander, Sally, *Becoming a Woman: And Other Essays in 19th and 20th Century Feminist History* (New York: New York University Press, 1995).

Allen, Frederick Lewis, *Since Yesterday: The 1930s in America* (New York: Harper and Row, 1986).

Allerfeldt, Kristofer, *Crime and the Rise of Modern America: A History from 1865–1941* (London and New York: Routledge, 2011).

Anderson, Margaret and Howard Taylor, *Sociology: Understanding a Diverse Society* (Belmont, CA: Thomson Wadsworth, 2006).

Andrews, Maggie and Mary M. Talbot (eds.), *All the World and Her Husband* (London and New York: Cassel, 2000).

Apollonio, Umbro (ed.), *Futurist Manifestos,* trans. Robert Brain et. al. (London: Tate, 2009).

Ariès, Philippe, *Images of Man and Death*, trans. Janet Lloyd (Cambridge, MA, and London: Harvard University Press, 1985).

Ariès, Philippe, *The Hour of Our Death*, trans. Helen Weaver, (London: Allen Lane, 1981).

Ariès, Philippe, *Western Attitudes to Death*, trans. Patricia M. Ranum, (Baltimore and London: Johns Hopkins University Press, 1974).

Armstrong, Timothy, Modernism, *Technology and the Body: A Cultural Study* (Cambridge and New York: Cambridge University Press, 1998).

Armstrong, Timothy, Modernism (ed.), *American Bodies: Cultural Histories of the Physique* (New York: New York University Press, 1996).

Arnold, Rebecca, *Fashion: A Very Short Introduction* (Oxford and New York: Oxford University Press, 2009).

Arnold, Rebecca, Fashion, *Desire and Anxiety: Image and Morality in the Twentieth Century* (London: I. B. Tauris, 2001).

Arnold, Rebecca, *The American Look: Fashion, Sportswear and the Image of Women in 1930s and 1940s America* (London: I.B. Tauris, 2009).

Atkins, Jacqueline M., *Wearing Propaganda: Textiles on the Home Front in Japan, Britain, and the United States, 1931–45* (New Haven and London: Yale University Press, 2005).

Auping, Michael (ed.), *Modern Art Museum of Fort Worth: 110* (London: Third Millennium Information Ltd).

Badger, Anthony J., *The New Deal: The Depression Years, 1933–40* (New York: Hill and Wang, 1993).

Bailly, Lionel, *Lacan* (Oxford: Oneworld, 2009).

Baldick, Chris, *Literature of the 1920s: Writers among the Ruins: Volume 3* (Edinburgh: Edinburgh University Press, 2012).

Bancroft, Alison, *Fashion and Psychoanalysis: Styling the Self* (London and New York: I. B. Tauris, 2012).

Banner, Lois, *American Beauty: A Social History through Two Centuries of the American Idea, Ideal, and Image of the Beautiful Woman* (New York: Alfred A. Knopf, 1983).

Banta, Martha, *Imaging American Women: Ideas and Ideals in Cultural History* (New York: Columbia University Press, 1987).

Barnard, Suzanne and Bruce Fink (eds.), *Reading Seminar XX: Lacan's Major Work on Love, Knowledge, and Feminine Sexuality* (Albany, NY: State University of New York Press, 2002).

Barnett, Homer Garner, *Innovation, The Basis of Cultural Change* (New York: McGraw-Hill, 1953).

Barrett, Henry and Majorie Annie Carpenter, *Colour: A Manual of Its Theory and Practice* (New York: B. T. Batsford Ltd., 1932).

Barthel, Diane, *Putting on Appearances: Gender and Advertising* (Philadelphia: Temple University Press, 1988).

Baskerville, Stephen W. and Ralph Willett (eds.), *Nothing Else to Fear: New Perspectives on America in the Thirties* (Dekalb: Northern Illinois University Press, 1988).

Batson, Charles R., *Dance, Desire and Anxiety in Early Twentieth-century French Theater: Playing Identities* (Aldershot: Ashgate, 2005).

Bauman, John F. and Thomas H. Coode, *In the Eye of the Depression: New Deal Reporters and the Agony of the American People* (Dekalb: Northern Illinois Press, 1992).

Beauman, Nicola, *A Very Great Profession: The Women's Novel, 1914–39* (London: Virago, 1989).

Beck, Ulrich, *Risk Society: Towards a New Modernity*, trans. Mark Ritter (London and Newbury Park, New Delhi: Sage, 1992).

Beckett, Ian Frederick William, *The Great War, 1914–1918* (London: Longman, 2001).

Beeler, Karin, *Tattoos, Desire and Violence: Marks of Resistance in Literature, Film and Television* (Jefferson, NC; London: McFarland, 2006).

Beizer, Janet L., *Ventriloquised Bodies: Narratives of Hysteria in Nineteenth Century France* (Ithaca, NY, and London: Cornell University Press, 1994).

Bendiner, Aaron, Daniel and Robert (eds.), *The Strenuous Decade: A Social and Intellectual Record of the 1930s* (Garden City, New York: Anchor Books, Doubleday and Co., 1970).

Benstock, Shari and Suzanne Ferriss (eds.), *On Fashion* (New Brunswick, New Jersey: Rutgers University Press, 1994).

Bentley, Eric (ed.), *The Theory of the Modern Stage* (London: Penguin Modern Classics, 1968).

Berman, Marshall, *All That Is Solid Melts into Air: The Experience of Modernity* (London: Verso, 1983).

Berry, Mary, *Screen Style: Fashion and Femininity in 1930s Hollywood* (Minneapolis and London: University of Minnesota Press, 2000).

Bland, Lucy, *Modern Women on Trial: Sexual Transgression in the Age of the Flapper* (Manchester: Manchester University Press, 2013).

Blau, Herbert, *Nothing in Itself: Complexions of Fashion* (Bloomington and Indianapolis: Indiana University Press, 1999).

Blum, Dilys E., *Shocking!: The Art and Fashion of Elsa Schiaparelli*, exh. cat. (Philadelphia: Philadelphia Museum of Art, September 2003–January 2004).

Bocock, Robert and Kenneth Thompson (eds.), *Social and Cultural Forms of Modernity* (Oxford and Cambridge: Polity Press in Association with Open University, 1992).

Bolt, Christine, *Feminist Ferment: The Women Question in the USA and England, 1870–1940* (London: University College London Press, 1995).

Bordo, Susan R., 'The Body and the Reproduction of Femininity: A Feminist Appropriation of Foucault', in Alison M. Jaggar and Susan R. Bordo (eds.), *Gender/Body/Knowledge: Feminist Reconstructions of Being and Knowing* (New Jersey: Rutgers University Press, 1989).

Bordo, Susan R., *Unbearable Weight: Feminism, Western Culture, and the Body* (Berkeley and London: University of California Press, 1993).

Bourke, Joanna, *Dismembering the Male: Men's Bodies, Britain, and the Great War* (Chicago: University of Chicago Press, 1996).

Bourke, Joanna, *Fear: A Cultural History* (2005).

Bourke, Joanna, *Rape: A History from 1860s to the Present* (2007).

Bowie, Malcolm, *Lacan* (Cambridge, MA, and London: Harvard University Press, 1991).

Bracher, Mark, *Lacan, Discourse, and Social Change: A Psychoanalytic Cultural Criticism* (Ithaca, NY, and London: Cornell University Press, 1993).

Bracher, Mark, *Lacanian Theory of Discourse: Subject, Structure, and Society* (New York and London: New York University Press, 1994).

Bradley, Fiona, *Surrealism* (London: Tate, 2005).

Bramlett, Frank, Roy Cook and Aaron Meskin (eds.), *The Routledge Companion to Comics* (New York: Routledge, 2017).

Braybon, Gail and Penny Summerfield, *Out of the Cage: Women's Experiences of the Two World Wars* (London: Pandora, 1987).

Brennan, Teresa, *Between Feminism and Psychoanalysis* (London and New York: Routledge, 1989).

Breward, Christopher and Caroline Evans, *Fashion* (Oxford and New York: Oxford University Press, 2003).

Breward, Christopher and Caroline Evans, *The Culture of Fashion: A New History of Fashionable Dress* (Manchester: Manchester University Press, 1995).

Breward, Christopher and Caroline Evans, *The Hidden Consumer: Masculinities, Fashion and City Life 1860–1914* (Manchester: Manchester University Press, 1999).

Breward, Christopher and Caroline Evans (eds.), *Fashion and Modernity* (Oxford and New York: Berg, 2005).

Bridge, Gary and Sophie Watson (eds.), *The Blackwell City Reader* (Oxford and Malden, MA: Wiley-Blackwell, 2002).

Briganti, Chiara and Kathy Mezei, *Domestic Modernism, the Interwar Novel, and E. H. Young* (Hampshire: Ashgate Publishing Company, 2006).

Broby-Johanson, Rudolf, *Body and Clothes: An Illustrated History of Costume* (New York: Reinhold Book Corporation, 1968).

Bronfen, Elisabeth, *Over Her Dead Body: Death, Femininity and the Aesthetic* (Manchester: Manchester University Press, 1992).

Bronfen, Elisabeth, *The Knotted Subject: Hysteria and Its Discontents* (Princeton, NJ, and Chichester: Princeton University Press, 1998).

Brooks, Peter and Alex Woloch (eds.), *Whose Freud? The Place of Psychoanalysis in Contemporary Culture* (New Haven: Yale University Press, 2000).

Brown, Judith, *Glamour in Six Dimensions: Modernism and the Radiance of Form* (New York: Cornell University Press, 2009).

Bruzzi, Stella, *Undressing Cinema, Clothing and Identity in the Movies* (London: Routledge, 1997).

Bryant Charles, Salome, 1923.

Buci-Glucksmann, Christine, *Baroque Reason: The Aesthetics of Modernity*, trans. Patrick Camiller, with an intro. by Bryan S. Turner (London and Thousand Oaks, New Delhi: Sage, 1994).

Buckley, Cheryl and Hilary Fawcett, *Fashioning the Feminine: Representation and Women's Fashion from the Fin de Siècle to the Present* (London: I.B. Tauris, 2002).

Buck-Morss, Susan, *The Dialectics of Seeing, Walter Benjamin and the Arcades Project* (Cambridge, MA: MIT Press, 1997).

Burckhardt, Jacqueline and Bice Curiger, *Meret Oppenheim: Beyond the Teacup* (New York: Independent Curators International, 1997).

Burman, Baines, Barbara, *Fashion Revivals: From the Elizabethan Age to the Present Day* (London: Batsford, 1981).

Burnham, Oliver, Valerie, *Fashion and Costume in American Popular Culture: A Reference Guide*, *Volume 45*. (CT: Greenwood Publishing Group, 1996).

Burris-Meyer, Elizabeth, *Color and Design in the Decorative Arts* (New Jersey: Prentice Hall, 1935), p. 159.

Butler, Judith, *Bodies That Matter: On the Discursive Limits of 'Sex'* (London and New York: Routledge, 1993).

Butler, Judith, *Gender Trouble: Feminism and the Subversion of Identity* (New York and London: Routledge, 1990).

Butler, Judith, *Precarious Life: The Power of Mourning and Violence* (London: Verso, 2004).

Butsch, Richard, 'American Movie Audiences of the 1930s', *International Labor and Working-Class History*, 'Workers and Film: As Subject and Audience' (Spring, 2001), pp. 106–120.

Cabanne, Pierre, *Dialogues with Marcel Duchamp*, trans. Ron Padgett (London: De Capo Press, 1971).

Calvocoressi, Richard, *Magritte* (London: Phaidon, 1994).

Campbell, Patrick and Adrian Kear, *Psychoanalysis and Performance* (London: Routledge, 2001).

Carle, Emmanuelle, 'Women, Anti-Fascism and Peace in Interwar France: Gabrielle Duchêne's Itinerary', *French History*, vol. 18, no. 3 (2004), pp. 291–314.

Carlyle, Thomas, *Sartor Resartus: The Life and Opinions of Herr Teufelsdröckh in Three Books* (London: Chapman and Hall, Limited, 1831).

Carter, Angela, *The Sadeian Woman: An Exercise in Cultural History* (London: Virago, 1979).

Cartwright, Duncan, *Psychoanalysis, Violence and Rage-Type Murder: Murdering Minds*, with a foreword by Peter Fonagy (Hove and New York: Brunner-Routledge, 2002).

Caruth, Cathy, *Trauma: Explorations in Memory* (Baltimore and London: Johns Hopkins University Press, 1995).

Casement, Ann, 'The Shadow', in Renos K. Papadopoulos (ed.), *The Handbook of Jungian Psychology* (Sussex and New York: Routledge, 2006), pp. 94–112.

Cassara, Beverley Beuner and Ethel Josephine Alpenfels (eds.), *American Women: The Changing Image* (Boston: Beacon, 1962).

Cassuto, Leonard (ed.), *The Cambridge History of the American Novel* (Cambridge: Cambridge University Press, 2011).

Castelbajac, Kate de, *The Face of the Century: One Hundred Years of Make Up and Style* (New York: Rizzoli, 1995).

Cavallro, Dani and Alexandra Warwick, *Fashioning the Frame: Boundaries, Dress and the Body* (Oxford: Berg, 1998).

Caws, Mary Ann, *Surrealism, Themes and Movements* (London: Phaidon, 2004).

Caws, Mary Ann, *The Surrealist Look: An Erotics of Encounter* (Cambridge, MA and London: The MIT Press, 1999).

Caws, Mary Ann et. al. (eds.), *Surrealism and Women* (Cambridge and London: MIT Press, 1993).

Celello, Kristin and Hanan Kholoussy (eds.), *Domestic Tensions, National Anxieties: Global Perspectives on Marriage Crisis* (Oxford: Oxford University Press, 2016).

Chadwick, Whitney, *Women Artists and the Surrealist Movement* (London: Thames & Hudson, 1992).

Chadwick, Whitney and Tirza True Latimer, *The Modern Woman Revisited: Paris between the Wars* (New Brunswick, NJ: Rutgers University Press, 2003).

Chafe, William H., *The American Woman: Her Changing Social, Economic and Political Roles, 1920–70* (New York: Oxford University Press, 1972).

Chafe, William H., *The Paradox of Change: American Women in the Twentieth Century* (New York: Oxford University Press, 1991).

Chambers, Iain, *Popular Culture: The Metropolitan Experience* (London: Routledge, 1982).

Charles-Roux, Edmonde, *Chanel and Her World*, trans. Daniel Wheeler (London: Weidenfeld & Nicolson, 1982).

Cheney, Liana De Girolami (ed.), *The Symbolism of Vanitas in the Arts, Literature and Music* (Lewiston, Queenston, Lampeter: Edwin Mellen Press, 1992).

Chickering, Roger and Stig Förster, *Great War, Total War, Combat and Mobilization on the Western Front, 1914–1918* (Cambridge: Cambridge University Press, 2006).

Chodorow, Nancy J., *Feminism and Psychoanalytic Theory* (New Haven, CT, and London: Yale University Press, 1989).

Cixous, Helene and Catherine Clement, *The Newly Born Woman*, trans. Betsy Wing (Manchester: Manchester University Press, 1986).

Claridge, Laura, *Emily Post: Daughter of the Gilded Age, Mistress of American Manners* (New York and London: Random House, 2008).

Clark, Anna, *Desire: A History of European Sexuality* (New York and London: Routledge, 2008).

Clark, Judith, *Spectres: When Fashion Turns Back* (London: V&A Publications, 2004).

Clark, T. J., *Farewell to an Idea: Episodes from a History of Modernism* (New Haven and London: Yale University Press, 1999).

Clark, T. J., *The Painting of Modern Life: Paris in the Art of Manet and His Followers* (London: Princeton University Press and Thames & Hudson, 1984).

Cohen, Arthur Allen, *Sonia Delaunay* (New York: H. N. Abrams, 1975).

Cohen, Margaret, *Profane Illumination: Walter Benjamin and the Paris of Surrealist Revolution* (Berkeley and London: University of California Press, 1993).

Coles, Alex and Alexia Defert (eds.), *The Anxiety of Interdisciplinarity* (London: BACKless Books and Black Dog, 1998).

Collard, A. with J. Contrucci, *Rape of the Wild, Man's Violence against Animals and the Earth* (London: The Women's Press, 1988).

Conley, Katharine, *Automatic Woman: The Representation of Woman in Surrealism* (Nebraska: University of Nebraska Press, 1996).

Conor, Liz, *The Spectacular Modern Woman: Feminine Visibility in the 1920s* (Bloomington: Indiana University Press, 2004).

Copjec, Joan, *Read My Desire: Lacan against the Historicists* (Cambridge, MA, and London: MIT Press, 1994).

Copsey, Nigel, 'Communists and the Inter-War Anti-Fascist Struggle in the United States and Britain', *Labour History Review* (Maney Publishing), vol. 76, no. 3 (December 2011).

Corbin, Alain, *The Foul and the Fragrant: Odor and the French Social Imagination* (Cambridge, MA: Harvard University Press, 1988).

Corbin, Alain, *Woman for Hire: Prostitution and Sexuality in France after 1850*, trans. Alan Sheridan (Cambridge, MA: Harvard University Press, 1990).

Cospey, Nigel and Andrzej Olechnowicz (eds.), *Varieties of Anti-Fascism: Britain in the Inter-War Period* (Basingstoke: Palgrave Macmillan, 2010).

Costello, John, *Love, Sex and War: Changing Values* (London: Harper Collins, 1985).

Cotton, Charlotte, *Imperfect Beauty: The Making of Contemporary Fashion Photographs* (London: Victoria & Albert Publications, 2000).

Crary, Jonathan, *Suspensions of Perception: Attention, Spectacle and Modern Culture* (Cambridge, MA and London: MIT Press, 2001).

Crary, Jonathan, *Techniques of the Observer: On Vision and Modernity in the Nineteenth Century* (Cambridge, MA and London: MIT Press, 1990).

Cross, Gary, *An All-Consuming Century: Why Commercialism Won in Modern America* (New York: Columbia University Press, 2000).

Cumming, Valerie and C.W. Cunnington, *The Dictionary of Fashion History* (London: Bloomsbury, 2010).

Cummins, Duane D. and William Gee White, *Contrasting Decades: The 1920s and 1930s* (Encino, CA: Glencoe Publishing Co. Inc., 1980).

Dali, Salvador, *The Secret Life of Salvador Dali*, trans. Haakon M. Chevalier (New York and London: Dial Press, 1961).

Darnton, Richard, *The Forbidden Best-Sellers of Pre-Revolutionary France* (New York: W.W. Norton & Co., 1995).

Dauton, Martin and Bernhard Rieger (eds.), *Meanings of Modernity: Britain from the Late-Victorian Era to World War I* (Oxford: Berg, 2001).

Davidson, Arnold Ira, *The Emergence of Sexuality: Historical Epistemology and the Formation of Concepts* (Cambridge, MA, and London: Harvard University Press, 2001).

Davis, Fred, *Fashion, Culture & Identity* (Chicago: Chicago University Press, 1994).

Davis, Mary E., *Classic Chic: Music, Fashion, and Modernism* (Berkeley, Los Angeles and London: University of California Press, 2006).

Dawson, Loleta I. and Marion Davis Huntting, *War Fiction and Personal Narratives* (Massachusetts: F. W. Faxon, 1921).

Dawson, William, *Colour* (London: The Baynard Press, 1929).

de Certeau, Michel, *The Practice of Everyday Life*, trans. Steven Rendall (Berkeley, Los Angeles, London: University of California Press, 2011).

De Grazia, Victoria and Ellen Furlough, *The Sex of Things: Gender and Consumption in Historical Perspective* (Berkeley and London: University of California Press, 1996).

De la Haye, Amy, *Chanel: Couturière at Work* (London: V&A Museum, 1997).

Dean, Carolyn J., *The Frail Social Body: Pornography, Homosexuality, and Other Fantasies in Interwar France (Studies on the History of Society and Culture)* (Berkeley and London: University of California Press, 2000).

Dean, Carolyn J., *The Self and Its Pleasures: Bataille, Lacan and the History of the Decentered Subject* (Ithaca and London: Cornell University Press, 1992).

Dean, Tim, *Beyond Sexuality* (Chicago and London: University of Chicago Press, 2000).

Delarue-Mardrus, Lucie, *Une Femme Mûre et l'Amour* (Paris: Ferenczi, 1935).

D'Harnoncourt, Anne and Kynaston McShine (eds.), *Marcel Duchamp* (New York: Museum of Modern Art, 1973).

Diamond, Elin (ed.), *Performance and Cultural Politics* (Oxford: Routledge, 1996).

Didi-Huberman, Georges, *Invention of Hysteria: Charcot and the Photographic Iconography of the Salpêtrière*, trans. Alisa Hartz (Cambridge, MA, and London: MIT Press, 2003).

Diedrich, Maria and Dorothea Fischer-Homung (eds.), *Women and War: The Changing Status of American Women from the 1930s to the 1950s* (New York and London: Berg, 1990).

Dijksra, Bram, *Idols of Perversity: Fantasies of Feminine Evil in Fin-de-Siecle Culture* (Oxford & New York: Oxford University Press, 1986).

Dingwall, Eric John, *The American Woman, a Historical Study* (London: Gerald Duckworth, 1956).

Doane, Mary Ann, *Femmes Fatales. Feminism, Film Theory, Psychoanalysis* (New York and London: Routledge, 1991).

Doane, Mary Ann, *The Desire to Desire: The Woman's Film of the 1940s* (Bloomington, IN: Indiana University Press, 1987).

Dodd, Nigel, *Social Theory and Modernity* (Cambridge: Polity Press, 1999).

Dollimore, Jonathan, *Death, Desire and Loss in Western Culture*, ed. Allen Lane (London: Penguin, 1998).

Dollimore, Jonathan, *Sexual Dissidence: Augustine to Wilde, Freud to Foucault* (Oxford: Clarendon Press, 1991).

Doherty, Thomas Patrick, *Pre Code Hollywood: Sex, Immorality and Insurrection in American Cinema, 1930–4* (New York: Columbia University Press, 2013).

Donald, James, *Imagining the Modern City* (London: The Athlone Press, 1999).

Dos Passos, John, *Manhattan Transfer* (Boston: Houghton Mifflin, 1925).

Douglas, Mary, *Purity and Danger: An Analysis of the Concepts of Pollution and Taboo* (London and New York: Routledge, 1992).

Douglas, Norman, *South Wind* (South Dakota: NuVision Publications, 1925).

Drowne, Kathleen Morgan and Patrick Huber, *The 1920's* (Westport, CT: Greenwood Publishing Group, 2004).

Dunant, Sarah and Roy Porter (eds.), *The Age of Anxiety* (London: Virago, 1996).

Duval, Pierre, *War Wounds of the Lung: Notes on Their Surgical Treatment at the Front* (Bristol, 1918).

E. Playne, Caroline, *Britain Holds on 1917, 1918* (London: Allen and Unwin, 1933), pp. 76–7.

Eagleton, Terry, *Sweet Violence: The Idea of the Tragic* (Oxford: Basil Blackwell, 2002).

Easthope, Antony and Kate McGowan, *A Critical and Cultural Theory Reader*, 2nd edn. (Toronto: University of Toronto Press, 2004).

Eburne, Jonathan P., *Surrealism and the Art of Crime* (Ithaca New York: Cornell University Press, 2008).

Eckert, Charles, 'The Carole Lombard in Macy's Window', in Christine Gledhill (ed.), *Stardom: Industry of Desire* (London: Routledge, 1991), p. 109.

Eksteins, Modris, *Rites of Spring: The Great War and the Birth of Modern Age* (New York, 1989).

Ellis, Albert, *The American Sexual Tragedy* (New York: Twayne, 1954).

Ellis, Edward Robb, *A Nation in Torment: The Great Depression, 1929–39* (New York, Tokyo and London: Kodansha International, 1995).

Ellman, Richard, *James Joyce* (Oxford: Oxford University Press, 1982).

Erenberg, Lewis A, *Steppin' Out: New York Nightlife and the Transformations of American Culture, 1890–1930* (Chicago: Chicago University Press, 1984).

Evans, Caroline and Christopher Breward (eds.), *Fashion and Modernity* (Oxford: Berg, 2005).

Evans, Caroline, *Fashion at the Edge: Spectacle, Modernity & Deathliness* (New Haven, CT, and London: Yale University Press, 2003).

Evans, Caroline and Minna Thornton, *Women and Fashion: A New Look* (London: Quartet, 1989).

Evans, M., *The Morality Gap* (Ohio: Alba Books, 1976).

Ewen, Stuart and Elizabeth, *Channels of Desire: Mass Images and the Shaping of American Consciousness* (New York: McGraw Hill Book Company, 1982).

Ewen, Stuart and Elizabeth, *Channels of Desire: Mass Images and the Shaping of America* (Minneapolis: University of Minnesota Press, 1992).

Ewing, William A., *Blumenfeld: A Fetish for Beauty* (London: Barbican Art Gallery and Thames & Hudson, 1996).

Faludi, S., Backlash, *The Undeclared War against Women* (London: Vintage, 1992).

Farrell, Kirkby, *Post-traumatic Culture: Imagery and Interpretation in the 1990s* (Baltimore: Johns Hopkins University Press, 1998).

Featherstone, Mike, Mike Hepworth and Bryan S. Turner (eds.), *The Body as Social Process and Cultural Theory* (London, Newbury Park and New Dehli: Sage, 1991).

Feher, M., R. Naddaff and N. Tazi (eds.), *Fragments for a History of the Human Body* [all vols.] (New York: Zone, 1989).

Felman, Shoshana (ed.), *Literature and Psychoanalysis. The Question of Reading: Otherwise* (Baltimore, MD, and London: Johns Hopkins University Press, 1982).

Ferenczi, Sándor, Karl Abraham, Ernst Simmel and Ernest Jones, *Psychoanalysis & War Neuroses* (London, Vienna and New York: The International Psycho-Analytical Press, 1921).

Fischer, Lucy, *Designing Women: Cinema, Art Deco, and the Female Form* (New York: Columbia University Press, 2003).

Fischer, Lucy, *Designing Women: Cinema, Art Deco, and the Female Form* (New York: Columbia University Press, 2013).

Fitzgerald, F. Scott, *The Great Gatsby* (Cambridge: Cambridge University Press, 1999).

Flanagan, John Clemans, *Factor Analysis in the Study of Personality* (Stanford: Stanford University Press, 1935).

Hal Foster, Rosalind Krauss, Yve-Alain Bois, Benjamin H. D. Buchloh and David Joselit, *Art since 1900* (London: Thames & Hudson, 2004).

Foster, Hal, *Compulsive Beauty* (Cambridge, MA: MIT Press, 1995).

Foster, Hal, *Prosthetic Gods* (Cambridge, MA: The MIT Press, 2004).

Foster, Hal, *The Return of the Real: The Avant-Garde at the End of the Century* (Cambridge, MA, and London: MIT Press, 1996).

Fotiade, Ramona, *Andre Breton, the Power of Language* (Wilmington: Intellect Books, 2000).

Foucault, Michel, *The Birth of the Clinic* (London: Routledge, 2003).

Fraser, John, *Violence in the Arts* (Cambridge: Cambridge University Press, 1974).

Freidman, Susan Stanford, *Psyche Reborn: The Emergence of H. D. Bloomington* (Indiana: Indiana University Press, 1981).

French, Karl (ed.), *Screen Violence* (London: Bloomsbury, 1996).

Friedan, Betty, *The Feminine Mystique* (London: Penguin, 1983).

Furedi, Frank, *Culture of Fear: Risk-Taking and the Morality of Low Expectation* (London: Cassell, 1997).

Fussell, Paul, *The Great War and Modern Memory* (London, 1975).

Gage, John, *Colour and Culture: Practice and Meaning from Antiquity to Abstraction* (California: University of California Press, 1999).

Gale, Matthew, *Dada and Surrealism* (London/New York, 2006).

Gamman, Lorraine and Merja Makinen, *Female Fetishism: A New Look* (London: Lawrence & Wishart, 1994).

Gane, Mike, *Baudrillard's Bestiary, Baudrillard and Culture* (London: Routledge, 1991).

Garb, Tamar, *Bodies of Modernity: Figure and Flesh in Fin-de-Siecle France* (London: Thames & Hudson, 1998).

Garb, Tamar, *The Painted Face: Portraits of Women in France, 1814–1914* (New Haven, CT; London: Yale University Press, 2007).

Garber, Marjorie, *Vested Interests: Cross-Dressing and Cultural Anxiety* (London: Penguin, 1993).

Garland, Madge, *The Indecisive Decade: The World of Fashion and Entertainment in the Thirties* (London: MacDonald, 1968).

Gay, Jules, *Bibliographie des ouvrages relatifs à l'amour, aux femmes au marriage*, IV table (Geneva: Slatkine Reprints).

Gertzman, Jay A., *Bookleggers and Smuthounds: The Trade in Erotica: 1920–1940* (Pennsylvania: University of Pennsylvania Press, 2001).

Giddens, Anthony, *Modernity and Self Identity: Self and Society in the Late Modern Age* (Cambridge: Polity Press, 1991).

Gilbert, Guilleminault, *Less Années folles* (Paris: editions Denöel, 1958).

Gilden, Charles T., *The Human Face: A Symposium* (Philadelphia: Philadelphia County Medical Society, 1935).

Giles, Judy, *Women, Identity and Private Life in Britain, 1900–50* (London: Palgrave Macmillan, 1995).

Gilman, Sander L., *Hysteria beyond Freud* (Berkeley, Los Angeles and London: University of California Press, 1993).

Gilman, Sander L., *Making the Body Beautiful: A Cultural History of Aesthetic Surgery* (Princeton and Oxford: Princeton University Press, 1999).

Girard, R., *Violence and the Sacred* (Baltimore, MD: Johns Hopkins University Press, 1981).

Gledhill, Christine (ed.), *Home Is Where the Heart Is: Studies in Melodrama and the Woman's Film* (London: BFI Publishing, 1987).

Gledhill, Christine, *Reframing British Cinema, 1918–1928: Between Restraint and Passion* (London: Palgrave, 2003), p. 132.

Gluck, Sherna Berger (ed.), *Rosie the Riveter Revisited: Women, the War and Social Change* (Longbeach, CA: School of Social and Behavioral Sciences, Oral History Resource Center, California State University, 1987).

Goethe, Johann Wolfgang von, *Conversations with Goethe* (London: J. M. Dent & Sons, Limited, 1935).

Golan, Romy, *Modernity and Nostalgia: Art and Politics in France between the Wars* (New Haven and London: Yale University Press, 1995).

Goodman, Paul and Frank O. Gatell, *America in the Twenties: The Beginnings of Contemporary America* (New York, London and Sydney: Holt, Rinehartand Winston, 1972).

Graham, Martha, *Blood Memory* (New York: Doubleday, 1992).

Gray, Colonel H. M. W., *The Early Treatment of War Wounds* (Oxford University Press, 1919).

Grayzel, Susan R., *Women and the First World War* (London: Longman, 2002).

Grazia, Victoria de and Ellen Furlough (eds.), *The Sex of Things: Gender and Consumption in Historical Perspective* (Berkeley, Los Angeles and London: University of California Press, 1996).

Green, Christopher, *Art in France: 1900–1940* (New Haven, CT; London: Yale University Press, 2000).

Green, Jonathon and Nicholas J. Karolides (eds.), *Enyclopedia of Censorship* (New York: Facts On File, 2005).

Grey, Zane, *The Call of the Canyon* (Maryland: Phoenix Rider, Arc Manor, 2008 [1923]).

Gronberg, Tag, *Designs on Modernity: Exhibiting the City in 1920s Paris* (Manchester and New York: Manchester University Press, 1998).

Gundle, Stephen, *Glamour: A History* (Oxford and New York: Oxford University Press, 2008).

Haiken, Beth, *Venus Envy* (Baltimore, MA: John Hopkins University Press, 1997).

Haine, W. Scott, *Culture and Customs of France* (Westport, CT: Greenwood, 2006).

Hall, Carolyn, *The Twenties in Vogue* (London: Octopus books, 1983).

Hall, Lesley A., *Sex, Gender and Social Change in Britain since 1880* (Basingstoke: Macmillan, 2000).

Hall Stuart and Tony Jefferson (eds.), *Resistance through Rituals, Youth Subcultures in Post-War Britain* (London: Routledge, 1996).

Hall, Stuart, 'Notes on Deconstructing the Popular', in Raphael Samuel (ed.) *People's History and Socialist Theory* (London: Routledge, 1981), pp. 227–240.

Hall, Stuart and Bram Gieben (eds.), *Formations of Modernity* (Cambridge and Oxford: Polity Press in association with the Open University, 1993).

Hall-Duncan, Nancy, *The History of Fashion Photography* (New York: Alpine Book Company, 1979).

Hansen, Miriam, *Babel and Babylon: Spectatorship in American Silent Film* (Cambridge, MA: Harvard University Press, 1991).

Haskell, Molly, *From Reverence to Rape: The Treatment of Women in the Movies* (University of Chicago Press, 1987).

Havelock, Ellis, *Studies in the Psychology of Sex: Vol. 5, Erotic Symbolism* (Philadelphia: F. A. Davis, 1927).

Haye, Amy de la and Elizabeth Wilson (eds.), *Defining Dress: Dress as Object, Meaning and Identity* (Manchester and New York: Manchester University Press, 1999).

Hebdige, Dick, *Subculture: The Meaning of Style* (London: Routledge, 1988 [1979]).

Heyer, Georgette, 'The Historical Romance and the Consumption of the Erotic', in Maggie Andrews and Mary M. Talbot (eds.), *All the World and Her Husband* (London and New York: Cassel, 2000).

Higonnet, Margaret Randolph, *Behind the Lines: Gender and the Two World Wars* (New Haven: Yale University Press, 1987).

Hitschmann, Dr. Eduard, *Freud's Theories of the Neuroses* (New York: New York Psychiatrical Society, 1913).

Hobsbawm, Eric, *Age of Extremes: The Short Twentieth Century 1914–1991* (London: Michael Joseph, 1994).

Hollander, Anne, *Feeding the Eye: Essays* (Berkeley, Los Angeles and London: University of California Press, 1999).

Hollander, Anne, *Seeing through Clothes* (Berkeley: University of California Press, 1993).

Hollander, Anne, *Sex and Suits: The Eroticism of Modern Dress* (New York: Kodansha, 1994).

Holt, Henry, *The Sinister Shadow* (New York: Caxton House, 1934).

Homey, Karen, *Feminine Psychology* (London: Routledge and Kegan Paul, 1967).

Hoobler, Dorothy and Thomas, *Vanity Rules: A History of American Fashion and Beauty* (Brookfield: Millbrook Press, 2000).

Horsley, Lee, *The Noir Thriller* (Palgrave, 2001).

Howes, David, 'Introduction' in Howes (ed.), *Empire of the Senses* (London: Bloomsbury, 2005).

Howlett, Jana and Rod Mengham, *The Violent Muse: Violence and Artistic Imagination in Europe 1910–39* (Manchester; New York: Manchester University Press Distributed exclusively in the USA and Canada by St. Martin's Press, 1994).

Howlett, Jana and Rod Mengham (eds.), *The Violent Muse: Violence and the Artistic Imagination in Europe, 1910–1939* (Manchester and New York: Manchester University Press, 1994).

Hoy, Suellen, *Chasing Dirt: The American Pursuit of Cleanliness* (New York and Oxford: Oxford University Press, 1995).

Huberman, Leo, *Man's Worldly Goods* (New York: New York University Press, 1936).

Humphreys, Nancy K., *American Women's Magazines: An Annotated Historical Guide* (New York: Garland, 1989).

Huyssen, Andreas, *After the Great Divide: Modernism, Mass Culture, Postmodernism* (Bloomington: Indiana University Press, 1986).

Huyssen, Andreas, *After the Great Divide: Modernism, Mass Culture and Postmodernism* (London: Macmillan, 1986).

Irigaray, Luce, *Speculum of the Other Woman*, trans. Gillian C. Gill (Ithaca, NY: Cornell University Press, 1985).

Jay, Martin, *Downcast Eyes: The Denigration of Vision in Twentieth-Century French Thought* (Berkeley: University of California Press, 1993).

Jelenski, Constantin, *Les Dessins de Hans Bellmer* (Paris: Denoel, 1966).

Jenson, Deborah, *Trauma and Its Representations: The Social Life of Mimesis in Post-Revolutionary France* (Maryland: The John Hopkins University Press, 2001).

Jiminez, Jill Berk (ed.), *Dictionary of Artists' Models* (London and Chicago: Fitzroy Dearborn Publishers, 2001).

Jones, Amelia, *Body Art/Performing the Subject* (Minneapolis and London: University of Minnesota Press, 1998).

Joyce, James, *The Little Review: Ulysses* (New Haven and London: Yale University Press, 2015).

Jupp, Peter C. and Tony Walter, 'The Healthy Society: 1918–98', in Peter C. Jupp and Clare Gittings (eds.), *Death in England: An Illustrated History* (Manchester: Manchester University Press, 1999).

Kachur, Lewis, *Displaying the Marvelous: Marcel Duchamp, Salvador Dali, and Surrealist Exhibition Installations* (MIT Press, 2003).

Kammen, Michael, *American Culture, American Tastes: Social Change and the Twentieth Century* (New York: Basic Books. 1999).

Kammeyer, Kenneth C. W., *A Hypersexual Society: Sexual Discourse, Erotica and Pornography in America Today* (New York: Palgrave Macmillan, 2008).

Kanin, Ruth, *The Manufacture of Beauty* (Boston: Brandon Publishing, 1990).

Kanta, Kochhar-Lindgren, Davis Schneiderman and Tom Denlinger, *The Exquisite Corpse: Chance and Collaboration in Surrealism's Parlor Game* (Lincoln: University of Nebraska Press, 2009).

Kaplan, Ann E., *Women and Film. Both Sides of the Camera* (London and New York: Methuen, 1983).

Kaplan, Louise J., *Female Perversions: The Temptations of Madame Bovary* (London: Pandora, 1991).

Kearney, Patrick J., *A History of Erotic Literature* (London: Parragon, 1982).

Keller, E., *Reflections on Gender and Science* (New Haven and London: Yale University Press, 1985).

Kember, Sarah, *Virtual Anxiety: Photography, New Technologies and Subjectivity* (Manchester University Press, 1998).

Kennedy, David M., *The American People in the Great Depression: Freedom from Fear* (Oxford and New York: Oxford University Press, 1999).

Kern, Stephen, *The Culture of Time and Space: 1880–1918* (Cambridge, MA: Harvard University Press, 1983).

Kidwell, Claudia Brush and Valerie Steele (eds.), *Men and Women: Dressing the Part* (Washington: Smithsonian Institution Press, 1989).

King, Laura, *Family Men: Fatherhood and Masculinity in Britain, 1914–1960* (Oxford: Oxford University Press, 2015).

Kirkham, Pat, ed., *Women Designers in the USA, 1900–2000* (New York: BCG and Yale, 2001).

Klüver, Billy and Julie Martin, *Kiki's Paris: Artists and Lovers 1900-30* (New York, 1989).

Knopf, Christina M., *The Comic Art of War: A Critical Study of Military Cartoons, 1805–2014* (North Carolina: McFarland, 2015).

Koda, Harold, *Extreme Beauty: The Body Transformed* (New Haven and London: Yale University Press, 2002).

Koda, Harold and Andrew Bolton (eds.), *Chanel*, exh. cat. (New York: Metropolitan Museum of Art, 2005).

Koureas, Gabriel, *Memory, Masculinity and National Identity in British Culture, 1914–1930: A Study of 'Unconquerable Manhood'* (Hampshire and Burlington, VT: Ashgate, 2007).

Krauss, Rosalind E., *The Optical Unconscious* (Cambridge, MA: MIT Press, 1993).

Krauss, Rosalind E., *The Originality of the Avant-Garde and Other Modernist Myths* (Cambridge, MA, and London: MIT Press, 1985).

Krauss, Rosalind E., 'Uncanny', in Yve-Alain Bois and Rosalind Krauss (eds.), *Formless: A User's Guide* (New York: Zone Books, 1997).

Krauss, Rosalind E. and Jane Livingston (eds.), *L'Amour Fou, Photography and Surrealism* (Corcoran Gallery of Art, 1985), pp. 15–56.

Krauss, Rosalind E., Jane Livingston and Dawn Ades, *L'amour Fou: Photography and Surrealism* (Washington, DC: Corcoran Gallery of Art and New York: Abbeville Press, 1985).

Kristeva, Julia, *Powers of Horror: An Essay on Abjection*, trans. Leon S. Roudiez (New York: Columbia University Press, 1982).

Kuhn, Annette, *The Power of Images: Essays on Representation and Sexuality* (New York and London: Routledge, 1985).

Kunzle, David, *Fashion and Fetishism: Corsets, Tight-Lacing and Other Forms of Body-Sculpture* (Stroud: Sutton, 2004).

Kyvig, David E., *Daily Life in the United States, 1920–1940: How Americans Lived through the 'Roaring Twenties' and the Great Depression* (Chicago: Ivarvan R. Dee, 2004).

Ladd-Franklin, Christine, *Colour and Colour Theories* (New York: American Psychological Association, 1932).

Lant, Antonia, *Blackout: Reinventing Women for Wartime British Cinema* (Princeton, NJ: Princeton University Press, 1991).

Lash, Scott and Jonathan Friedman (eds.), *Modernity and Identity* (Oxford: Basil Blackwell, 1992).

Latham, Anglea J., *Posing a Threat: Flappers, Chorus Girls, and Other Brazen Performers of the American 1920s* (Hanover, New Hampshire and London: Wesleyan University Press, 2000).

Leed, Eric J., *No Man's Land: Combat and Identity in World War I* (Cambridge, 1979).

Leslie, Esther, *Walter Benjamin: Overpowering Conformism* (London and Sterling, VA: Pluto Press, 2000).

Levy, Thomas (ed.), *From Breakfast in Fur and Back Again* (Hamburg: Levy Galerie, 2003).

Lichtenstein, Therese, *Behind Closed Doors: The Art of Hans Bellmer* (California: University of California Press, 2001).

Lidz, C. W. and A. Walker, *Heroin, Deviance and Morality* (London: Sage, 1980).

Light, Alison, *Forever England: Femininity, Literature and Conservatism between the Wars* (London and New York: Routledge, 1991).

Linker, Beth, *War's Waste: Rehabilitation in World War I* (Chicago: University of Chicago Press, 2011).

Lipovetsky, Gilles, *The Empire of Fashion, Dressing Modern Democracy* (Princeton, NJ: Princeton University Press, 1994).

Lomas, David, *The Haunted Self: Surrealism, Psychoanalysis, Subjectivity* (New Haven and London: Yale University Press, 2000).

Lovibond, Joseph W., *Light and Colour Theories* (London and New York: E. & F. N. Spon, 1921).

Low, Barbara, *Psycho-Analysis: A Brief Account of the Freudian Theory* (New York: Harcourt, Brace and Company, 1920).

Lucic, Karen, *Charles Sheeler and the Cult of the Machine* (Cambridge, MA: Harvard University Press, 1991).

Lupton, Ellen, *Mechanical Brides: Women and Machines from Home to Office* (New York: Cooper Hewitt National Museum of Design, Smithsonian Institution and Princeton Architectural Press, 1993).

Lurie, Alison, *The Language of Clothes* (London: Heinemann, 1981).

Lusty, Natalya, *Surrealism, Feminism, Psychoanalysis* (Hampshire and Burlington, VT: Ashgate, 2007).

Lyford, Amy, *Surrealist Masculinities: Gender Anxiety and the Aesthetics of Post-World War I Reconstruction in France* (California: University of California Press, 2007).

Mackrell, Alice, *Art and Fashion: The Impact of Art on Fashion and Fashion on Art* (London: Batsford, 2005).

Madden, David, *Tough Guy Writers of the Thirties* (Carbondale: Southern Illinois University Press, 1968).

Madsen, Axel, *Chanel: A Woman of Her Own* (New York: Henry Holt & Company Inc, 1991).

Mahon, Alyce, *Surrealism and the Politics of Eros, 1938–1968* (London: Thames & Hudson, 2005).

Malt, Johanna, *Obscure Objects of Desire: Surrealism, Fetishism, and Politics* (Chicago: The University of Chicago Press, 2005).

Marcoci, Roxana and Geoffrey Batchen, *The Original Copy: Photography of Sculpture, 1839 to Today* (New York: Museum of Modern Art, 2010).

Marshall, P. J. (ed.), *The Cambridge History of the British Empire* (Cambridge: Cambridge University Press, 1996).

Martin, Richard, *Fashion and Surrealism* (New York: Rizzoli, 1987).

Mary, Alden, Hopkins, 'Do Women Dress for Men?' *Delineator*, vol. 98 (July 1921), p. 3.

Matthews, G. and S. Goodman (eds.), *Violence and the Limits of Representation* (London: Palgrave Macmillan, 2013).

Matthews, John Herbert, *The Imagery of Surrealism* (Syracuse, New York: Syracuse University Press, 1977).

McLaren, Angus, *Twentieth Century Sexuality: A History* (Oxford: Blackwell, 1999).

McQuaid, Matilda and Susan Brown (eds.), *Color Moves: Art & Fashion by Sonia Delaunay* (New York: Cooper Hewitt, Smithsonian Design Museum, 2011).

McQuire, Scott, *Visions of Modernity: Representation, Memory, Time and Space in the Age of the Camera* (London, Thousand Oaks and New Delhi: Sage, 1998).

Mehring, Christine, *Wols Photographs*, exh. cat. (Cambridge, MA: Busch-Reisinger Museum, 1999).

Mendes, Valerie D., *Black in Fashion* (London: V&A Publications, 1999).

Merck, Mandy, *Perversions* (London: Virago, 1993).

Merck, Mandy (ed.), *The Sexual Subject: A Screen Reader in Sexuality* (London: Routledge, 1992).

Merleau-Ponty, Maurice, *Phenemology of Perception* (Oxford: Taylor & Francis, Psychology Press, 2002).

Metz, Christian, *Psychoanalysis and Cinema: The Imaginary Signifier, Language, Discourse, Society Series* (London: Macmillan, 1982).

Meyerstein, E. H. W., 'Landscape in English Art and Poetry', *Saturday Review of Politics, Literature, Science and Art* (23rd May 1931), p. 764; *Country Life* (11th July 1936).

Micale, Mark S., *Approaching Hysteria: Disease and Its Interpretations* (Princeton, NJ: Princeton University Press, 1995).

Micale, Mark S., *Hysterical Men: The Hidden History of Male Nervous Illness* (Harvard, CT: Harvard University Press, 2008).

Michelle Tolini, Finamore, *Hollywood before Glamour: Fashion in American Silent Film* (London: Palgrave Macmillan, 2013), p. 22.

Miller, Tyrus, *Late Modernism: Politics, Fiction and the Arts between the World Wars* (Berkeley, Los Angeles and London: University of California Press, 1999).

Minsky, Rosalind, *Psychoanalysis and Gender: An Introductory Reader* (London: Routledge, 1996).

Morgan, Philip, *Fascism in Europe, 1919–1945* (Oxford and New York: Routledge, 2007).

Müller, Florence, *Art and Fashion (Fashion Memoir)*, trans. Anne Rubin (London: Thames & Hudson, 2000).

Mundy, Jennifer (ed.), *Man Ray: Writing on Art* (Los Angeles, CA: Getty Research Institute, 2015).

Nead, Lynda, *The Female Nude: Art, Obscenity and Sexuality* (London and New York: Routledge, 1992).

Nicola, White and Ian Griffiths (eds.), *The Fashion Business: Theory, Practice, Image* (Oxford and New York: Berg, 2000).

Nochlin, Linda, *The Body in Pieces: The Fragment as a Metaphor of Modernity* (London: Thames & Hudson, 1994).

Nomis, Anne O., *The History and Arts of the Dominatrix* (London and Melbourne: Anna Nomis Ltd., 2013).

Nussbaum, Martha C., *Hiding from Humanity: Disgust, Shame and the Law* (Princeton, NJ: Princeton University Press, 2004).

Overy, Richard, *The Origins of the Second World War* (London and New York: Routledge, 2009).

Owen, Jonathan L., *Avant-garde to New Wave: Czechoslovak Cinema, Surrealism and the Sixties* (New York and Oxford: Berghahn, 2011).

Pacteau, Francette, *The Symptom of Beauty* (London: Reaktion, 1994).

Parker-Smith, Caroline, *Race with Death: A Collection of Poems with Caroline Parker-Smith* (New York: Hastings House, 1939).

Parrott, Nicole (ed.), *Mannequins*, trans. Sheila De Vallee (London: Academy Editions, 1982).

Parsons, Deborah L., *Streetwalking the Metropolis: Women, the City, and Modernity* (Oxford: Oxford University Press, 2000).

Parsons, Sir John Herbert, *Introduction to the Study of Colour Vision* (Cambridge: Cambridge University Press, 1924).

Paskauskas, R. Andrew (ed.), *The Complete Correspondance of Sigmund Freud and Ernest Jones* (Cambridge, MA: Harvard University Press, 1993).

Pease, Allison, *Modernism, Mass Culture, and the Aesthetics of Obscenity* (Cambridge: Cambridge University Press, 2009).

Peiss, Kathy, *Hope in a Jar, the Making of America's Beauty Culture* (New York: Metropolitan Books, 1998).

Peiss, Kathyand Christina Simmons (ed.), *Passion and Power: Sexuality in History* (Philadelphia: Temple University Press, 1989).

Pelletier, Madeleine, *L'Émancipation sexuelle de la femme* (Paris: Brochure Mensuelle, 1926).

Perec, George, *Species of Space and Other Pieces* (London: Penguin, 1991).

Peterson, Amy T. (ed.), *The Greenwood Encyclopedia of Clothing through American History 1900 to the Present, vol. 1, 1900–1949* (Westport, CT: Greenwood Press, 2008).

Phelan, Peggy, *Mourning Sex: Performing Public Memories* (London and New York: Routledge, 1997).

Phelan, Peggy, *Unmarked: Politics of Performance* (London: Routledge, 1993).

Pollock, Griselda, *Vision and Difference: Femininity, Feminism, and Histories of Art* (London/New York: Routledge, 1988).

Post, Emily and Elizabeth L. Post, *The New Emily Post's Etiquette* (New York: Funk & Wagnalls, 1975).

Potvin, John (ed.), *The Places and Spaces of Fashion, 1800–2007* (London: Routledge, 2009).

Projansky, Sarah, *Watching Rape: Film and Television in Postfeminist Culture* (New York: New York University Press, 2001).

Rabaté, Jean-Michel, *The Cambridge Introduction to Literature and Psychoanalysis* (Cambridge: Cambridge University Press, 2014).

Rabate, Jean-Michel, *The Ghosts of Modernity* (Gainsville: University Press of Florida, 1996).

Ragland, Ellie, *The Logic of Sexuation: From Aristotle to Lacan* (New York: SUNY Albany, 2004).

Rainey, Lawrence, *Modernism: An Anthology* (Malden, MA and Oxford: Blackwell Publishing, 2005).

Rappaport, Erica, *Shopping for Pleasure: Women in the Making of London's West End* (New Jersey: Princeton University Press, 2000).

Reed, Christopher, *A Roger Fry Reader* (Chicago and London: The University of Chicago Press, 1996).

Reeder, Jan Giler, *High Style: Masterworks from the Brooklyn Museum Costume Collection at the Metropolitan Museum of Art* (New York: Metropolitan Museum of Art, 2010).

Remington, R. Roger and Barbara J. Hodik, *Nine Pioneers in American Graphic Design* (Cambridge, MA: MIT, 1989).

Ribeiro, Aileen, *Dress and Morality* (London, Oxford and New York: Berg, 2003).

Ribeiro, Aileen, *Dress and Morality* (London: Bloomsbury, 2003).

Ribeiro, Aileen, *The Gallery of Fashion* (London: National Portrait Gallery, 2000).

Rice, John R. (ed.), *The Best of Billy Sunday: 17 Burning Sermons from the Most Spectacular Evangelist the World Has Ever Known* (Murfreesboro, Tennessee: Sword of the Lord Publishers, 1965).

Rifkin, Adrian, *Street Noises: Parisian Pleasure, 1900–40* (Manchester: Manchester University Press, 1993).

Riley, Denise, *War in the Nursery: Theories of the Child and Mother* (London: Virago, 1983).

Roberts, Elizabeth, *A Woman's Place: An Oral History of Working Class Women 1890–1940* (Oxford: Wiley-Blackwell, 1995).

Roberts, John, *The Art of Interruption: Realism, Photography and the Everyday* (Manchester and London: Manchester University Press, 1998).

Roberts, John, *The Art of Interruption: Realism, Photography, and the Everyday* (Manchester: Manchester University Press, 1998).

Roberts, Mary Louise, *Civilization without Sexes: Reconstructing Gender in Postwar France, 1917–1927* (Chicago and London: Chicago University Press, 1994).

Robins, Kevin, *Into the Image: Culture and Politics in the Field of Vision* (London and New York: Routledge, 1996).

Rodgers, Daniel T., *Atlantic Crossings: Social Politics in a Progressive Age* (Cambridge, MA: Harvard University Press, 1998).

Ronen, Ruth, *Aesthetics of Anxiety* (New York: State University of New York Press, 2010).

Rose, Jacqueline, *Sexuality in the Field of Vision* (London: Verso, 2005).

Rose, Jacqueline, *Why War? Psychoanalysis, Politics and the Return to Melanie Klein* (Bucknell Lectures in Literary Theory) (Oxford, UK; Cambridge, MA, USA: Blackwell, 1993).

Rosenberg, Rosalind, *Divided Lives: American Women in the Twentieth Century* (London: Penguin, 1993).

Roth, Michael S., *Rediscovering History: Culture, Politics, and the Psyche* (Stanford: Stanford University Press, 1994).

Rothermund, Dietmar, *The Global Impact of the Great Depression 1929–1939* (Routledge: London and New York, 1996).

Roudinesco, Élisabeth, *Jacques Lacan: An Outline of a Life and a History of a System of Thought* (Cambridge, Oxford and Boston: Polity Press, 1999).

Rowbotham, Sheila, *A Century of Women: The History of Women in Britain and the United States in the Twentieth Century* (New York: Penguin, 1999).

Rubinstein, Ruth P., *Dress Codes: Meanings and Messages in American Culture* (Boulder, San Francisco and Oxford: Westview, 1995).

Rustin, Michael, *The Good Society and the Inner World: Psychoanalysis, Politics and Culture* (London: Verso, 1991).

Samuel, Raphael, *Theatres of Memory: Past and Present in Contemporary Culture* (London: Verso, 1994).

Sawday, Jonathan, *The Body Emblazoned: Dissection and the Human Body; Renaissance Culture* (London and New York: Routledge, 1995).

Schiaparelli, Elsa, *Shocking Life: The Autobiography of Elsa Schiaparelli* (London: V&A Museum, 2007).

Schilder, Paul, *The Image and Appearance of the Human Body* (London: Routledge, 1999).

Scranton, Philip (ed.), *Beauty and Business: Commerce, Gender, and Culture in Modern America* (London and New York: Routledge, 2001).

Secrest, Meryle, *Elsa Schiaparelli: A Biography* (New York: Random House, 2014).

Segal, Hannah, *Introduction to the Work of Melanie Klein* (London: The Hogarth Press, 2008).

Segal, Lynne and Mary Mcintosh (eds.), *Sex Exposed, Sexuality & the Pornography Debate* (London: Virago, 1992).

Seller, Conrad, *Good Night, Caroline* (New York: Dramatists Play Service, 1938).

Seltzer, Mark, *Bodies and Machines* (New York and London: Routledge, 1992).

Seltzer, Mark, *Serial Killers: Death and Life in Americas Wound Culture* (London and New York: Routledge, 1998).

Selzer, Richard, *Mortal Lessons* (New York: Touchstone, 1987).

Sennett, Richard, *Flesh and Stone: The Body and the City in Western Civilization* (New York: Norton, 1994).

Sennett, Richard, *The Fall of Public Man* (New York and London: W. W. Norton, 1992).

Shannon, David A., *Between the Wars: America 1919–1941* (Boston: Houghton Mifflin Company, 1979).

Shapira, Michal, *The War Inside: Psychoanalysis, Total War and the Making of the Democratic Self in Postwar Britain* (Cambridge: Cambridge University Press, 2013).

Shephard, Ben, *A War of Nerves: Soldiers and Psychiatrists in the Twentieth Century* (Cambridge, MA: Harvard University Press, 2000).

Shohat, Ella, *Taboo Memories, Diasporic Voices* (Durham: Duke University Press, 2006).

Shorter, Edward, *A History of Psychiatry: From the Era of the Asylum to the Age of Prozac* (New York, Brisbane, Toronto: John Wiley and Sons, 1997).

Showalter, Elaine, *Sexual Anarchy, Gender and Culture at the Fin de Siecle* (London: Virago, 1992).

Showalter, Elaine, *The Female Malady, Women, Madness, and English Culture, 1830–1980* (London: Virago, 1985).

Showalter, Elaine, *Sexual Anarchy: Gender and Culture at the Fin de Siecle* (London: Bloomsbury, 1991).

Showalter, Elaine, *These Modern Women: Autobiographical Essays from the Twenties* (New York: The Feminist Press City University of New York, 1989).

Silver, Kenneth E., *Espirit de Corps: The Art of the Parisian Avant-Garde and the First World War, 1914–1925* (Princeton 1989).

Silver, Kenneth E., *Making Paradise: Art, Modernity and the Myth of the French Riviera* (2001).

Silverman, Kaja, *Male Subjectivity at the Margins* (New York and London: Routledge, 1992).

Silverman, Kaja, *The Acoustic Mirror: The Female Voice in Psychoanalysis and Cinema* (Bloomington: Indiana University Press, 1988).

Simpson, Mark, *Male Impersonators: Performing Masculinity* (London: Cassell, 1994).

Sinclair, Iain, *Lights Out for the Territory: Nine Excursions into the Secret History of London* (London: Granta, 1997).

Slade, Joseph W., *Pornography and Sexual Representation: A Reference Guide* [all vols.] (Westport, CT: Greenwood Press, 2001).

Smelik, Anneke, 'Feminist Film Theory' in Pam Cook (ed.), *The Cinema Book*, 3rd edn. (London: BFI Publishing, 2007), pp. 491–504, p. 491.

Smith, Gervase, 'Taste for Nature', *The English Review* (November 1936).

Snowman, Daniel, *America since 1920* (London: Hiennemann, 1980).

Sonn, Richard David, *Sex, Violence and the Avant-Garde: Anarchism in Interwar France* (University Park: Pennsylvania State University Press, 2010).

Sontag, Susan, *Illness as Metaphor; Aids and Its Metaphors* (London: Penguin, 1991).

Sontag, Susan, *Regarding the Pain of Others* (London: Penguin, 2003).

Spiteri, Raymond and Donald LaCosse (eds.), *Surrealism, Politics and Culture* (Aldershot and Burlington, VT: Ashgate Publishing, 2003).

Steele, Valerie, *Fashion and Eroticism* (Oxford: Berg, 1999).

Steele, Valerie, *Paris Fashion: A Cultural History* (Oxford; New York: Berg, 1999).

Steele, Valerie, *The Corset: A Cultural History* (New Haven, CT, and London: Yale University Press, 2001).

Steele, Valerie and Jennifer Park, *Gothic: Dark Glamour* (New Haven and London: Yale University Press, 2008).

Steiner, Riccardo, 'Some Thoughts about Tradition and Change Arising from an Examination of the British Psycho-Analytical Society's Controversial Discussions', *International Review of Psychoanalysis*, vol. 12, no. 27 (1985).

Stewart, Mary Lynn, *For Health and Beauty: Physical Culture for French Women, 1880s–1930s* (Baltimore and London: The Johns Hopkins University Press, 2001).

Stich, Sidra, *Anxious Visions: Surrealist Art* (New York, 1990).

Stimpson, Catharine R., *Women and the American City* (Chicago and London: University of Chicago Press, 1981).

Stoichita, Victor I., *A Short History of the Shadow* (Chicago: Reaktion Books, 1997).

Stone, Alluquere Rosanne, *The War of Desire and Technology at the Close of the Mechanical Age* (Cambridge, MA, and London: MIT Press, 1995).

Stoneley, Peter, *Consumerism and American Girl's Literature, 1860–1940* (Cambridge and New York: Cambridge University Press, 2002).

Strong, Sir Roy C., *The Spirit of Britain: A Narrative History of the Arts* (New York: Fromm International Publishing Corporation, 2000).

Studlar, Gaylyn, *In the Realm of Pleasure: Von Sternberg, Dietrich, and the Masochistic Aesthetic* (New York: Columbia University Press, 1988).

Studlar, Gaylyn, *This Mad Masquerade: Stardom and Masculinity in the Jazz Age* (New York, 1996).

Sumner, Colin, *The Sociology of Deviance, an Obituary* (Buckingham: Open University Press, 1996).

Sumner, Colin (ed.), *Violence, Culture and Censure* (London and Bristol, PA: Taylor & Francis, 1997).

Svendsen, Lars, *Fashion: A Philosophy,* trans. John Irons (London: Reaktion Books, 2006).

Szreter, Simon and Kate Fisher, *Sex before the Sexual Revolution: Intimate Life in England 1918–1963* (Cambridge: Cambridge University Press, 2010).

Taylor, Lucien (ed.), *Visualizing Theory: Selected Essays from V.A.R* (New York and Oxford: Routledge, 2009).

Taylor, Sue, *Hans Bellmer: The Anatomy of Anxiety* (Cambridge, MA: MIT Press, 2002).

Tepperman, Charles, 'Color Unlimited: Amateur Color Cinema in the 1930s', in Simon Brown, Sarah Street, Liz Watkins (eds.), *Color and the Moving Image: History, Theory, Aesthetics, Archive* (New York and London: Routledge, 2013), pp. 138–49, p. 138.

The 10s, the 20s, the 30s: Inventive Clothes, 1909–1939 (New York: Metropolitan Museum of Art, 1973).

Théberge, Jean Clair and Pierre, *The 1930s: The Making of 'the New Man* (Ottowa: National Gallery of Canada, 2008).

Theodore, Peterson, *Magazines in the Twentieth Century* (Illinois: University of Illinois Press, 1964).

Thesander, Marianne, *The Feminine Ideal* (London: Reaktion, 1997).

Thompson, Kristin and David Bordwell, *Film History: An Introduction*, 3rd edn. (Columbus, OH.: McGraw Hill, 2010).

Thornham, Sue (ed.), *Feminist Film Theory: A Reader* (Edinburgh: Edinburgh University Press, 1999).

Tickner, Lisa, *Modern Lives and Modern Subjects* (New Haven and London: Yale University Press, 2000).

Tickner, Lisa, *The Spectacle of Women: Imagery of the Suffragette Campaign* (London: Chatto & Windus, 1987).

Trotter, David, *Paranoid Modernism* (Oxford: Oxford University Press, 2001).

Troy, Nancy J., *Couture Culture: A Study in Modern Art and Fashion* (Cambridge, MA, and London: MIT Press, 2003).

Tseelon, Efrat, *The Masque of Femininity: The Presentation of Woman in Everyday Life* (London, Thousand Oaks and New Delhi: Sage, 1995).

Tucker, Andrew, *The London Fashion Book* (London: Thames & Hudson, 1998).

Tucker, Susan, Katherine Ott, and Patricia Buckler (eds.), *The Scrapbook in American Life* (Philadelphia, PA: Temple University Press, 2006).

Vance, Carol S. (ed.), *Pleasure and Danger: Exploring Female Sexuality* (London: Routledge & Kegan Paul, 1984).

Veillon, Dominique, *Fashion under the Occupation* (New York and Oxford: Berg, 2002).

Veith, Ilsa, *Hysteria: The History of a Disease* (Chicago: University of Chicago Press, 1965).

Vessels, Joel E., *Drawing France: French Comics and the Republic* (Oxford and Mississippi: University Press of Mississippi, 2012).

Vigarello, Georges, *La silhouette du XVIIIe siècle à nos jours: naissance d'un défi* (Paris: Éditions de Seuil, 2012).

Wagner, Peter, *A Sociology of Modernity: Liberty and Discipline* (London and New York: Routledge, 1994).

Waldberg, Patrick (ed.), *Surrealism* (New York: Oxford University Press, 1965).

Walz, Robin, *Pulp Surrealism: Insolent Popular Culture in Early Twentieth-Century Paris* (California: University of California Press, 2000).

Ward, David and Olivier Zunz, *The Landscape of Modernity: Essays on New York City, 1900–1940* (New York: Russell Sage Foundation, 1992).

Ware, Susan, *Beyond Suffrage: Women in the New Deal* (Cambridge, MA and London: Harvard University Press, 1981).

Ware, Susan, *Holding Their Own: American Women in the 1930s* (Boston: Twayne, 1982).

Warner, Marina, *Monuments and Maidens: The Allegory of the Female Form* (London: Vintage, 1996).

Watts, Jill, *Mae West: An Icon in Black and White* (Oxford: Oxford University Press, 2001).

Weber, Samuel, 'The Sideshow, or Remarks on a Canny Moment', *MLN*, vol. 88, no. 26 (December 1973).

Weeks, Jeffrey, *Inventing Moralities: Sexual Values in an Age of Uncertainty* (New York: Columbia University Press, 1995).

Werner, Spies, *Max Ernst Collages: The Invention of the Surrealist Universe* (New York: Harry N. Abrams, 1991).

White, Nancy and John Esten, *Style in Motion: Munkacsi Photography '20s, 30s, '40s* (New York: Clarkson N. Potter Inc, 1979).

White, Palmer, *Elsa Schiaparelli: Empress of Paris Fashion* (London: Aurum, 1986).

Wilcox, Claire (ed.), *Radical Fashion* (London: Victoria & Albert Publications, 2001).

Wilkes, A. (ed.), *The Idealising Vision: The Art of Fashion Photography* (New York: Aperture Foundation Inc., 1991).

William, Fox, *Salome*, 1918.

Williams, Rosalind H., *Dream Worlds: Mass Consumption in Late Nineteenth-Century France* (Berkeley, and Los Angeles: University of California Press, 1982).

Williamson, Judith, *Consuming Passions: The Dynamics of Popular Culture* (London and New York: Marion Boyars, 1986).

Wilson, Elizabeth and J. Ash, *Chic Thrills, a Fashion Reader* (London: Pandora, 1992).

Wilson, Elizabeth, *Adorned in Dreams, Fashion & Modernity* (London: Virago, 1987).

Wilson, Elizabeth, *The Sphinx in the City: Urban Life, the Control of Disorder, and Women* (London: Virago, 1991).

Wilson, Simon, *Surrealist Painting* (London: Phaidon, 1982).

Winkler, Mary G. and Letha B. Cole (eds.), *The Good Body: Asceticism in Contemporary Culture* (New Haven and London: Yale, 1994).

Winter, Jay, *Sites of Memory, Sites of Mourning* (Cambridge: Cambridge University Press, 1998).

Wolf, Naomi, *The Beauty Myth* (New York: Vintage, 1991).

Wollen, Peter, *Addressing the Century: 100 Years of Art and Fashion* (London: Hayward Gallery, 1998).

Wolveridge, Jim, *Ain't It Grand (or This Was Stepney)* (London: The Journeyman Press, 1981).

Wood, Ghislaine, *Surreal Things: Surrealism and Design* (London: V&A Publishing, 2014).

Wood, Ghislaine, *The Surreal Body: Fetish and Fashion* (New York: Harry N. Abrams, 2007).

Wood, Ghislaine (ed.), *Surreal Things: Surrealism and Design* (London: V&A Publishing, 2007).

Woodhead, Lindy, *War Paint: Elizabeth Arden and Helena Rubinstein: Their Lives, Their Times, Their Rivalry* (London: Virago, 2012).

'World Urbanisation Trends as Measured in Agglomerations, 1920–1960' and Alternative Estimates and Trends Derived from 'Metropolitan Area ... 1920–1960', *UN Dept. of Economic and Social Affairs, Population Studies*, no. 44 (New York: United Nations, 1969), pp. 19–38, 44–9.

Wosk, Julie, *Women and the Machine: Representations from the Spinning Wheel to the Electronic Age* (Baltimore: John Hopkins University Press, 2003).

Wright, Elizabeth, *Feminism and Psychoanalysis: A Critical Dictionary* (Oxford: Blackwell, 1992).

Wright, Kenneth, *Mirroring and Attunement: Self-Realization in Psychoanalysis and Art* (London: Routledge, 2009).

Yates, L.B., *Picking Winners with Major Miles* (Bobbs-Merrill Company, 1922).

Young, Caroline, *Classic Hollywood Style* (London: Frances Lincoln, 2012).

Zalman, Sandra, *Consuming Surrealism in American Culture* (Surrey: Ashgate, 2015).

Zenderland, Leila (ed.), *Recycling the Past: Popular Uses of American History* (Philadelphia: University of Pennsylvania Press, 1978).

Ziegler, Benjamin Munn, *The International Law of John Marshall* (New Jersey: The Lawbook Exchange, Ltd., 2006).

Miscellaneous

Dixon, Bryony, 'Surveying the Screen: Fashion and Film 1896 to 1929', lecture, The Courtauld Institute of Art, The Courtauld Spring 2014 Friends Lecture Series, 28th January 2014.

Elman, Laura, 'Freudian Fashion: Freud, Psychoanalysis and the Fashions of the Inter-war Years', MA thesis, The Courtauld Institute of Art, University of London, 2005.

Finlay, John, 'Violence and Destruction in the Collages and Papiers Collés of Pablo Picasso, 1926 and 1912–12', MA thesis, The Courtauld Institute of Art, University of London, 1993.

Follo, Valentina, 'The Power of Images in the Age of Mussolini', PhD thesis, University of Pennsylvania, 2013.

Pass, Victoria Rose, 'Strange Glamour: Fashion and Surrealism between the World Wars', PhD thesis, University of Rochester, New York, 2011.

Ring, Nancy, 'New York Dada and the Crisis of Masculinity: Man Ray, Francis Picabia, and Marcel Duchamp in the United States, 1913–1921', PhD thesis, Northwestern University, 1991.

'The First World War in France', British Library French Collections Highlights, www.bl.uk/reshelp/findhelpregion/europe/france/france/ww1/frenchww1.html, accessed March 2013.

Thinking in Fragments, Romanticism and Beyond [Conference], 16th–17th December 2010, Leopardi Centre, University of Birmingham (UK).

Index